"This book appears not a moment too soon. As liberalism is scorned, here is liberalism made radiant...philosophy bursting with life...the history of ideas at its most vivid. Here is a free mind, learned and fearless and humane, teaching by example. I hope that *The Crooked Timber of Humanity* falls promptly into the hands of a new generation. For, like all of Berlin's writings, this will remind its readers of the charisma of the intellect."
—Leon Wieseltier

"Few writers and intellectuals command the awe and admiration accorded to Sir Isaiah Berlin, and with good reason. His wide-ranging erudition, humane skepticism and elegant prose set him apart."
—*Economist*

"A collection of essays in 'political philosophy' should not, on the face of it perhaps, be expected to offer thrilling vistas, aesthetic delights, but that is what Sir Isaiah Berlin delivers....The pleasure to be had from his bracing and accessible prose, from being invited to see what he has seen...is keen indeed."
—*Washington Times*

"Sir Isaiah Berlin...comes as close to being the intellectual high priest of humane Western liberalism as that secular worldview permits. This is entirely appropriate, for, more successfully than any other modern thinker, Berlin has succeeded in expressing in his work the great, if provisional, beliefs of classical liberalism.... Isaiah Berlin has no equal."
—*Newsday*

Isaiah Berlin
THE CROOKED TIMBER
OF HUMANITY

Sir Isaiah Berlin was born in Riga, Latvia, in 1909. In 1915, his family moved to Petrograd, where in 1917 he witnessed both the February and October revolutions. He came to England in 1919 and was educated at St. Paul's School and Corpus Christi College, Oxford. At Oxford, he has been and is a Fellow of All Souls College and was a Fellow of New College (1938–1950), Chichele Professor of Social and Political Theory (1957–1967), and first president of Wolfson College (1966–1975). He was president of the British Academy from 1974 to 1978. In 1941, during World War II, he was sent to New York by the British Ministry of Information; in 1942 he was transferred to the Foreign Office, which he served in the British embassies in Washington and Moscow.

Berlin's achievements as a historian and exponent of ideas has earned him the Erasmus, Lippincott, and Agnelli prizes. He has also received the Jerusalem Prize for his lifelong defense of civil liberties. His address on receiving the Agnelli Prize is the opening chapter of this book.

THE CROOKED TIMBER
OF HUMANITY

THE CROOKED TIMBER OF HUMANITY

Chapters in the History of Ideas

ISAIAH BERLIN

Edited by
Henry Hardy

VINTAGE BOOKS
A DIVISION OF RANDOM HOUSE, INC.
NEW YORK

FIRST VINTAGE BOOKS EDITION, MAY 1992

Copyright © 1959, 1972, 1975, 1978, 1980, 1983, 1990 by Isaiah Berlin
This section and editorial matter copyright © 1990 by Henry Hardy

Library of Congress Cataloging-in-Publication Data
Berlin, Isaiah, Sir.
The crooked timber of humanity: chapters in the history of ideas
/ Isaiah Berling; edited by Henry Hardy. — 1st Vintage Books ed.
p.   cm.
ISBN 0-679-73576-3
1. Philosophy.   2. Civilization, Modern.   I. Hardy, Henry.
II. Title.
[B29.B4465   1992]
190—dc20   91-50490
CIP

Manufactured in the United States of America
10 9 8 7 6 5 4 3 2

EDITOR'S PREFACE

THIS IS in effect the fifth of four volumes, though it appears under a different imprint and thus in independent livery. Some ten years ago, in the four-volume series collectively entitled *Selected Writings*,[1] I brought together most of the essays thus far published by Isaiah Berlin which had not hitherto been made available in a collected form. His many writings had been scattered, often in obscure places, most were out of print, and only half a dozen essays had previously been collected and reissued.[2] Those four volumes, together with the list of his publications which one of them (*Against the Current*) contains, made much more of his work readily accessible than before.

This new volume – devoted, like *Against the Current*, to the history of ideas – contains one early essay which has never previously been published, three essays written in the last decade, and four essays excluded from *Against the Current* for various reasons explained in my preface to that volume: three of these four have now happily become available for collective reissue; the fourth, 'The Bent Twig', omitted only because it was too similar to another essay in the volume on the same topic (nationalism), nevertheless contains much that is distinctive, and fully earns its place in this different company.

---

[1] *Russian Thinkers* (London and New York, 1978), *Concepts and Categories: Philosophical Essays* (London, 1978; New York, 1979), *Against the Current: Essays in the History of Ideas* (London, 1979; New York, 1980), and *Personal Impressions* (London, 1980; New York, 1981).

[2] *Four Essays on Liberty* (London and New York, 1969) and *Vico and Herder: Two Studies in the History of Ideas* (London and New York, 1976). Other collections had appeared only in translation.

The essay published here for the first time, on Joseph de Maistre, was put aside in 1960 as needing further revision. However, it was so nearly ready for publication, and contained so much of value, that it seemed right to include it here. Although the author has added a few new passages, and redrafted others, it has not been revised in any systematic way to take full account of subsequent work on Maistre, which in any case does not affect its central theses.

The details of original publication of the essays reprinted from elsewhere are as follows: 'The pursuit of the Ideal', an abbreviated version of which was read on 15 February 1988 at the ceremony in Turin at which the author was awarded the first Senator Giovanni Agnelli International Prize 'for the ethical dimension in advanced societies', was published privately by the Agnelli Foundation (in English and Italian), and also appeared in the *New York Review of Books*, 17 March 1988; 'The Decline of Utopian Ideas in the West' was published in Tokyo in 1978 by the Japan Foundation, and reprinted in J. M. Porter and Richard Vernon (eds), *Unity, Plurality and Politics: Essays in Honour of F. M. Barnard* (London and Sydney, 1986: Croom Helm); 'Giambattista Vico and Cultural History' was a contribution to Leigh S. Cauman and others (eds), *How Many Questions? Essays in Honor of Sidney Morgenbesser* (Indianapolis, 1983: Hackett); 'Alleged Relativism in Eighteenth-Century European Thought' first appeared in the *British Journal for Eighteenth-Century Studies* 3 (1980), and was reprinted with revisions in L. Pompa and W. H. Dray (eds), *Substance and Form in History: A Collection of Essays in Philosophy of History* (Edinburgh, 1981: University of Edinburgh Press); 'European Unity and its Vicissitudes', an address read on 21 November 1959 at the third Congress of the Fondation Européenne de la Culture in Vienna, was published by the Foundation in Amsterdam in the same year; 'The Apotheosis of the Romantic Will: The Revolt against the Myth of an Ideal World' was published in an Italian translation in *Lettere italiane* 27 (1975), and appears here in its original English form for the first time; 'The Bent Twig:

On the Rise of Nationalism' appeared in *Foreign Affairs* 51 (1972).

Because the same or similar topics turn up in different contexts, some of the discussions in these essays, as in the case of those in *Selected Writings*, inevitably overlap to some degree. Each essay was written as a self-contained item, not leaning on preceding chapters or anticipating subsequent ones. Apart from necessary corrections, the previously published essays appear here essentially in their original form, without the addition of references (the article on relativism, exceptionally in this context, was referenced on first publication, and in this case some missing sources have been provided).

The volume takes its title from Isaiah Berlin's preferred rendering of his favourite quotation, from Kant: 'Out of the crooked timber of humanity no straight thing was ever made.'[1] He has always ascribed this translation to R. G. Collingwood, but it turns out that he has not left Collingwood's version untouched. The quotation does not appear in Collingwood's published writings, but among his unpublished papers there is a lecture on the philosophy of history, dating from 1929, in which the following rendering appears: 'Out of the cross-grained timber of human nature nothing quite straight can be made.'[2] It seems likely that Isaiah Berlin attended the lecture

[1] The original German, together with a more literal translation, appears as an epigraph on p. xi.

[2] It must be added that Collingwood did originally write 'crooked', but then crossed this out (it is still legible) and substituted 'cross-grained'. The substitution may post-date the delivery of the lecture; or the same passage may have been used in another version in another lecture which does not survive. The truth is probably not definitively recoverable. I should like to thank W. J. van der Dussen for pointing me to the right place in Collingwood's manuscripts, and Teresa Smith, Collingwood's daughter and literary executor, for allowing me to quote this sentence. Collingwood's papers are in the Bodleian Library, Oxford: the lecture in question, headed 'II (T.T. 1929)', is in Box 12 (shelfmark Ms. Collingwood 12), and the quotation appears on the third folio.

and was struck by this passage, which then matured in his memory.

I have again received generous help from a number of scholars. Roger Hausheer, without whose advocacy the essay on Maistre would not have been included, has also assisted in other ways too many and various to specify. Leofranc Holford-Strevens gave immediate answers to several arcane queries on which I should otherwise have had to spend many hours, in some cases fruitlessly. Richard Lebrun gave with astonishing generosity and effectiveness from his store of expert knowledge of Maistre. Frederick Barnard has helped prodigiously with Herder and Locke. For solutions of individual problems I am indebted to John Batchelor, Clifford Geertz, David Klinck, Jean O'Grady, John M. Robson and Cedric Watts. My wife, Anne, has kindly double-checked the proofs. Pat Utechin, the author's secretary, has as before given unstinting and indispensable support and assistance.

May 1990   HENRY HARDY

CONTENTS

[A]us so krummem Holze, als woraus der Mensch gemacht ist, kann nichts ganz Gerades gezimmert werden.

(Out of timber so crooked as that from which man is made nothing entirely straight can be built.)

—Immanuel Kant, 'Idee zu einer allgemeinen Geschichte in welbürgerlicher Absicht' (1784)

THE CROOKED TIMBER
OF HUMANITY

THE PURSUIT OF THE IDEAL

I

THERE ARE, in my view, two factors that, above all others, have shaped human history in this century. One is the development of the natural sciences and technology, certainly the greatest success story of our time – to this, great and mounting attention has been paid from all quarters. The other, without doubt, consists in the great ideological storms that have altered the lives of virtually all mankind: the Russian Revolution and its aftermath – totalitarian tyrannies of both right and left and the explosions of nationalism, racism and, in places, of religious bigotry, which, interestingly enough, not one among the most perceptive social thinkers of the nineteenth century had ever predicted.

When our descendants, in two or three centuries' time (if mankind survives until then), come to look at our age, it is these two phenomena that will, I think, be held to be the outstanding characteristics of our century, the most demanding of explanation and analysis. But it is as well to realise that these great movements began with ideas in people's heads: ideas about what relations between men have been, are, might be and should be; and to realise how they came to be transformed in the name of a vision of some supreme goal in the minds of the leaders, above all of the prophets with armies at their backs. Such ideas are the substance of ethics. Ethical thought consists of the systematic examination of the relations of human beings to each other, the conceptions, interests and ideals from which human ways of treating one another spring, and the systems of value on which such ends of life are based. These beliefs about how life should be lived, what men and women should be and do, are objects of moral inquiry; and when applied to groups and nations, and, indeed, mankind as a whole, are called political philosophy, which is but ethics applied to society.

If we are to hope to understand the often violent world in which we live (and unless we try to understand it, we cannot expect to be able to act rationally in it and on it), we cannot confine our attention to the great impersonal forces, natural and man-made, which act upon us. The goals and motives that guide human action must be looked at in the light of all that we know and understand; their roots and growth, their essence, and above all their validity, must be critically examined with every intellectual resource that we have. This urgent need, apart from the intrinsic value of the discovery of truth about human relationships, makes ethics a field of primary importance. Only barbarians are not curious about where they come from, how they came to be where they are, where they appear to be going, whether they wish to go there, and if so, why, and if not, why not.

The study of the variety of ideas about the views of life that embody such values and such ends is something that I have spent forty years of my long life in trying to make clear to myself. I should like to say something about how I came to become absorbed by this topic, and particularly about a turning-point which altered my thoughts about the heart of it. This will, to some degree, inevitably turn out to be somewhat autobiographical – for this I offer my apologies, but I do not know how else to give an account of it.

II

When I was young I read *War and Peace* by Tolstoy, much too early. The real impact on me of this great novel came only later, together with that of other Russian writers, both novelists and social thinkers, of the mid-nineteenth century. These writers did much to shape my outlook. It seemed to me, and still does, that the purpose of these writers was not principally to give realistic accounts of the lives and relationships to one another of individuals or social groups or classes, not psychological or social analysis for its own sake – although, of course, the best of them achieved precisely this, incomparably. Their approach seemed to me essentially moral: they were concerned most deeply with what was responsible for injustice, oppression, falsity in human relations, imprisonment whether by stone walls or conformism – unprotesting submission to man-made yokes – moral blindness, egoism, cruelty, humiliation, ser- vility, poverty, helplessness, bitter indignation, despair, on the part of so many. In short, they were concerned with the nature of these experiences and their roots in the human condition; the condition of Russia in the first place, but, by implication, of all mankind. And conversely they wished to know what would bring about the opposite of this, a reign of truth, love, honesty, justice, security, personal relations based on the possibility of human dignity, decency, independence, freedom, spiritual fulfilment.

Some, like Tolstoy, found this in the outlook of simple people, unspoiled by civilisation; like Rousseau, he wished to believe that the moral universe of peasants was not unlike that of children, not distorted by the conventions and institutions of civilisation, which sprang from human vices – greed, egoism, spiritual blindness; that the world could be saved if only men saw the truth that lay at their feet; if they but looked, it was to be found in the Christian gospels, the Sermon on the Mount. Others among these Russians put their faith in scientific rationalism, or in social and political revolution founded on a true theory of historical change. Others again looked for answers in the teachings of the Orthodox theology, or in liberal western democracy, or in a return to ancient Slav values, obscured by the reforms of Peter the Great and his successors.

What was common to all these outlooks was the belief that

solutions to the central problems existed, that one could discover them, and, with sufficient selfless effort, realise them on earth. They all believed that the essence of human beings was to be able to choose how to live: societies could be transformed in the light of true ideals believed in with enough fervour and dedication. If, like Tolstoy, they sometimes thought that man was not truly free but determined by factors outside his control, they knew well enough, as he did, that if freedom was an illusion it was one without which one could not live or think. None of this was part of my school curriculum, which consisted of Greek and Latin authors, but it remained with me.

When I became a student at the University of Oxford, I began to read the works of the great philosophers, and found that the major figures, especially in the field of ethical and political thought, believed this too. Socrates thought that if certainty could be established in our knowledge of the external world by rational methods (had not Anaxagoras arrived at the truth that the moon was many times larger than the Peloponnese, however small it looked in the sky?) the same methods would surely yield equal certainty in the field of human behaviour – how to live, what to be. This could be achieved by rational argument. Plato thought that an élite of sages who arrived at such certainty should be given the power of governing others intellectually less well endowed, in obedience to patterns dictated by the correct solutions to personal and social problems. The Stoics thought that the attainment of these solutions was in the power of any man who set himself to live according to reason. Jews, Christians, Muslims (I knew too little about Buddhism) believed that the true answers had been revealed by God to his chosen prophets and saints, and accepted the interpretation of these revealed truths by qualified teachers and the traditions to which they belonged.

The rationalists of the seventeenth century thought that the answers could be found by a species of metaphysical insight, a special application of the light of reason with which all men were endowed. The empiricists of the eighteenth century, impressed by the vast new realms of knowledge opened by the natural sciences based on mathematical techniques, which had driven out so much error, superstition, dogmatic nonsense, asked themselves, like Socrates, why the same methods should not succeed in establishing similar irrefutable laws in the realm of human affairs. With the new methods discovered by natural science, order could be introduced into the social sphere as well – uniformities could be observed, hypotheses formulated and tested by experiment; laws could be based on them, and then laws in specific regions of experience could be seen to be entailed by wider laws; and these in turn to be entailed by still wider laws, and so on upwards, until a great harmonious system, connected by unbreakable logical links and capable of being formulated in precise – that is, mathematical – terms, could be established.

The rational reorganisation of society would put an end to spiritual and intellectual confusion, the reign of prejudice and superstition, blind obedience to unexamined dogmas, and the stupidities and cruelties of the oppressive regimes which such intellectual darkness bred and promoted. All that was wanted was the identification of the principal human needs and discovery of the means of satisfying them. This would create the happy, free, just, virtuous, harmonious world which Condorcet so movingly predicted in his prison cell in 1794. This view lay at the basis of all progressive thought in the nineteenth century, and was at the heart of much of the critical empiricism which I imbibed in Oxford as a student.

III

At some point I realised that what all these views had in common was a Platonic ideal: in the first place, that, as in the sciences, all genuine questions must have one true answer and one only, all the rest being necessarily errors; in the second place, that there must be a dependable path towards the discovery of these truths; in the third place, that the true answers, when found, must necessarily be compatible with one another and form a single whole, for one truth cannot be incompatible with another – that we knew *a priori*. This kind of omniscience was the solution of the cosmic jigsaw puzzle. In the case of morals, we could then conceive what the perfect life must be, founded as it would be on a correct understanding of the rules that governed the universe.

True, we might never get to this condition of perfect knowledge – we may be too feeble-witted, or too weak or corrupt or sinful, to achieve this. The obstacles, both intellectual and those of external nature, may be too many. Moreover, opinions, as I said, had widely differed about the right path to pursue – some found it in churches, some in laboratories; some believed in intuition, others in experiment, or in mystical visions, or in mathematical calculation. But even if we could not ourselves reach these true answers, or indeed, the final system that interweaves them all, the answers must exist – else the questions were not real. The answers must be known to someone: perhaps Adam in Paradise knew; perhaps we shall only reach them at the end of days; if men cannot know them, perhaps the angels know; and if not the angels, then God knows. These timeless truths must in principle be knowable.

Some nineteenth-century thinkers – Hegel, Marx – thought it was not quite so simple. There were no timeless truths. There was historical development, continuous change; human horizons altered with each new step in the evolutionary ladder; history was a drama with many acts; it was moved by conflicts of forces in the realms of both ideas and reality, sometimes called dialectical, which took the form of wars, revolutions, violent upheavals of nations, classes, cultures, movements. Yet after inevitable setbacks, failures, relapses, returns to barbarism, Condorcet's dream would come true. The drama would have a happy ending – man's reason had achieved triumphs in the past, it could not be held back for ever. Men would no longer be victims of nature or of their own largely irrational societies:

reason would triumph; universal harmonious cooperation, true history, would at last begin.

For if this was not so, do the ideas of progress, of history, have any meaning? Is there not a movement, however tortuous, from ignorance to knowledge, from mythical thought and childish fantasies to perception of reality face to face, to knowledge of true goals, true values as well as truths of fact? Can history be a mere purposeless succession of events, caused by a mixture of material factors and the play of random selection, a tale full of sound and fury signifying nothing? This was unthinkable. The day would dawn when men and women would take their lives in their own hands and not be self-seeking beings or the playthings of blind forces that they did not understand. It was, at the very least, not impossible to conceive what such an earthly paradise could be; and if conceivable we could, at any rate, try to march towards it. That has been at the centre of ethical thought from the Greeks to the Christian visionaries of the Middle Ages, from the Renaissance to progressive thought in the last century; and indeed, is believed by many to this day.

IV

At a certain stage in my reading, I naturally met with the principal works of Machiavelli. They made a deep and lasting impression upon me, and shook my earlier faith. I derived from them not the most obvious teachings – on how to acquire and retain political power, or by what force or guile rulers must act if they are to regenerate their societies, or protect themselves and their states from enemies within or without, or what the principal qualities of rulers on the one hand, and of citizens on the other, must be, if their states are to flourish – but something else. Machiavelli was not a historicist: he thought it possible to restore something like the Roman Republic or Rome of the early Principate. He believed that to do this one needed a ruling class of brave, resourceful, intelligent, gifted men who knew how to seize opportunities and use them, and citizens who were adequately protected, patriotic, proud of their state, epitomes of manly, pagan virtues. That is how Rome rose to power and conquered the world, and it is the absence of this kind of wisdom and vitality and courage in adversity, of the qualities of both lions and foxes, that in the end brought it down. Decadent states were conquered by vigorous invaders who retained these virtues.

But Machiavelli also sets, side by side with this, the notion of Christian virtues – humility, acceptance of suffering, unworldliness, the hope of salvation in an afterlife – and he remarks that if, as he plainly himself favours, a state of a Roman type is to be established, these qualities will not promote it: those who live by the precepts of Christian morality are bound to be trampled on by the ruthless pursuit of power by men who alone can re-create and dominate the republic which he wants to see. He does not condemn Christian virtues. He merely points out that the two moralities are incompatible, and he does not recognise any overarching criterion whereby we are enabled to decide the right life for men. The combination of *virtù* and Christian values is for him an impossibility. He simply leaves you to choose – he knows which he himself prefers.

The idea that this planted in my mind was the realisation, which came as something of a shock, that not all the supreme values pursued by mankind now and in the past were necessarily compatible with one another. It undermined my earlier assumption, based on the *philosophia perennis*, that there could be no conflict between true ends, true answers to the central problems of life.

Then I came across Giambattista Vico's *La scienza nuova*. Scarcely anyone in Oxford had then heard of Vico, but there was one philosopher, Robin Collingwood, who had translated Croce's book on Vico, and he urged me to read it. This opened my eyes to something new. Vico seemed to be concerned with the succession of human cultures – every society had, for him, its own vision of reality, of the world in which it lived, and of itself and of its relations to its own past, to nature, to what it strove for. This vision of a society is conveyed by everything that its members do and think and feel – expressed and embodied in the kinds of words, the forms of language that they use, the images, the metaphors, the forms of worship, the institutions that they generate, which embody and convey their image of reality and of their place in it; by which they live. These visions differ with each successive social whole – each has its own gifts, values, modes of creation, incommensurable with one another: each must be understood in its own terms – understood, not necessarily evaluated.

The Homeric Greeks, the master class, Vico tells us, were cruel, barbarous, mean, oppressive to the weak; but they created the *Iliad* and the *Odyssey*, something we cannot do in our more enlightened day. Their great creative masterpieces belong to them, and once the vision of the world changes, the possibility of that type of creation disappears also. We, for our part, have our sciences, our thinkers, our poets, but there is no ladder of ascent from the ancients to the moderns. If this is so, it must be absurd to say that Racine is a better poet than Sophocles, that Bach is a rudimentary Beethoven, that, let us say, the Impressionist painters are the peak to which the painters of Florence aspired but did not reach. The values of these cultures are different, and they are not necessarily compatible with one another. Voltaire, who thought that the values and ideals of the enlightened exceptions in a sea of darkness – of classical Athens, of Florence of the Renaissance, of France in the *grand siècle* and of his own time – were almost identical, was mistaken.[1] Machiavelli's Rome did not, in fact, exist. For Vico there is a plurality of civilisations (repetitive cycles of them, but that is unimportant), each with its own unique pattern.

---

[1] Voltaire's conception of enlightenment as being identical in essentials wherever it is attained seems to lead to the inescapable conclusion that, in his view, Byron would have been happy at table with Confucius, and Sophocles would have felt completely at ease in quattrocento Florence, and Seneca in the *salon* of Madame du Deffand or at the court of Frederick the Great.

Machiavelli conveyed the idea of two incompatible outlooks; and here were societies the cultures of which were shaped by values, not means to ends but ultimate ends, ends in themselves, which differed, not in all respects – for they were all human – but in some profound, irreconcilable ways, not combinable in any final synthesis.

After this I naturally turned to the German eighteenth-century thinker Johann Gottfried Herder. Vico thought of a succession of civilisations, Herder went further and compared national cultures in many lands and periods, and held that every society had what he called its own centre of gravity, which differed from that of others. If, as he wished, we are to understand Scandinavian sagas or the poetry of the Bible, we must not apply to them the aesthetic criteria of the critics of eighteenth-century Paris. The ways in which men live, think, feel, speak to one another, the clothes they wear, the songs they sing, the gods they worship, the food they eat, the assumptions, customs, habits which are intrinsic to them – it is this that creates communities, each of which has its own 'life-style'. Communities may resemble each other in many respects, but the Greeks differ from Lutheran Germans, the Chinese differ from both; what they strive after and what they fear or worship are scarcely ever similar.

This view has been called cultural or moral relativism – this is what that great scholar, my friend Arnaldo Momigliano, whom I greatly admired, supposed both about Vico and about Herder. He was mistaken. It is not relativism. Members of one culture can, by the force of imaginative insight, understand (what Vico called *entrare*) the values, the ideals, the forms of life of another culture or society, even those remote in time or space. They may find these values unacceptable, but if they open their minds sufficiently they can grasp how one might be a full human being, with whom one could communicate, and at the same time live in the light of values widely different from one's own, but which nevertheless one can see to be values, ends of life, by the realisation of which men could be fulfilled.

'I prefer coffee, you prefer champagne. We have different tastes. There is no more to be said.' That is relativism. But Herder's view, and Vico's, is not that: it is what I should describe as pluralism – that is, the conception that there are many different ends that men may seek and still be fully rational, fully men, capable of understanding each other and sympathising and deriving light from each other, as we derive it from reading Plato or the novels of medieval Japan – worlds, outlooks, very remote from our own. Of course, if we did not have any values in common with these distant figures, each civilisation would be enclosed in its own impenetrable bubble, and we could not understand them at all; this is what Spengler's typology amounts to. Intercommunication between cultures in time and space is only possible because what makes men human is common to them, and acts as a bridge between them. But our values are ours, and theirs are theirs. We are free to criticise the values of other cultures, to condemn them, but we cannot pretend not to understand them at all, or to regard them simply as subjective, the products of creatures in different circumstances with different tastes from our own, which do not speak to us at all.

There is a world of objective values. By this I mean those ends that men pursue for their own sakes, to which other things are means. I am not blind to what the Greeks valued – their values may not be mine, but I can grasp what it would be like to live by their light, I can admire and respect them, and even imagine myself as pursuing them, although I do not – and do not wish to, and perhaps could not if I wished. Forms of life differ. Ends, moral principles, are many. But not infinitely many: they must be within the human horizon. If they are not, then they are outside the human sphere. If I find men who worship trees, not because they are symbols of fertility or because they are divine, with a mysterious life and powers of their own, or because this grove is sacred to Athena – but only because they are made of wood; and if when I ask them why they worship wood they say 'Because it is wood' and give no other answer; then I do not know what they mean. If they are human, they are not beings with whom I can communicate – there is a real barrier. They are not human for me. I cannot even call their values subjective if I cannot conceive what it would be like to pursue such a life.

What is clear is that values can clash – that is why civilisations are incompatible. They can be incompatible between cultures, or groups in the same culture, or between you and me. You believe in always telling the truth, no matter what; I do not, because I believe that it can sometimes be too painful and too destructive. We can discuss each other's point of view, we can try to reach common ground, but in the end what you pursue may not be reconcilable with the ends to which I find that I have dedicated my life. Values may easily clash within the breast of a single individual; and it does not follow that, if they do, some must be true and others false. Justice, rigorous justice, is for some people an absolute value, but it is not compatible with what may be no less ultimate values for them – mercy, compassion – as arises in concrete cases.

Both liberty and equality are among the primary goals pursued by human beings through many centuries; but total liberty for wolves is death to the lambs, total liberty of the powerful, the gifted, is not compatible with the rights to a decent existence of the weak and the less gifted. An artist, in order to create a masterpiece, may lead a life which plunges his family into misery and squalor to which he is indifferent. We may condemn him and declare that the masterpiece should be sacrificed to human needs, or we may take his side – but both attitudes embody values which for some men or women are ultimate, and which are intelligible to us all if we have any sympathy or imagination or understanding of human beings. Equality may demand the restraint of the liberty of those who wish to dominate; liberty – without some modicum of which there is no choice and therefore no possibility of remaining human as we understand the word – may have to be curtailed in order to make room for social welfare, to feed the hungry, to clothe the naked, to shelter the homeless, to leave room

pessimism of the bourgeoisie made uneasy by consciousness of, but unable to face, its inescapably approaching doom. Since then the 'perennial philosophy', with its unalterable objective truths founded on the perception of an eternal order behind the chaos of appearances, has been thrown on the defensive in the face of the attacks of relativists, pluralists, irrationalists, pragmatists, subjectivists, and certain types of empiricism; and with its decline, the conception of the perfect society, which derives from this great unitary vision, loses its persuasive power. From this time onwards, believers in the possibility of social perfection tend to be accused by their opponents of trying to foist an artificial order on a reluctant humanity, of trying to fit human beings, like bricks, into a preconceived structure, force them into Procrustean beds, and vivisect living men in the pursuit of some fanatically held schema. Hence the protest – and anti-Utopias – of Aldous Huxley, or Orwell, or Zamyatin (in Russia in the early 1920s), who paint a horrifying picture of a frictionless society in which differences between human beings are, as far as possible, eliminated, or at least reduced, and the multi-coloured pattern of the variety of human temperaments, inclinations, ideals – in short, the flow of life – is brutally reduced to uniformity, pressed into a social and political straitjacket which hurts and maims and ends by crushing men in the name of a monistic theory, a dream of a perfect, static order. This is the heart of the protest against the uniformitarian despotism which Tocqueville and J. S. Mill felt to be advancing upon mankind.

Our times have seen the conflict of two irreconcilable views: one is the view of those who believe that there exist eternal values, binding on all men, and that the reason why men have not, as yet, all recognised or realised them is a lack of the capacity, moral, intellectual or material, needed to compass this end. It may be that this knowledge has been withheld from us by the laws of history itself: on one interpretation of these laws it is the class war that has so distorted our relations to each other as to blind men to the truth, and so prevented a rational organisation of human life. But enough progress has occurred to enable some persons to see the truth; in the fullness of time the universal solution will be clear to men at large; then prehistory will end and true human history will begin. Thus contend the Marxists, and perhaps other socialist and optimistic prophets. This is not accepted by those who declare that men's temperaments, gifts, outlooks, wishes permanently differ one from another, that uniformity kills; that men can live full lives only in societies with an open texture, in which variety is not merely tolerated but is approved and encouraged; that the richest development of human potentialities can occur only in societies in which there is a wide spectrum of opinions – the freedom for what J. S. Mill called 'experiments in living' – in which there is liberty of thought and of expression, views and opinions clash with each other, societies in which friction and even conflict are permitted, albeit with rules to control them and prevent destruction and violence; that subjection to a single ideology, no matter how reasonable and imaginative, robs men of freedom and vitality. It may be this that Goethe meant when, after reading Holbach's *Système de la nature* (one of the most famous works of eighteenth-century French materialism, which looked to a kind of rationalist Utopia), he declared that he could not understand how anyone could accept such a grey, Cimmerian, corpse-like affair, devoid of colour, life, art, humanity. For those who embrace this romantically tinged individualism, what matters is not the common base but the differences, not the one but the many; for them the craving for unity – the regeneration of mankind by recovery of a lost innocence and harmony, the return from a fragmented existence to the all-embracing whole – is an infantile and dangerous delusion: to crush all diversity and even conflict in the interest of uniformity is, for them, to crush life itself.

These doctrines are not compatible with one another. They are ancient antagonists; in their modern guise both dominate mankind today, and both are resisted: industrial organisation versus human rights, bureaucratic rules versus 'doing one's own thing'; good government versus self-government; security versus freedom. Sometimes a demand turns into its opposite: claims to participatory democracy turn into oppression of minorities, measures to establish social equality crush self-determination and stifle individual genius. Side by side with these collisions of values there persists an age-old dream: there is, there must be – and it can be found – the final solution to all human ills; it can be achieved; by revolution or peaceful means it will surely come; and then all, or the vast majority, of men will be virtuous and happy, wise and good and free; if such a position can be attained, and once attained will last for ever, what sane man could wish to return to the miseries of men's wanderings in the desert? If this is possible, then surely no price is too heavy to pay for it; no amount of oppression, cruelty, repression, coercion will be too high, if this, and this alone, is the price for ultimate salvation of all men? This conviction gives a wide licence to inflict suffering on other men, provided it is done for pure, disinterested motives. But if one believes this doctrine to be an illusion, if only because some ultimate values may be incompatible with one another, and the very notion of an ideal world in which they are reconciled to be a conceptual (and not merely practical) impossibility, then, perhaps, the best that one can do is to try to promote some kind of equilibrium, necessarily unstable, between the different aspirations of differing groups of human beings – at the very least to prevent them from attempting to exterminate each other, and, so far as possible, to prevent them from hurting each other – and to promote the maximum practicable degree of sympathy and understanding, never likely to be complete, between them. But this is not, *prima facie*, a wildly exciting programme: a liberal sermon which recommends machinery designed to prevent people from doing each other too much harm, giving each human group sufficient room to realise its own idiosyncratic, unique, particular ends without too much interference with the ends of others, is not a passionate battle-cry to inspire men to sacrifice and martyrdom and heroic feats. Yet if it were adopted, it might yet prevent mutual destruction, and, in the end, preserve the world. Immanuel Kant, a man very remote from irrationalism, once observed that 'Out of the crooked timber of humanity no straight thing was ever made.' And for that reason no perfect solution is, not merely in practice, but in principle, possible in human affairs, and any determined attempt to produce it is likely to lead to suffering, disillusionment and failure.

GIAMBATTISTA VICO
AND CULTURAL HISTORY

I

THE STUDY of their own past has long been one of the major preoccupations of men. There have been many motives for this, some of them discussed by Nietzsche in a famous essay: pride, the desire to glorify the achievements of tribe, nation, church, race, class, party; the wish to promote the bonds of solidarity in a given society – 'We are all sons of Cadmus'; faith in the sacred traditions of the tribe – to our ancestors alone has been vouchsafed the revelation of the true ends of life, of good and evil, right and wrong, how one should live, what to live by; and, associated with this, a sense of collective worth, the need to know and teach others to understand the kind of society that we are and have been, the texture of relationships through which our collective genius has expressed itself, and by which alone it can function.

There is the ethical approach: history provides us with authentic examples – and exemplars – of virtue and vice, with vivid illustrations of what to do and what to avoid – a gallery of portraits of heroes and villains, the wise and the foolish, the successful and the failures; here history is seen as being in the first place a school of morals, as, for example, Leibniz declared, or of experimental politics, as Joseph de Maistre (and perhaps Machiavelli) believed.

Then again, there are those who look for a pattern in history, the gradual realisation of a cosmic plan, the work of the Divine Artificer who has created us, and all there is, to serve a universal purpose, hidden from us, perhaps, because we are too weak or sinful or foolish, but real and unalterable, with lineaments which can be discerned, however imperfectly, by those who have eyes to see. One of the forms of this vision is the conception of history as a cosmic drama, which, according to some doctrines, must culminate in a final denouement beyond the frontiers of history and time, in a total spiritual transfiguration not to be fully grasped by the finite human intellect. According to others history is a cyclical process which leads to a peak of human achievement, then to decadence and collapse, after which the entire process begins afresh. It is held that such patterns alone give meaning to the historical process, else what can it be – the mere play of chance combinations and divisions, a mechanical succession of causes and effects?

Then again, there are those who believe in the possibility of a sociological science for which historical facts are the data, which, once we have discovered the laws that govern social change, will enable us to predict the future and retrodict the past – this is the conception of history as a systematic collection of observations that stands to a developed scientific sociology much as the observations of the heavens by Tycho Brahe stood to the laws discovered by Kepler or Galileo, a new and powerful instrument which makes return to the mere accumulation of such data unnecessary save to verify specific hypotheses. That was the hope of such nineteenth-century positivists as Comte and Buckle, who believed in the possibility of, and need for, a natural science of history created by methods in essence analogous to those of, if not physics, at any rate the biological sciences.

Again, there are those who own to no better motive for studying history than simple curiosity about the past, the quest for knowledge for its own sake, the wish to know what happened, and when and why, without necessarily drawing general conclusions or formulating laws.

Last but not least is the ambition of those who wish to know how we, the present generation, came to be what we are, who our ancestors have been, what they have done, what were the consequences of their activities, what was the nature of the interplay between these activities, what were their hopes and fears and goals, and the natural forces with which they had to contend; for it seems obvious that only barbarians feel no curiosity about the sources of their own forms of life and civilisation, their place in the world order as determined by the antecedent experiences of their ancestors, as well as the very identity of these ancestors, which alone can give a sense of identity to their successors.

This last motive for the study of history springs from a desire for self-knowledge – something which, however implicit in earlier writers, came to the surface only in the eighteenth century, principally among thinkers in the west who reacted against a central doctrine of the French Enlightenment, then the dominant influence on the majority of European intellectuals. This was the belief that a universally valid method had finally been found for the solution of the fundamental questions that had exercised men at all times – how to establish what was true and what was false in every province of knowledge; and, above all, what was the right life that men should lead if they were to attain those goals which men had always pursued – life, liberty, justice, happiness, virtue, the fullest development of human faculties in a harmonious and creative way. This method consisted in the application of those rational (that is, scientific) rules which had in the previous century produced such magnificent results in the fields of mathematics and the natural sciences to the moral, social, political, economic problems of mankind, so long bedevilled by ignorance and error, superstition and prejudice, much of it deliberately spread by priests, princes, ruling classes, bureaucrats, and ambitious adventurers who disseminated falsehoods as a means of keeping men obedient to their will.

The greatest publicist of the Enlightenment, Voltaire, even while he advocated the widening of historical inquiry to embrace social and economic activities and their effects, strongly believed that the only objects worthy of historical study were the peaks, not the valleys, of the achievements of mankind. He had no doubt about what they were: Periclean Athens, Rome of the late republic and early principate, Renaissance Florence, and France during the reign of Louis XIV. These were the finest hours of mankind, when the true, the only true, ends that all wise men sought at all times – in art, in thought, in morals and manners – determined the lives of states and individuals alike. These ends were timeless and universal, known to all reasonable men – those who had eyes to see – not touched by change or any kind of historical evolution. Just as answers to the problems of the natural sciences could be solved once and for all, just as the theorems of geometry, the laws of physics and astronomy, were unaffected by changes in human opinion or ways of life, so, at any rate in principle, equally clear and final answers could be found to human problems also.

Even Montesquieu, who believed in the unavoidable variety of customs and outlooks, due largely to the influence both of physical factors and human institutions determined by them, nevertheless assumed that the fundamental goals of mankind were identical at all times, everywhere, even if the particular forms they took in various climates and societies necessarily differed, so that no uniform legislation for all human societies could be successfully devised. The very conception of progress among the *philosophes* in the eighteenth century, whether its champions were optimistic, like Condorcet or Helvétius, or assailed by doubts about its prospects, like Voltaire and Rousseau, entailed the view that the light of the truth, *lumen naturale*, is everywhere and always the same, even if men were often too wicked or stupid or weak to discover it, or, if they did, to live their lives by its radiance.

The dark periods of human history were, for Voltaire, simply not worthy of the attention of intelligent men. The purpose of history is to impart instructive truths, not to satisfy idle curiosity, and this can only be done by studying the triumphs of reason and imagination, not the failures. 'If you have no more to tell us', Voltaire declared, 'than that one barbarian succeeded another on the banks of the Oxus or the Ixartes, what use are you to the public?' Who wants to know that 'Quancum succeeded Kincum, and Kicum succeeded Quancum'? Who wants to know about Shalmaneser or Mardokempad? Historians must not clutter the minds of their readers with the absurdities of religion, the ravings of idiots and savages, or the inventions of knaves, unless it be as cautionary tales to warn mankind of the horrors of barbarism and tyranny. This deeply unhistorical approach to the nature of men and societies is common enough in the eighteenth century, and derives in part from the phenomenal success of the exact sciences in the previous century, which led Descartes, for example, to look on the study of history as unworthy of intelligent men interested in the advancement of objective knowledge, which in such muddy waters could scarcely be hoped for. The view that the truth is one and undivided, and the same for all men everywhere at all times, whether one finds it in the pronouncements of sacred books, traditional wisdom, the authority of churches, democratic majorities, observation and experiment conducted by qualified experts, or the convictions of simple folk uncorrupted by civilisation – this view, in one form or another, is central to western thought, which stems from Plato and his disciples.

It did not go entirely unchallenged. Apart from the sceptics in ancient Greece and Rome, the revolt against papal authority led some of the reformers in the sixteenth century (particularly the Protestant jurists among them) to claim that the differences between various cultural traditions were as important as, if not more so than, that which was common to them. Jurists like Hotman in France and Coke and Matthew Hale in England, who rejected the universal authority of Rome, developed the beginnings of the view that, as customs, ways of life, outlooks differed, so, necessarily, did the laws and rules by which various societies lived, and that this expressed deep and basic differences in their growth as distinct and at times widely dissimilar social entities. Thereby these lawyers contributed to the notion of cultural diversity.

The very notion of cultures – of the interconnection of diverse activities on the part of members of a given community – of the links that exist between legal systems, religions, arts, sciences, customs and, above all, languages, as well as myths and legends and ritual forms of behaviour, and bind them into identifiable ways of life with differing ideals and values – this entire notion, in its fully conscious, explicit form, is not very old. It owes a great deal to the rise of interest in the classical world of Greece and Rome during the Italian Renaissance, when the obvious and profound differences between their own societies and those of the classical period drew the attention of scholars and those influenced by them to the possibility of more than one true human civilisation. Paradoxically, the very idea of a restoration, the wish to revive the splendours of Greece and Rome after the dark night of the Middle Ages, to reorganise life on the eternally valid principles that were held to govern classical civilisation, gave way gradually, as knowledge of the past increased, to its very opposite, the perception of the irreconcilable differences of outlook and behaviour – and rules and principles – between ancient and modern societies.

A number of historical writers in France in the sixteenth century, men like Vignier, La Popelinière, Le Caron, Bodin, maintained that the study of antiquities – customs, myths, religious rites, languages, as well as inscriptions, coins, works of art and, of course, literary monuments – provided the evidence on which reconstruction of entire cultures could be based. Nevertheless, the view according to which all high cultures were so many branches of the same great tree of enlightenment – that human progress was basically a single forward movement, broken by periods of retrogression and collapse, but never destroyed, constantly renewed, drawing ever nearer to the final victory of reason – continued in general to dominate western thought. Historians and jurists, mainly Protestant, who stressed the all but unbridgeable differences between the old and the new, Romans and Franks, continued to question this assumption. The remote, the exotic, began to be studied seriously and sympathetically. The differences between East and West, for example, or Europe and the Americas, were noted, but little was done by way of producing actual histories or analyses of these dissimilar societies, which fascinated scholars and travellers by their very unlikeness to their own.

A major advance in this direction was made by the early opponents of the literary mandarins of Paris in the eighteenth century, critical of those who took it for granted that the past was to be judged by the degree of the proximity of its theory and practice to the canons of taste of our own enlightened day. Thus we find British and Swiss scholars in the early years of the century who began to investigate legends, sagas, early poetry historically, as the vehicles of the self-expression of particular peoples. Such critics held that the Homeric poems, the songs of the Niebelungs, the Norse sagas, owed their power and beauty to the peculiar traits of the societies by which, in their own times and places, they were generated. The Regius Professor of Hebrew at Oxford University, Bishop Lowth, spoke of the Old Testament as the national epic of the inhabitants of ancient Judaea, not to be judged by the criteria derived from the study of Sophocles or Virgil, Racine or Boileau.

The most famous proponent of this approach is the German poet and critic Johann Gottfried Herder, who insisted upon and celebrated the uniqueness of national cultures, above all their incommensurability, the differences in the criteria by which they could be understood and judged. He was fascinated all his life by the very variety of the paths of development of civilisation, past and present, European and Asian, of which the new interest in oriental scholarship, the languages of India and Persia, provided much convincing concrete evidence. This, in its turn, animated the German historical school of juris-prudence, itself directed against the claims to timeless ration-ality, the assertion of universal validity, whether of Roman law, or the *Code Napoléon*, or the principles proclaimed by the ideologues of the French Revolution and their allies in other lands. At times opposition to the authority of a single immutable natural law, whether as formulated by the Roman Church or the French *lumières*, tended to take highly reactionary forms, justifying oppression, arbitrary rule, and inequalities and injustices of various kinds. Nevertheless, the obverse side of this coin was the attention it attracted to the rich diversity of human institutions and the deep differences of outlook and experience which informed and divided them, and, above all, the impossibility of reducing them to a single pattern, or indeed even to deviations from such a pattern of a systematic kind.

It is worth remarking, in this connection, that the history of ideas offers few examples of so dramatic a change of outlook as the birth of the new belief, not so much in the inevitability, as in the value and importance, of the singular and the unique, of variety as such; and the corresponding conviction that there is something repressive and deeply unattractive in uniformity; that whereas variety is a symptom of vitality, the opposite is a dreary and dead monotony. Indeed, this notion, this feeling, which seems so natural to us now, is not compatible with a view of the world according to which truth is everywhere one, while error is multiple; that the ideal state is one of total harmony, while apparently irreconcilable differences of outlook or opinion are a symptom of imperfection – of incoherence due to error or ignorance or weakness or vice. Yet that kind of worship of oneness is the basis of Platonism and of much subsequent thought, in both Judaism and Christianity, and no less so in the Renaissance and in the Enlightenment, deeply influenced as it was by the triumphant progress of the natural sciences. Even Leibniz, who believed in plenitude, in the value of the greatest possible variety of species, supposed that they must be compatible with one another; even Pericles, who in Thucydides' version of his funeral oration compares the rigid discipline of the militarised state of Sparta unfavourably with the looser texture of Athenian life, nevertheless wanted a harmonious city, to the preservation and enhancement of which all its members should consciously bend their energies. Aristotle conceded that some differences in outlook and character were unavoidable, but did not celebrate this as a virtue and merely recognised it as a part of unalterable human nature. As for the greatest champion in the eighteenth century of variety, Herder, who passionately believed that every culture has its own irreplaceable contribution to make to the progress of the human race, even he believed that there need be – indeed, there should be – no conflict between these dissimilar contributions, that their function is to enrich the universal harmony between nations and institutions, for which men have been created by God or nature. No doctrine that has at its heart a monistic conception of the true and the good and the beautiful, or a teleology according to which everything conspires towards a final harmonious resolution – an ultimate order in which all the apparent confusions and imperfections of the life of the world will be resolved – no doctrine of this kind can allow variety as an independent value to be pursued for its own sake; for variety entails the possibility of the conflict of values, of some irreducible incompatibility between the ideals, or, indeed, the immediate aims, of fully realised, equally virtuous men.

Yet it is this worship of rich variety which was at the centre of the romantic movement, both in the arts and in philosophy. This seems to me to have led to something like the melting away of the very notion of objective truth, at least in the normative sphere. However it might be in the natural sciences, in the realm of ethics, politics, aesthetics it was the authenticity and sincerity of the pursuit of inner goals that mattered; this applied equally to individuals and groups – states, nations, movements. This is most evident in the aesthetics of romanticism, where the notion of eternal models, a Platonic vision of ideal beauty, which the artist seeks to convey, however imperfectly, on canvas or in sound, is replaced by a passionate belief in spiritual freedom, individual creativity. The painter, the poet, the composer do not hold up a mirror to nature, however ideal, but invent; they do not imitate (the doctrine of mimesis), but create not merely the means but the goals that they pursue; these goals represent the self-expression of the artist's own unique, inner vision, to set aside which in response to the demands of some 'external' voice – church, state, public opinion, family, friends, arbiters of taste – is an act of betrayal of what alone justifies their existence for those who are in any sense creative.

This voluntarism and subjectivism, of which the most passionate prophet is the true father of romanticism, Johann Gottlieb Fichte, did, of course, in the end lead to wild anarchy and irrationality, Byronic self-intoxication, the worship of the gloomy outcast, sinister and fascinating, the enemy of settled society, the satanic hero, Cain, Manfred, the Giaour, Melmoth, whose proud independence is purchased at the cost of no matter how much human happiness or how many human lives. In the case of nations, this rejection of the very notion of universally valid values tended at times to inspire nationalism and aggressive chauvinism, the glorification of uncompromising individual or collective self-assertion. In its extreme forms it took criminal and violently pathological forms and culminated in the abandonment of reason and all sense of reality, with often monstrous moral and political consequences.

Yet in its earlier phase this very movement marked the birth of a great extension of historical understanding, whereby the development of human civilisation was conceived not as a single linear movement, now rising, now declining, nor as a dialectical movement of clashing opposites always resolved in a higher synthesis, but as the realisation that cultures are many and various, each embodying scales of value different from those of other cultures and sometimes incompatible with them, yet capable of being understood, that is, seen by observers endowed with sufficiently acute and sympathetic historical insight, as ways of living which human beings could pursue and remain fully human. The principal, officially recognized exponent of this view was Herder; but it may be that the man who first gave it flesh and substance was Walter Scott. The best of Scott's historical novels for the first time presented individuals, classes, and indeed entire societies, in the round, as fully realised characters, not as figures on a stage, the two-dimensional, generalised types of Livy or Tacitus and even Gibbon and Hume. Scott's characters are, as a rule, men and women into whose outlook and feelings and motives the reader can enter; Scott is the first writer to achieve what Herder preached: the conveying of a world that the reader apprehends as being as full as his own, equally real yet profoundly different, but not so remote as not to be understood as we understand contemporaries whose characters and lives differ greatly from our own. The influence of Scott on the writing of history has not been sufficiently investigated. To see the past through the eyes of those who lived through it, from the inside, as it were, and not merely as a succession of distant facts and events and figures in a procession to be described from some external vantage-point as so much material for narrative or statistical treatment — to be able to achieve this kind of understanding, even though with considerable effort, is a claim to a capacity that could scarcely have been made before the modern age by historians concerned with the truth.

Herder may have been the effective discoverer of the nature of this kind of imaginative insight, but the man who first conceived, in concrete terms, the possibility of it, and provided examples of how such a method could be employed, was the early-eighteenth-century Italian thinker Giambattista Vico. Vico's principal work remained unread save by a handful of Italians and those few Frenchmen to whom, years later, the Italians spoke of him, until, at the beginning of the last century, Jules Michelet came upon him, caught fire, and celebrated his achievements across Europe.

II

Vico is the true father both of the modern concept of culture and of what one might call cultural pluralism, according to which each authentic culture has its own unique vision, its own scale of values, which, in the course of development, is superseded by other visions and values, but never wholly so: that is, earlier value-systems do not become totally unintelligible to succeeding generations. Unlike such relativists as Spengler or Westermarck, Vico did not suppose that men are encapsulated within their own epoch or culture, insulated in a box without windows and consequently incapable of understanding other societies and periods whose values may be widely different from theirs and which they may find strange or repellent. His deepest belief was that what men have made, other men can understand. It may take an immense amount of painful effort to decipher the meaning of conduct or language different from our own. Nevertheless, according to Vico, if anything is meant by the term 'human', there must be enough that is common to all such beings for it to be possible, by a sufficient effort of imagination, to grasp what the world must have looked like to creatures, remote in time or space, who practised such rites, and used such words, and created such works of art as the natural means of self-expression involved in the attempt to understand and interpret their worlds to themselves.

Fundamentally, Vico's is the same sort of method as that used by most modern social anthropologists in seeking to understand the behaviour and imagery of primitive tribes (or what there is left of them), whose myths and tales and metaphors and similes and allegories they do not dismiss as so much nonsense, confusion in the heads of irrational, childlike barbarians (as the eighteenth century was apt to do): rather they seek for a key to enable them to enter into their worlds, to see through their eyes, remembering that men (as a later philosopher has said) are at once subjects and objects to themselves. They look upon the primitives, therefore, not as so many creatures who can only be described, but whose motives cannot be fathomed – plants or animals, with only the laws of physics or biology to account for their behaviour – but as beings akin to ourselves, inhabitants of a world in which such behaviour and such words can be interpreted as intelligible responses to the natural conditions in which they find themselves and which they seek to understand.

In a sense, the mere existence of an extraordinary variety of very dissimilar languages – sometimes among neighbouring societies (as, for example, in the Caucasus or in Pacific islands) – is itself an index or, one might say, a model of the irreducible variety of human self-expression, such that even in the case of cognate languages, complete translation of one into any other is in principle impossible; and the gap – indicative of differences in ways of perceiving and acting – is at times very wide indeed.

In a sense this approach is not so very different from what is involved in any act of understanding others, their words, their looks, their gestures, which convey to us their intentions and aspirations. We have recourse to purely scientific methods of decipherment only when communication breaks down; we formulate hypotheses and seek to verify them, to establish the authenticity of documents, the dates of antiquities, the analysis of the materials of which they are made, the degree of reliability of testimony, sources of information, and the like. For all of this we have recourse to normal scientific methods, and not to the kind of inspired guesswork that must inevitably enter to some extent into any attempt to understand what it must have been like to have lived in a given situation at a particular time, to have to cope with the forces of nature or other men, to grasp what things must have seemed like to those who believed in the efficacy of witchcraft, incantations, sacrifices to placate the gods or to make nature more amenable to human will.

Because our ancestors were men, Vico supposes that they knew, as we know, what it is to love and hate, hope and fear, to want, to pray, to fight, to betray, to oppress, to be oppressed, to revolt. Roman law and Roman history are what Vico knew best; consequently many of his examples come from the history and legislation of early Rome. His etymologies are often fanciful, but his account of the economic circumstances which, in his view, led to this or that type of legislation in what he regards as continuing class warfare between plebeians and patricians is a great advance on earlier theories. The historical details may be wrong, even absurd, the knowledge may be defective, the critical methods insufficient – but the approach is bold, original and fruitful. Vico never tells us what he means by what he calls 'entering into' or 'descending to' the minds of primitive men, but from his practice in the *Scienza nuova* it is plain that it is imaginative insight that he demands, a gift which he calls *fantasia*. Later German thinkers spoke of *verstehen* – to under-stand – as opposed to *wissen*, the kind of knowledge we have in the natural sciences, where 'entering' is not in question, since one cannot enter into the hopes and fears of bees and beavers. Vico's *fantasia* is indispensable to his conception of historical knowledge; it is unlike the knowledge that Julius Caesar is dead, or that Rome was not built in a day, or that thirteen is a prime number, or that a week has seven days; nor yet is it like knowledge of how to ride a bicycle or engage in statistical research or win a battle. It is more like knowing what it is to be poor, to belong to a nation, to be a revolutionary, to be converted to a religion, to fall in love, to be seized by nameless terror, to be delighted by a work of art. I give these examples only as analogies, for Vico is interested not in the experience of individuals but in that of entire societies. It is this kind of collective self-awareness – what men thought, imagined, felt, wanted, strove for in the face of physical nature at a particular stage of social development, expressed by institutions, monu-ments, symbols, ways of writing and speech, generated by their efforts to represent and explain their condition to themselves – that he wished to analyse, and he thought he had found a path to it not trodden by others. The door that he opened to the understanding of cultural history by the 'decoding' of myths, ceremonies, laws, artistic images, he regarded as his major achievement. No wonder that Karl Marx, in a well-known letter to Lassalle, said that Vico had moments of genius as a writer on social evolution.

No one has stronger claims than Vico to be considered as the begetter of historical anthropology. Jules Michelet, who re-garded himself as his disciple, was right: Vico was indeed the forgotten anticipator of the German historical school, the first and in some ways the most formidable opponent of unhistorical doctrines of natural law, of timeless authority, of the assumption made by, for example, Spinoza, that any truth could have been discovered by anyone, at any time, and that it is just bad luck that men have stumbled for so long in darkness because they did not or could not employ their reason correctly. The idea of historical development in this large sense, as a succession of cultures, each of which stems from its predecessor in the course of men's constant struggle against the forces of nature, which at a certain stage of social development generates the war between economic classes, themselves formed by the very process of production, is a major event in the history of the growth of human self-understanding. This conception of the nature of historic change (whatever adumbrations of it are to be found in social thought from Hesiod to Harrington) had never before been so fully stated.

Vico's critics in modern times have pointed out that his doctrine that man can understand only what he makes is insufficient for the discovery and analysis of cultures – are there not unconscious drives, irrational factors, of which we are not aware, even retrospectively? Do acts not often lead to unintended consequences, unforeseen accidental results not 'made' by the actors? Is not Providence, on Vico's view – his form of Hegel's 'cunning of reason' – using our very vices to create forms of life which are to mankind's benefit (a somewhat similar idea was advanced by Vico's contemporary Bernard Mandeville), something that cannot be 'understood' by men, since, according to Vico, it springs from the will of God, a spirit to whose workings we are not privy? Moreover, are we not unavoidably committed to importing some of our own concepts and categories into our understanding of the past? Did not the great classical scholar Ulrich von Wilamowitz-Moellendorff tell us (alluding to Homer's account of Achilles, whose ghost was summoned from the nether regions by Odysseus) that the dead cannot speak until they have drunk blood? But since it is our blood that we offer them it is with our own voices that they talk to us, and in our words, not theirs; and, if this is so, is not our claim to understand them and their worlds to some degree always illusory?

All these considerations are doubtless valid, and an obstacle to the idea that, since human history is made by men, it can therefore, even in principle, be wholly understood by 'entering' into the minds of our ancestors. Yet even though human history is more than an account of men's hopes or ideas and the actions that embody them, and not solely an account of human experience or stages of consciousness (as, at times, both Hegel and Collingwood seemed to believe), and even though Marx is right in saying that it is men, indeed, who make human history (not out of whole cloth, however, but in conditions provided by nature and by earlier human institutions, which may lead to situations not necessarily related to the purpose of the actors) – even though Vico's claims now seem overambitious, yet something of importance survives despite these qualifications. Everyone is today aware of the fundamental difference between, on the one hand, those historians who paint portraits of entire societies or groups within them that are rounded and three-dimensional, so that we believe, whether rightly or mistakenly, that we are able to tell what it would have been like to have lived in such conditions, and, on the other, antiquaries, chroniclers, accumulators of facts or statistics on which large generalisations can be founded, learned compilers, or theorists who look on the use of imagination as opening the door to the horrors of guesswork, subjectivism, journalism, or worse.

This all-important distinction rests precisely on the attitude to the faculty that Vico called *fantasia*, without which the past cannot, in his view, be resurrected. The crucial role he assigns to the imagination must not blind us – and did not blind him – to the necessity for verification; he allows that critical methods of examining evidence are indispensable. Yet without *fantasia* the past remains dead; to bring it to life we need, at least ideally, to hear men's voices, to conjecture (on the basis of such evidence as we can gather) what may have been their experience, their forms of expression, their values, outlook, aims, ways of living; without this we cannot grasp whence we came, how we come to be as we are now, not merely physically or biologically and, in a narrow sense, politically and institutionally, but socially, psychologically, morally; without this there can be no genuine self-understanding. We call great historians only those who not only are in full control of the factual evidence obtained by the use of the best critical methods available to them, but also possess the depth of imaginative insight that characterises gifted novelists. Clio, as the English historian G. M. Trevelyan pointed out long ago, is, after all, a muse.

III

One of the most interesting corollaries of the application of Vico's method of reconstructing the past is what I have called cultural pluralism – a panorama of a variety of cultures, the pursuit of different, and sometimes incompatible, ways of life, ideals, standards of value. This, in its turn, entails that the perennial idea of the perfect society, in which truth, justice, freedom, happiness, virtue coalesce in their most perfect forms, is not merely Utopian (which few deny), but intrinsically incoherent; for if some of these values prove to be incompatible, they cannot – conceptually cannot – coalesce. Every culture expresses itself in works of art, of thought, in ways of living and action, each of which possesses its own character which can neither be combined nor necessarily form stages of a single progress towards a single universal goal.

The conception of different visions of life and their values, which cannot be represented as capable of fitting into one great harmonious structure, is illustrated vividly in that part of Vico's *Scienza nuova* which deals with Homer. His views stand in sharp contrast to the prevalent aesthetic doctrines of his time, according to which, despite some deviations towards relativism, standards of excellence are objective, universal and timeless, *quod semper*, *quod ubique*, *quod ab omnibus*. Thus, to give a well-known example, while some held that the ancients were better poets than the moderns, others maintained the opposite – it was over this that the famous Battle of the Ancients and Moderns was fought in Vico's younger days. The relevant point is that the opponents in this conflict defended their positions in terms of identical values which both sides considered to be eternally applicable to all times and all forms of art.

Not so Vico. He tells us that 'in the world's childhood men were by nature sublime poets'. For imagination is strong in primitive peoples, thinking power feeble. Homer, Vico believed, lived towards the end of the civilisation that he described with a degree of genius that no later writer had been able to approach, let alone equal. Homeric men are 'crude, boorish, savage, proud, stubborn'. Achilles is cruel, violent, vindictive, concerned only with his own feelings; yet he is depicted as a blameless warrior, the ideal hero of the Homeric world. The values of that world have passed away; Vico was living in a more humane age. But this does not mean, so he maintained, that the art of this later day is necessarily superior to that of the most sublime of all poets. Homer clearly admired the values of these frightful men; his marvellous celebration of savage and truculent warriors engaged in cruel butchery, his account of the Olympian gods which had so shocked Plato and caused Aristotle to wish to 'correct' him, could not have been composed by the cultivated poets of the Renaissance or of Vico's own times.

Vico is clear that this is an irremediable loss. So, too, he speaks of Roman writers who hold up men like Brutus, Mucius Scaevola, Manlius, the Decii for our admiration – men who, as he points out, ruined, robbed, crushed the poor unhappy Roman *plebs*. He reminds us that when, in an even earlier age, King Agis of Sparta tried to help the oppressed, he was executed as a traitor. Yet it is grim, ferocious men of this kind by and for whom unsurpassed masterpieces were written – works that we cannot rival. We may be superior to these barbarians (Vico believes) in rational thought, knowledge, humanity, but we do not, for that very reason, possess the marvellous, elemental power of imagination or language of the magnificent epics and sagas which only a brutal and primitive culture can produce. For Vico there is no true progress in the arts; the genius of one age cannot be compared with that of another. He would have thought it idle to ask whether Sophocles is not a better poet than Virgil or Virgil than Racine. Each culture creates masterpieces that belong to it and it alone, and when it is over one can admire its triumphs or deplore its vices: but they are no more; nothing can restore them to us. If this is so, it follows that the very notion of a perfect society, in which all the excellences of all cultures will harmoniously coalesce, does not make sense. One virtue may turn out to be incompatible with another. The uncombinable remains uncombinable. The virtues of the Homeric heroes are not the virtues of the age of Plato and Aristotle in the name of which they attacked the morality of the Homeric poems; nor are the virtues of fifth-century Athens, for all that Voltaire thought otherwise, similar to those of Renaissance Florence or the Court of Versailles. There is both loss and gain in the passing from one stage of civilisation to another, but, whatever the gain, what is lost is lost for ever and will not be restored in some earthly paradise.

There is something boldly original about a thinker who, in so self-satisfied a civilisation as that into which Vico was born, one which saw itself as a vast improvement on the brutality, absurdity, ignorance of earlier times, dared maintain that an unapproachably sublime poem could have been produced only by a cruel, savage and, to later generations, morally repellent age. This amounts to a denial of the very possibility of a harmony of all excellences in an ideal world. From this it follows that to judge the attainments of any one age by applying to them a single absolute criterion – that of the critics and theorists of a later period – not only is unhistorical and anachronistic, but rests on a fallacy, the assumption of the existence of timeless standards – the ideal values of an ideal world – when in fact some of the most greatly admired works of men are organically bound up with a culture some aspects of which we may – perhaps cannot help but – condemn, even while claiming to understand why it is that men situated as these were must have felt, thought and acted as they did.

The notion of a perfect society in which all that men have striven for finds total fulfilment is consequently perceived to be incoherent, at any rate in terrestrial terms: Homer cannot coexist with Dante; nor Dante with Galileo. This is a truism now. But the anti-Utopian implications of the section on Homer in the *Scienza nuova*, largely neglected as they were in the author's time, have lessons for our own day. The unparalleled services of the Enlightenment in its battle against obscurantism, oppression, injustice and irrationality of every kind are not in question. But it may be that all great liberating movements, if they are to break through the resistance of accepted dogma and custom, are bound to exaggerate, and be blind to the virtues of that which they attack. The proposition that man is at once subject and object to himself does not lie easily with the views of the *philosophes* of Paris, for whom mankind is, in the first place, an object of scientific investigation. The underlying assumption that human nature is basically the same at all times, everywhere, and obeys eternal laws beyond human control, is a conception that only a handful of bold thinkers have dared to question. Yet to accept it in the name of science is, in effect, to ignore and downgrade man's role as creator and destroyer of values, of entire forms of life, of man as a subject, a creature with an inner life denied to other inhabitants of the universe. The most celebrated Utopians of modern times, from Thomas More to Mably, Saint-Simon, Fourier, Owen and their followers, provided a somewhat static picture of men's basic attributes, and, in consequence, an equally static description of an attainable perfect society. Thereby they ignored the character of men as self-transforming beings, able to choose freely, within the limits imposed by nature and history, between rival, mutually incompatible ends.

The conception of man as an actor, a purposive being, moved

by his own conscious aims as well as causal laws, capable of unpredictable flights of thought and imagination, and of his culture as created by his effort to achieve self-knowledge and control of his environment in the face of material and psychic forces which he may use but cannot evade – this conception lies at the heart of all truly historical study. To exercise their proper function, historians require the capacity for imaginative insight, without which the bones of the past remain dry and lifeless. To deploy it is, and always has been, a risky business.

ALLEGED RELATIVISM IN
EIGHTEENTH-CENTURY
EUROPEAN THOUGHT

IT IS an accepted truth that the central view of the French
philosophes (whatever their, often very sharp, differences) is that
(in the words of the eminent American anthropologist Clifford
Geertz) man is 'of a piece with nature': there is a human nature
'as invariant . . . as Newton's universe'.[1] The laws that govern
it may be different, but they exist. Manners, fashions, tastes
may differ, but the same passions which move men everywhere,
at all times, cause the same behaviour. Only 'the constant, the
general, the universal' is real, and therefore only this is 'truly
human'.[2] Only that is true which any rational observer, at any
time, in any place, can, in principle, discover. Rational
methods – hypothesis, observation, generalisation, deduction,
experimental verification where it is possible – can solve social
and individual problems, as they have triumphantly solved
those of physics and astronomy, and are progressively solving
those of chemistry, biology and economics; philosophy, that is
ethics, politics, aesthetics, logic, theory of knowledge, can and
should be transformed into a general science of man – the
natural science of anthropology; once knowledge of man's true
nature is attained, men's real needs will be clear: the only
remaining tasks are to discover how they may be satisfied, and to
act upon this knowledge. The majority of human ills – hunger,

[1] Clifford Geertz, *The Interpretation of Cultures* (New York, 1973; London,
1975), p. 34.
[2] ibid., p. 35.

disease, insecurity, poverty, misery, injustice, oppression – are due to ignorance, indolence and error, consciously or unconsciously fomented by those whose interests are served by this reign of darkness; the triumph of the scientific spirit will sweep away the forces of prejudice, superstition, stupidity and cruelty, too long concealed by the mumbo-jumbo of theologians and lawyers.

Some *philosophes* were pessimistic about the prospects of universal enlightenment, at any rate in a foreseeable future; but none among them denied that it was in principle, if not in practice, attainable. They knew, of course, that there had always existed those who had been sceptical about the central thesis itself – that it was possible, even in principle, to discover such final solutions: relativists, such as the Greek sophists assailed by Plato, or those who agreed with Aristotle that 'fire burns both here and in Persia, but what is thought just changes before our very eyes'.[1] There were sceptics from Aenesidemus, Carneades and Sextus Empiricus to their modern disciples – Montaigne and his followers – who had maintained that in the vast welter of diverse human beliefs and practices (described as early as Herodotus, and by Voltaire's time much added to by the great increase in the number of travellers' tales and historical investigations) no universal rules could possibly be found. There were Christian thinkers, whether Bossuet or Pascal, who held that man in his fallen state had no means of establishing the full truth, which only God possessed. The majority of the French *philosophes* reacted against this outlook: for them the Christian view of man was demonstrably false. As for the doubts of Montaigne or Charron or La Mothe Le Vayer, these had been understandable in a confused, prescientific age, but could now be dissolved, as those of the old natural philosophers had been, by the application of Newtonian methods.

Nor were such contemporary doubters as Montesquieu or Hume a source of danger; Montesquieu did not doubt the

[1] Aristotle, *Nicomachean Ethics*, $1134^{b}26$.

universality of ultimate human values, founded, as they were, unlike passing tastes or conventions, on eternal reason or nature;[1] all men by nature sought security, justice, social stability, happiness; only means differed according to natural, environmental and social conditions and the institutions, habits, tastes, conventions, resulting from them. In morals and politics and even aesthetic judgements, Montesquieu is no less objectivist about men's central ends than Helvétius: he merely probed and analysed more and preached less.

As for Hume, he did away with the notion of natural necessity, and thereby did, indeed, destroy the metaphysical cement which had hitherto held the objective world together as a system of logically linked relations within, and between, facts and events; but even he did not seek to disrupt the accepted patterns of these relations, but merely transposed them into the empirical mode, from *a priori* necessity to *de facto* probability. A man who, in a famous passage, said 'human nature remains still the same, in its principles and operations . . . Ambition, avarice, self-love, vanity, friendship, generosity, public spirit', or again, that if a traveller brought us 'an account of men, wholly different from any with whom we were ever acquainted' – far nicer than any we have met – 'we should immediately . . . detect the falsehood, and prove him a liar, with the same certainty as if he had stuffed his narration with stories of

[1] In his *Spicilège* (554), before describing the plot of a Chinese play, the first he had come across, Montesquieu remarks, 'Elle m'a paru contre nos mœurs, mais non pas contre la raison'; so too in his *Pensées* (122) he distinguishes *mœurs*, which vary widely, from *la nature*, which is immutable; accordingly (in *pensée* 817) he declares that modern comedies are at fault in seeking to ridicule human passions (which are natural and can never be ridiculous) as opposed to manners, which can be absurd. The limits of relativism are here firmly established: the context is aesthetic, but examples show that the principle extends to the whole of experience. My thanks are due to Professor Charles Jacques Beyer, who drew my attention to these passages: see his article, 'Montesquieu et le relativisme esthétique', *Studies on Voltaire and the Eighteenth Century* 24 (1963), 171–82. In *Œuvres complètes de Montesquieu*, ed. A. Masson, 3 vols (Paris, 1950–55), the passages are to be found in vol. 2, pp. 846, 42 and 239 respectively.

centaurs and dragons, miracles and prodigies'[1] – such a thinker offered no serious threat to the programme of the *philosophes*, *pace* Carl Becker's over-dramatised account of Hume's alleged subversion of the heavenly city of the eighteenth century.[2]

Nor were Diderot's speculations on how the world of the blind and deaf would differ from that of the healthy a form of relativism; for differences of climate, legislation, education, physique only dictated different paths to the same goals, which nature and reason had set for all men, everywhere. Locke, despite his celebrated long list of societies which looked without disapproval on parricide, infanticide, cannibalism and other monstrous practices, nevertheless held that *'Vertues* and *Vices* . . .* for the most part [are] the same everywhere', inasmuch as they are 'absolutely necessary to hold Society together', which amounts to a very strong form of utilitarianism.[3] Among eighteenth-century writers perhaps Sade and Deschamps uttered genuinely relativist opinions about ends as well as means, but they were marginal figures and disregarded. When Racine says 'The taste of Paris conforms to that of Athens. My spectators have been moved by the same things which, in other times, brought tears to the eyes of the most cultivated classes of Greece',[4] he is echoed equally by Voltaire and Dr Johnson.[5] When cultural differences are stripped off, what remains, at least until Burke, is Rousseau's natural man. So, too, within

[1] David Hume, *An Enquiry concerning Human Understanding*, section 8, part 1: pp. 83–4 in David Hume, *Enquiries*, ed. L. A. Selby-Bigge, 3rd ed., revised by P. H. Nidditch (Oxford, 1975). For discussion see Lester G. Crocker, *An Age of Crisis: Man and World in Eighteenth-Century French Thought* (Baltimore, 1959), pp. 186-7.

[2] Carl L. Becker, *The Heavenly City of the Eighteenth-Century Philosophers* (New Haven, 1932).

[3] *An Essay concerning Human Understanding*, book 1, chapter 3 ('No Innate Practical Principles'), sections 9, 10; book 2, chapter 28 ('Of Other Relations'), section 11.

[4] Jean Racine, Preface to *Iphigénie* – vol. 1, p. 671 in Racine, *Œuvres complètes*, ed. Raymond Picard, 2 vols ([Paris], 1969, 1966) – quoted by Geertz, op. cit. (p. 70 above, note 1), p. 35.

[5] Geertz, loc. cit.

every kind of civilised man there is Diderot's immutable natural man struggling to get out: the two are everywhere locked in a civil war that is the permanent condition of human culture everywhere.

This position, perhaps the deepest single assumption of western thought, was attacked by two of the fathers of modern historicism,[1] Vico and Herder. We all know that these thinkers denied the possibility of establishing the final truth in all the provinces of human thought by the application of the laws of the natural sciences. Both Vico and Herder are sometimes described as relativists. In this connection one thing ought to be made clear. There are at least two types of relativism, that of judgements of fact, and that of judgements of values. The first, in its strongest form, denies the very possibility of objective knowledge of facts, since all belief is conditioned by the place in the social system, and therefore by the interests, conscious or not, of the theorist, or of the group or class to which he belongs. The weaker version (for example that of Karl Mannheim) exempts the natural sciences from this predicament, or identifies a privileged group (in Mannheim's view, the intelligentsia) as being, somewhat mysteriously, free from these distorting factors.

Whether the first, or stronger, version is ultimately self-refuting (as I am inclined to believe) is a philosophical crux that cannot be discussed here. It is, however, only the second type of relativism, that of values or entire outlooks, that is in question here. No one, so far as I know, has ascribed relativism regarding factual knowledge to Vico or Herder. Their critique of the unhistorical approach which they attribute to the French *lumières* is confined to the interpretation and evaluation of past attitudes and cultures. I wonder how much *Wissenssoziologie* (radical sociology of knowledge) as we know it today is to be found before Marx and the Young Hegelians. Vico regarded

---

[1] I use the term not in Karl Popper's sense, but in the more usual one employed by Meinecke, Troeltsch and Croce.

each stage of the historical cycle of cultures (through which each gentile nation was bound to pass) as embodying its own autonomous values, its own vision of the world, in particular its own conception of the relations of men to one another and to the forces of nature; and he believed that it was in terms of this alone that their culture, that is, the significance attached by these men themselves to what they did and what was done to them, could be understood by us, their descendants. He maintained that men at each stage of this process generated their own expressions and interpretations of their experience – indeed, that their experience *was* these expressions and interpretations, which took the form of words, images, myths, ritual, institutions, artistic creation, worship. Only the study of these could convey what the human past was like, and enable posterity not merely to record it, which could be accomplished by a mere description of the regularities of behaviour, but also to understand it, that is, to grasp what these men were at – not merely to describe the gestures, but to reveal the intention behind them – that is, tell us what their words, movements, gestures meant to themselves; only so could we avoid being totally at sea about them. To understand what our ancestors saw, felt, thought, it is not enough merely to record, and offer causal explanations for, observed human behaviour, as zoologists record the behaviour of animals – which, for example, Condorcet regarded as basically the correct approach to human societies. For Vico, each of these cultures, or stages of development, is not just a link in a causal chain or contingent sequence, but a phase in a providential plan governed by divine purpose. Each phase is incommensurable with the others, since each lives by its own light and can be understood only in its own terms, even though these terms form a single intelligible process, which is not wholly, or, perhaps, even largely, intelligible to us. If a civilisation is interpreted or, worse still, evaluated by the application of criteria that hold only for other civilisations, its character will be misunderstood – by a form of what is nowadays attacked as cultural imperialism; and the account presented will, at best, be a systematically misleading, at worst a scarcely coherent story, a haphazard succession of events, somewhat like Voltaire's entertaining parodies of the Dark Ages.

Neither Vico nor Herder is a Humean empiricist: human history for them is not a mere set of *de facto* regularities; the pattern – every section of it – serves God's purposes; the different characters of each culture are imposed by this pattern – a species of temporalised natural law. Hence the constant warnings by both against cultural egocentricity and anachronism, and their appeals (whether valid or not) to the use of a special imaginative faculty to enable historians to enter, with whatever difficulty, into outlooks which they perceive, even while understanding ('entering into') them, to be unlike our own. This doctrine, whether, as in the case of Vico, it is applied to the past stages of a recurrent cycle, or, as it was by Herder, to differences of national culture, is wholly incompatible with that expressed in Racine's lines quoted above, or that of Voltaire, who seemed to be convinced that the central values of civilised men everywhere, and at all times, were, more or less, identical; it was still less compatible, if that is possible, with the position of those Encyclopedists who believed in linear progress – a single upward movement of mankind from darkness to light, which, rising in ignorance, brutish savagery, superstition, delusion, after much stumbling, many detours and retrogressions, finally culminated in the ideal reign of knowledge, virtue, wisdom and happiness.

I come to my central point. Because of their conception of the cultural autonomy of different societies (whether divided by space or time) and the incommensurability of their systems of values, Vico's and Herder's opposition to the central tenets of the French Enlightenment have commonly been described as a form of relativism. This *idée reçue* seems to me now to be a widespread error, like the label of relativism attached to Hume and Montesquieu, an error which, I must admit, I have in the past perpetrated myself. A distinguished and learned critic has wondered if I fully appreciate the implications of the historical relativism of Vico and Herder which, unacknowledged by them, dominated the historical outlook of these Christian thinkers, and constituted a problem which has persisted to this day.[1] If we grant the assumption that Vico and Herder were in fact relativists – that is, not merely historicists who hold that human thought and action are fully intelligible only in relation to their historical context, but upholders of a theory of ideology according to which the ideas and attitudes of individuals or groups are inescapably determined by varying conditioning factors, say, their place in the evolving social structures of their societies, or the relations of production, or genetic, psychological or other causes, or combinations of these – on an assumption of that kind, the point made by my critic was valid. But I now believe this to be a mistaken interpretation of Vico and Herder, although I have, in my time, inadvertently contributed to it myself. Doubts about the possibility of objective knowledge of the past, about changing perspectives on it determined by transient, culture-conditioned attitudes and values, such as are said to have oppressed Mommsen towards the end of his life, and troubled Wilamowitz in his prime, problems anxiously discussed principally by German thinkers – Max Weber, Troeltsch, Rickert, Simmel – and leading to the radical conclusions of Karl Mannheim and his school – these problems seem to me to have originated in the nineteenth century. When Voltaire said that history was a pack of tricks which we played upon the dead, that cynical witticism can hardly be regarded as contradicting his general moral and cultural objectivism. True relativism developed from other and later sources: German romantic irrationalism, the metaphysics of Schopenhauer and Nietzsche, the growth of schools of social anthropology, the doctrines of William Graham Sumner and Edward Westermarck, above all the influence of thinkers who were not necessarily relativists themselves – Marx, for example, or Freud, whose analyses of

---

[1] Arnaldo Momigliano, 'On the Pioneer Trail', *New York Review of Books*, 11 November 1976, pp. 33–8.

appearance or illusion and reality entailed belief in the objectivity of their own disciplines, without, perhaps, awareness of at any rate some of their full implications.[1]

I may be speaking in ignorance, and stand ready to be corrected, but I know of no consistent effort by any influential thinker in the eighteenth century to put forward relativist views. Some leading French *philosophes* certainly declared that passions and 'interest' could unconsciously mould values and entire outlooks; but they also believed that critical reason could dissipate this and remove obstacles to objective knowledge both of fact and of value. So too Lessing, who believed that values alter as mankind progresses, was not troubled by relativist doubts, any more than the leading historians of the first half of the nineteenth century – Ranke, Macaulay, Carlyle, Guizot, Michelet (the self-confessed disciple of Vico), Taine, Fustel de Coulanges; not even the early nationalists influenced by Herder. There is, so far as I can see, no relativism in the best-known attacks on the Enlightenment by reactionary thinkers – Hamann, Justus Möser, Burke, Maistre. Relativism, in its modern form, tends to spring from the view that men's outlooks are unavoidably determined by forces of which they are often unaware – Schopenhauer's irrational cosmic force; Marx's class-bound morality; Freud's unconscious drives; the social anthropologists' panorama of the irreconcilable variety of customs and beliefs conditioned by circumstances largely uncontrolled by men.

Let me return to the alleged relativism of Vico and Herder. Perhaps I can make my point best by giving as an example their aesthetic views. When Vico speaks of the splendour of the Homeric poems and gives reasons why they could only have been produced in a society dominated by a violent, ambitious,

---

[1] This is not a philosophical essay, and therefore not the place to discuss such problems as whether relativism, if its full implications are drawn out, is self-refuting, or, even if true, incapable of being stated without self-contradiction.

cruel and avaricious élite of 'heroes', so that such epics could not be generated in his own 'enlightened' times; when Herder tells us that to understand the Bible we must try to enter the world of nomadic Judaean shepherds, or that men who have seen sailors struggling with the waters of the Skagerrak can better understand the stern beauty of the old Scandinavian sagas and songs; when both thinkers maintain that unless we succeed in doing this we shall not understand what these earlier men lived by, spiritually as well as materially, they are not telling us that the values of these societies, dissimilar to ours, cast doubts on the objectivity of our own, or are undermined by them, because the existence of conflicting values or incompatible outlooks must mean that at most only one of these is valid, the rest being false; or, alternatively, that none belong to the kind of judgements that can be considered either valid or invalid. Rather, they are inviting us to look at societies different from our own, the ultimate values of which we can perceive to be wholly understandable ends of life for men who are different, indeed, from us, but human beings, *semblables*, into whose circumstances we can, by a great effort which we are commanded to make, find a way, 'enter', to use Vico's term. We are urged to look upon life as affording a plurality of values, equally genuine, equally ultimate, above all equally objective; incapable, therefore, of being ordered in a timeless hierarchy, or judged in terms of some one absolute standard. There is a finite variety of values and attitudes, some of which one society, some another, have made their own, attitudes and values which members of other societies may admire or condemn (in the light of their own value-systems) but can always, if they are sufficiently imaginative and try hard enough, contrive to understand – that is, see to be intelligible ends of life for human beings situated as these men were. In the house of human history there are many mansions: this view may be un-Christian; yet it appears to have been held by both these pious eighteenth-century thinkers.

This doctrine is called pluralism. There are many objective ends, ultimate values, some incompatible with others, pursued by different societies at various times, or by different groups in the same society, by entire classes or churches or races, or by particular individuals within them, any one of which may find itself subject to conflicting claims of uncombinable, yet equally ultimate and objective, ends. Incompatible these ends may be; but their variety cannot be unlimited, for the nature of men, however various and subject to change, must possess some generic character if it is to be called human at all. This holds, *a fortiori*, of differences between entire cultures. There is a limit beyond which we can no longer understand what a given creature is at; what kinds of rules it follows in its behaviour; what its gestures mean. In such situations, when the possibility of communication breaks down, we speak of derangement, of incomplete humanity. But within the limits of humanity the variety of ends, finite though it is, can be extensive. The fact that the values of one culture may be incompatible with those of another, or that they are in conflict within one culture or group or in a single human being at different times – or, for that matter, at one and the same time – does not entail relativism of values, only the notion of a plurality of values not structured hierarchically; which, of course, entails the permanent possibility of inescapable conflict between values, as well as incompatibility between the outlooks of different civilisations or of stages of the same civilisation.

Relativism is something different: I take it to mean a doctrine according to which the judgement of a man or a group, since it is the expression or statement of a taste, or emotional attitude or outlook, is simply what it is, with no objective correlate which determines its truth or falsehood. I like mountains, you do not; I love history, he thinks it is bunkum: it all depends on one's point of view. It follows that to speak of truth or falsehood on these assumptions is literally meaningless. But the values of each culture or phase of a culture are (for Vico or Herder or their disciples) not mere psychological, but objective facts, although not therefore necessarily commensurable, either within a culture or (still less) as between cultures. Let me offer an illustration of this view. The English critic Wyndham Lewis, in a work named *The Demon of Progress in the Arts*,[1] pointed out that it is absurd to speak, as many have, and still do, of progress between one style of art and another. His principal point was that it was absurd to range artists in a linear series – to think of, let us say, Dante as a more developed Homer, or of Shakespeare as an inferior Addison (as Voltaire thought), or of Phidias as a rudimentary Rodin. Are the paintings of Lascaux superior or inferior to those of Poussin? Is Mozart a less developed forerunner of *musique concrète*? The Battle of the Ancients and Moderns was based on the presupposition that such questions were answerable; perhaps even Montesquieu thought so. Vico and Herder did not. For them, values are many; some of the most fascinating come to light in the course of voyages, both in time and space; some among them cannot, in principle, be harmonised with one another. This leads to the conclusion, not explicitly formulated by either thinker, that the ancient ideal, common to many cultures and especially to that of the Enlightenment, of a perfect society in which all true human ends are reconciled, is conceptually incoherent. But this is not relativism. That doctrine, in all its versions, holds that there are no objective values; some varieties of it maintain that men's outlooks are so conditioned by natural or cultural factors as to render them incapable of seeing the values of other societies or epochs as no less worthy of pursuit than their own, if not by themselves then by others. The most extreme versions of cultural relativism, which stress the vast differences of cultures, hold that one culture can scarcely begin to understand what other civilisations lived by – can only describe their behaviour but not its purpose or meaning, as some early anthropologists described the behaviour of savage societies. If this were true (as, for example, Spengler, and at some moments even Dilthey, seemed to say) the very idea of the history of civilisation becomes an insoluble puzzle.

[1] (London, 1954).

At the heart of the best-known type of modern historical relativism lies the conception of men wholly bound by tradition or culture or class or generation to particular attitudes or scales of value which cause other outlooks or ideals to seem strange and, at times, even unintelligible; if the existence of such outlooks is recognised, this inevitably leads to scepticism about objective standards, since it becomes meaningless to ask which of them is correct. This is not at all Vico's position; nor, despite one or two remarks,[1] is it in general that of Herder either. This would indeed have been, to say the least, a strange doctrine for Christian thinkers, however unorthodox, to hold: paradoxes are not unknown in the history of ideas; but no such oddity arises in this case. Both thinkers advocate the use of the historical imagination, which can enable us to 'descend to' or 'enter' or 'feel oneself into' the mentality of remote societies; thereby we understand them, that is grasp (or believe that we grasp, for we cannot ever be certain, even though Vico and Herder seem to speak as if we can) what the acts of the men in question, the sounds or marks on stone or papyrus that they make, or their bodily movements, mean: that is, what they are signs of, what part they play in the conceptions of their worlds held by these men and women themselves, how they interpret what goes on; we are urged (to quote Clifford Geertz again) to achieve 'familiarity with the imaginative universe within which their acts are signs'.[2] This is the goal, he tells us, of social anthropology; it is certainly the conception of historical understanding of the past held by both Vico and Herder. If the quest is successful,

---

[1] As when he says 'Mother Nature . . . has put tendencies towards diversity in our hearts; she has placed part of the diversity in a close circle around us; she has restricted man's view so that by force of habit the circle became a horizon, beyond which he could not see nor scarcely speculate': J. G. Herder, *Sämmtliche Werke*, ed. Bernhard Suphan, 33 vols (Berlin, 1877–1913), vol. 5, pp. 509–10. Where the passages I quote are included in his selection, I have followed the translations by F. M. Barnard in his *J. G. Herder on Social and Political Culture* (Cambridge, 1969) (hereafter Barnard): this passage appears on p. 186.

[2] op. cit. (p. 70 above, note 1), p. 13.

we shall see that the values of these remote peoples are such as human beings like ourselves – creatures capable of conscious intellectual and moral discrimination – could live by. These values may attract or repel us: but to understand a past culture is to understand how men like ourselves, in a particular natural or man-made environment, could embody them in their activities, and why; by dint of enough historical investigation and imaginative sympathy, to see how human (that is, intelligible) lives could be lived by pursuing them.

Pluralism in this sense actually antedates the new historicism of the eighteenth century. It is manifest in the polemics against Rome of the jurists among the Reformers in the sixteenth century. Men like the Chancelier Pasquier or Dumoulin or Hotman argued that while ancient Roman law or custom was relevant to Rome, ancient or modern, it would not do for the descendants of Franks or Gauls; they insisted on the equally objective validity of different sets of values for dissimilar societies and conditions; and believed that the appropriateness of a particular code to a particular society and form of life could be demonstrated by universally valid, that is non-relativist, factual and logical considerations. This is Herder's (and Chairman Mao's) garden of many flowers. When Herder says 'each nation' (and elsewhere 'each age') 'has its centre of happiness within itself, just as every sphere has its centre of gravity',[1] he recognises a single principle of 'gravitation': the anthropology which Herder wishes to develop is one which would enable one to tell what creates the happiness of what social whole, or of what kinds of individuals; 'general, progressive amelioration of the world' is a 'fiction'. No 'true student of history and the human heart' could believe this. Each stage of development has its own value: 'The youth is not happier than the innocent, contented child; nor is the peaceful old man unhappier than the energetic man in his prime.' There is an order, a growth, a dependence of each stage, each human group, on another –

[1] op. cit. (p. 82 above, note 1), vol. 5, p. 509 ('age' p. 512); Barnard p. 186 (188).

but no progress towards an optimum.[1] But for Herder all the various peaks of human endeavour, based on differences in needs and circumstances, are equally objective and knowable. This is anything but relativism.

There are many kinds of happiness (or beauty or goodness or visions of life) and they are, at times, incommensurable: but all respond to the real needs and aspirations of normal human beings; each fits its circumstances, its country, its people; the relation of fitting is the same in all these cases; and members of one culture can understand and enter the minds of, and sympathise with, those of another.[2] When Herder attacks Voltaire's dogmatic assumption that the values of civilised societies – his own – of a few selected cultures in the past – in Athens, Rome, Florence, Paris – are alone true, he uses all his considerable creative gifts to bring to life the aims and outlooks of many cultures, eastern and western, and contrasts them with those of the Enlightenment: not simply as a matter of brute fact – of variety as such – of the prevalence of *sic volo, sic jubeo* – but as the ways of life which, no matter how different from our own, normal men could find it natural to pursue; such ways of life as we, armed as we are (for both Vico and Herder) with the capacity to perceive the (objectively) good, beautiful and just, in all their guises and transformations,[3] should not find it too strange to pursue in similar conditions, even if we do not ourselves accept them. We are called upon to exercise our imaginative powers to the utmost; but not to go beyond them; not to accept as authentic values anything that we cannot understand, imaginatively 'enter' into.

[1] ibid., pp. 511–13; Barnard pp. 187–8.
[2] ibid., pp. 502–3, 509–11; Barnard pp. 181–2, 185–7.
[3] In his Journal of 1769 Herder wrote that 'There is not a man, a country, a people, a national history, a state, which resemble each other; hence truth, goodness and beauty differ from one another' ('Journal of my Voyage in the Year 1769', ibid., vol. 4, p. 472). Yet they must all be recognisable as possible ends of beings whom we recognise to be men and women like ourselves.

Relativism is not the only alternative to universalism – what Lovejoy called 'uniformitarianism' – nor does incommensurability entail relativism. There are many worlds, some of which overlap. The world of the Greeks is not that of the Jews nor of eighteenth-century Germans or Italians; nor is the world of the rich the world of the poor, nor that of the happy the world of the unhappy; but all such values and ultimate ends are open to human pursuit, as the comparative study of history and literature and philosophy and *Völkerpsychologie* and religion reveals. This is what Vico and Herder mean when they tell us not to judge past cultures by the measuring-rods of our own civilisation, not to perpetuate anachronisms under the influence of what Vico attacks as national or philosophical vanity. Both thinkers insist on our need and ability to transcend the values of our own culture or nation or class, or those of whatever other windowless boxes some cultural relativists wish to confine us to. Herder's writings teem with contemporary examples of disdain for non-European cultures or the European Middle Ages (in some respects, he tells us, superior to our own), due to the tendency of the *lumières*, both French and English, to see the past through the distorting spectacles of what Vico, with similar irony, calls 'our own enlightened times'. Herder's theses are among the earliest – if not the earliest – antidotes to Gibbon's or Hume's or Macaulay's blindness to medieval civilisation, to Russell's dismissal of Byzantium, or Voltaire's antipathy to the Bible or Cromwell or learning for learning's sake. However, unlike later thinkers, both Vico and Herder attribute such attitudes not to the influence of inescapable impersonal forces, but, like the sceptics of the sixteenth and seventeenth centuries, to bias or ignorance or lack of integrity, from which anyone can be saved by the use of the normal powers of the imagination, greater knowledge and closer regard for the truth – virtues open to all. There is nothing here about the mazes of false consciousness.

The fact that they are not cultural relativists of an insulated kind is shown by this alone. For it is idle to tell men to learn to see other worlds through the eyes of those whom they seek to understand, if they are prevented by the walls of their own culture from doing so. Unless we are able to escape from the ideological prisons of class or nation or doctrine, we shall not be able to avoid seeing alien institutions or customs as either too strange to make any sense to us, or as tissues of error, lying inventions of unscrupulous priests; the doors which, according to Vico, myth and fable and language open to us will remain romantic delusions.

What are the alternatives to such ability to see beyond the bounds of one's own *Kulturkreis*? In the first place, attribution to members of other civilisations of motives, goals, values, ways of thinking prevalent in one's own: this is the anachronistic disregard of historical change against which our two thinkers warn us, and of which they offer us glaring examples intended to make us aware of its dangers. Secondly, an anthropology modelled on the biological sciences, an attempt to construct a science of man characterised by the neutral objectivity of other natural sciences, at the price of regarding mankind as being no more than a species of the animal kingdom: this, for Vico and Herder, is gratuitously to treat human beings as less than human; to pretend that we know less than we do, if only from our own experience, of what it is to be human and conscious of having purposes, of the differences between action and be-haviour. The last possibility is an all-pervasive scepticism: what is beyond the ken of our culture cannot be known or speculated about; *ignoramus et ignorabimus*; history and anthropology may be pure culture-conditioned fictions. So, indeed, they may; but why should we attend to this wild piece of subjective idealism? The onus of proof is on the sceptics; to say that the past is completely unknowable robs the concept of the past of all meaning: it is thus a strictly self-annihilating notion.

So much for doubts about the possibility of understanding the past. But to understand is not to accept. Vico experiences no intellectual discomfort — nor need he do so — when he damns in absolute terms the social injustice and brutality of Homeric society. Herder is not being inconsistent when he denounces the great conquerors and destroyers of local cultures – Alexander, Caesar, Charlemagne – or glorifies Oriental literature or primitive song. This would not be consistent with conscious (or, shall I say, conscientious) relativism of values, but is compatible with pluralism, which merely denies that there is one, and only one, true morality or aesthetics or theology, and allows equally objective alternative values or systems of value. One can reject a culture because one finds it morally or aesthetically repellent, but, on this view, only if one can understand how and why it could, nevertheless, be acceptable to a recognisably human society. Only if its behaviour is not intelligible at all are we reduced to a mere 'physicalist' description and prediction of gestures; the code, if there is one, which would yield their meaning remains unbroken. Such men are not fully human for us; we cannot imaginatively enter their worlds; we do not know what they are up to; they are not brothers to us (as Vico and Herder supposed that all human beings were); we can at most only dimly guess at what the point of their acts, if they are acts, may be. Then truly do we have to confine ourselves to mere behaviourist reports of unexplained brute fact, or, at best, resort to the language of pure relativism, to the extent that these men's ends, somehow grasped as ends, seem wholly unrelated to our own. I repeat, pluralism – the incommensurability and, at times, incompatibility of objective ends – is *not* relativism; nor, *a fortiori*, subjectivism, nor the allegedly unbridgeable differences of emotional attitude on which some modern positivists, emotivists, existentialists, nationalists and, indeed, relativistic sociologists and anthropologists found their accounts. This is the relativism from which I hold Montesquieu, Vico and Herder to have been free.[1] This is no less true of other, more reactionary, critics of the Enlightenment: of Justus Möser, for example,

---

[1] Plainly thinkers like those Renaissance critics who, by historical and philological analysis, exposed the forged Donation of Constantine, or like Vico, who similarly discredited the fable of the Athenian origin of the Twelve Tables of early Rome, can scarcely be accused of the cruder forms of

in his polemic against Voltaire's disparaging references to the absurd variety of laws and customs in the various little German principalities; or Burke, in his indictment of Warren Hastings for trampling on the traditional ways of life of the natives of India. I am not attempting to judge the validity of their objectivism or their pluralism, only to report it. *Je ne suppose rien, je ne propose rien, je n'impose rien, j'expose.*

If these fathers of cultural history are not relativists in the sphere of values and action, they are not even pluralists in that of knowledge. Vico nowhere supposes that we cannot reach even certainty (*certum* – let alone *verum*, demonstrable truth) in some sphere because our categories and conceptions and methods of investigation are hopelessly culture-bound, as are those of other cultures, and therefore neither more nor less valid than theirs. This is equally true of Herder. For all their erudition, they were philosophers of history rather than historical researchers; they did not possess the latest critical weapons even of their own time – they were not meticulous scholars like Muratori in Vico's day, or Michaelis, Schlözer and Heyne in Herder's. They neither used nor questioned the latest methods of scientific reconstruction of their own day. Vico conceded that Herodotus was full of fables and legends (which, of course, provided wonderful grist to the decoding mill of the *Scienza nuova*), whereas Thucydides was far more accurate and reliable. Herder was not concerned with the factual truth of the Bible or the Eddas, only with the kind of social and spiritual experience of which they were the natural expression. There is no suggestion of *Wissenssoziologie* in the writings of either. On the issue of factual truth they are at

---

culture-bound misinterpretation. Indeed, the very formulation of the central principle of such relativism, which claims to cover all possible assertions of fact, leaves no possibility of determining the status of the principle itself, since it must fall outside all the categories which it regards as together being exhaustive of all that can be asserted. Further discussion of the issue of such self-referential generalisations raises philosophico-logical issues outside the scope of this paper.

one with the Enlightenment: there is only one truth, not many, the same for all men universally, and it is what rational men affirm it to be, that which their critical methods uncover. Fable, legends, poetry, ritual, formulas, doors to past cultures, are therefore not literally (as opposed to poetically) true, and there is no more pluralism in the ideas of either thinker, let alone relativism, so far as the realms of facts and events are concerned than in those of the most doctrinaire Encyclopedist. The idea that the concept of fact is itself problematic, that all facts embody theories (as enunciated by, for example, Goethe) or socially conditioned, ideological attitudes, seems as remote from them as it is from the outlook of Ranke. His view that every age is equal in the sight of God could have been uttered by Herder: for it is an undeniably pluralist sentiment.

For the full development of the ideas of false consciousness, of ideological or psychological distortion of the nature of objective truth, of the complex relationships between fact and interpretation, reality and myth, theory and practice, for the distinction between the unbreakable laws of nature and the 'reified' but breakable man-made laws and rules which govern conduct, one has to wait for Hegel and his left-wing disciples, including the early Marx. It may seem odd to us, who live after Marx and Max Weber, that the issue of the relativism of the knowledge of the past should not have occurred to the historicist critics of the French Enlightenment; but such surprise is itself anachronistic. Categories of knowledge may have been distinguished earlier; but not varieties of knowledge as resembling styles of life and thought wholly or partially determined by climate, race, class, or any other social or psychological formation.

I return to my original thesis: relativism is not the only alternative to what Lovejoy called uniformitarianism. The attribution of relativism to the critics who charged the *philosophes* of Paris with anachronism seems to me to be itself anachronistic. The relativism which has so deeply troubled historians, sociologists, anthropologists and philosophers of history during the last hundred years is, in the main, if not entirely, a legacy of the schools of thought which look upon human activity as being largely caused by occult and inescapable forces of which explicit social beliefs and theories are rationalisations – disguises to be penetrated and exposed. This is the heritage of Marxism, of depth psychology, of the sociology of Pareto or Simmel or Mannheim – ideas of which, even in their embryonic form, the leading thinkers of the eighteenth century, in Paris and London and their cultural dependencies, as well as their critics in Italy and Germany, seem to have showed scarcely any systematic awareness.

John Stuart Mill once observed: 'It is hardly possible to overrate the value, in the present low state of human improvement, of placing human beings in contact with persons dissimilar to themselves, and with modes of thought and action unlike those with which they are familiar . . . Such communication has always been, and is peculiarly in the present age, one of the primary sources of progress.'[1] This amounts to a thesis, particularly if for 'progress' we substitute 'knowledge', with which some critics of the thinkers of the Enlightenment (and perhaps a good many of us today) might not disagree.

[1] John Stuart Mill, *Principles of Political Economy*, book 3, chapter 17, section 5: vol. 3, p. 594 in *Collected Works of John Stuart Mill*, ed. J. M. Robson (Toronto/London, 1981–).

JOSEPH DE MAISTRE
AND THE ORIGINS OF FASCISM

Un roi, c'est un homme équestre,
Personnage à numéro,
En marge duquel de Maistre
Écrit: Roi, lisez: Bourreau.

Victor Hugo, *Chansons des Rues et des Bois*[1]

Mais il n'est pas temps d'insister sur ces
sortes de matières, notre siècle n'est pas mûr
encore pour s'en occuper . . .

Joseph de Maistre, *Les Soirées de Saint-Pétersbourg*[2]

I

THE PERSONALITY and the outlook of Joseph de Maistre are not normally considered to be puzzling or problematic by historians of political or religious thought. In an age when the confluence of apparently incompatible ideas and attitudes, deriving from heterogeneous historical traditions, generated a number of protean personalities, too complex and contradictory

[1] Book 1 ('Jeunesse'), VI, 17 ('A un visiteur parisien'), 2nd stanza: p. 958 in *Œuvres complètes: Poésie II*, ed. Jean Gaudon (Paris, 1985).
[2] Hereafter usually *Soirées*. References for quotations from Maistre are by volume and page to *Œuvres complètes de J. de Maistre*, 14 vols and index (Lyon/Paris, 1884–7 and later unchanged impressions), thus: V 26, the reference for this epigraph.

to be fitted into the familiar categories, Maistre is regarded as being exceptionally simple, solid and clear.

Historians, biographers, political theorists, historians of ideas, theologians have expended much subtlety upon conveying the political and social atmosphere of the late eighteenth century and the early nineteenth, the peculiar quality characteristic of a time of transition between sharply divergent outlooks, of which such psychologically complex figures as Goethe and Herder, Schleiermacher and Friedrich Schlegel, Fichte and Schiller, Benjamin Constant and Chateaubriand, Saint-Simon and Stendhal, Tsar Alexander I of Russia and indeed Napoleon himself are typical representatives. The feeling of some contemporary observers is perhaps to some degree conveyed by the celebrated painting by Baron Gros, now in the Louvre, of Napoleon at Eylau. It represents a horseman of indeterminate origin, a strange, mysterious rider set against an equally mysterious background, *l'homme fatal*, in touch with secret forces, a man of destiny, coming from nowhere, moving in accordance with occult laws to which all humanity and indeed all nature is subject, the exotic hero of the baroque novels of the time – *Melmoth*, *The Monk*, *Obermann* – new, hypnotic, sinister and deeply disturbing.

This period is usually conceived in the history of western culture as at once the culmination of a long period of elaboration of classical patterns in thought and art, founded upon observation and rational reflection and experiment; and at the same time as infected by – and indeed more than infected, as an embodiment of – a new and restless spirit, seeking violently to burst through old and cramping forms, a nervous preoccupation with perpetually changing inner states of consciousness, a longing for the unbounded and the indefinable, for perpetual movement and change, an effort to return to the forgotten sources of life, a passionate effort at self-assertion both individual and collective, a search after means of expressing an unappeasable yearning for unattainable goals. This is the world of German romanticism – of Wackenroder and Schelling, Tieck and Novalis, of illuminists and Martinists. It is dedicated to a rejection of all that is tranquil, solid, luminous, intelligible, and is infatuated with darkness, the night, the unconscious, the hidden powers which reign equally within the individual soul and in external nature. It is a world possessed by a craving for the mystical identification of the two, an irresistible gravitation towards the unattainable centre of the universe – the heart of all created and uncreated things; a condition both of ironical detachment and of violent discontent, melancholy and exalted, fragmented, despairing and yet the source of all true insight and inspiration, at once destructive and creative. This is a process which alone solves (or dissolves) all seeming contradictions by removing them out of, and beyond, the framework of normal thought and sober reasoning, and so transforms them by an act of special vision, sometimes identified with the creative imagination, at other times with special powers of philosophical insight, into the 'logic' or the 'inner essence' of history – the 'exfoliation' of a metaphysically conceived process of growth, concealed from the superficial thinking of materialists, empiricists and ordinary men. This is the world of *Le Génie du christianisme*, of *Obermann* and *Heinrich von Ofterdingen* and *Woldemar*, of Schlegel's *Lucinde* and Tieck's *William Lovell*, of Coleridge and the new biology and physiology said to have been inspired by Schelling's doctrine of nature.

To this world, so we are told by virtually all his biographers and commentators, Joseph de Maistre did not belong. He detested the romantic spirit. Like Charles Maurras and T. S. Eliot, he stood for the trinity of classicism, monarchy and the church. He is the embodiment of the clear Latin spirit, the very antithesis of the moody German soul. In a world of half-lights he appears definite and unproblematical; in a society in which religion and art, history and mythology, social doctrine, metaphysics and logic seem inextricably confused, he classifies, discriminates and clings to his distinctions rigorously and consistently. He is a Catholic reactionary, a scholar and an aristocrat – *français, catholique, gentilhomme* – outraged alike by

the doctrines and the acts of the French Revolution, opposed
with equal firmness to rationalism and empiricism, liberalism,
technocracy and egalitarian democracy, hostile to secularism
and all forms of non-denominational, non-institutional religion, a powerful, retrograde figure, deriving his faith and his
method from the Church Fathers and the teaching of the Jesuit
order. 'A fierce absolutist, a furious theocrat, an intransigent
legitimist, apostle of a monstrous trinity composed of Pope,
King, and Hangman, always and everywhere the champion of
the hardest, narrowest, most inflexible dogmatism, a dark
figure out of the Middle Ages, part learned doctor, part
inquisitor, part executioner.'[1] That is Émile Faguet's characteristic summing-up. 'His Christianity is terror, passive obedience, and the religion of the state';[2] his faith is 'a slightly
touched-up paganism'.[3] He is a Roman of the fifth century,
baptised, but Roman; or alternatively a 'Praetorian of the
Vatican'.[4] His admirer Samuel Rocheblave speaks of his 'christianisme de la Terreur'.[5] The famous Danish critic Georg
Brandes, who devotes a careful study to Maistre and his times,
calls him a kind of literary colonel of the Papal Zouaves and a
Christian only in the sense that a man might be a freetrader or a
protectionist.[6] Edgar Quinet speaks of Maistre's 'inexorable
God aided by the hangman; the Christ of a permanent Committee of Public Safety'.[7] Stendhal (who may or may not have read

---

[1] Émile Faguet, *Politiques et moralistes du dix-neuvième siècle*, 1st series
(Paris, 1899), p. 1.

[2] ibid., p. 59.

[3] ibid. ('un paganisme un peu "nettoyé"').

[4] ibid., p. 60.

[5] S. Rocheblave, 'Étude sur Joseph de Maistre', *Revue d'histoire et de
philosophie religieuses* 2 (1922), p. 312.

[6] Georg Brandes, *Main Currents in Nineteenth-Century Literature,* English
trans. (London, 1901-5), vol. 3, *The Reaction in France,* p. 112.

[7] E. Quinet, *Le Christianisme et la Révolution française* (Paris, 1845), pp.
357–8.

him) calls him the 'hangman's friend';[1] René Doumic 'a spoilt theologian'.[2]

All these are in fact variants of the stock portrait, largely invented by Sainte-Beuve,[3] perpetuated by Faguet and faithfully reproduced by writers of textbooks of political thought. Maistre is painted as a fanatical monarchist and a still more fanatical supporter of papal authority, proud, bigoted and inflexible, with a strong will and an uncommon power of rigorous deduction from dogmatic premises to extreme and unpalatable conclusions; a brilliant, embittered composer of Tacitean paradoxes, a peerless master of French prose, a medieval doctor born out of his time, an exasperated reactionary, a ferocious opponent who aimed to kill, vainly seeking by the sole power of his superb prose to arrest the progress of history, a distinguished anomaly, formidable, solitary, fastidious, sensitive and ultimately pathetic; at best a tragic patrician figure, defying and denouncing a shifty and vulgar world into which he has been incongruously born; at worst an unbending, fanatical diehard, pouring curses upon the marvellous new age which he is too self-blinded to see, and too wilful to feel.

Maistre's works are regarded as interesting rather than important, the last despairing effort of feudalism and the dark ages to resist the march of progress. He excites the sharpest reactions: scarcely any of his critics can repress their feelings. He is represented by conservatives as a brave but doomed paladin of a lost cause, by liberals as a foolish or odious survival of an older and more heartless generation. Both sides agree that his day is done, his world has no relevance to any contemporary or any

[1] *Correspondance de Stendhal (1800–1842)*, ed. Ad. Paupe and P.-A. Cheramy (Paris, 1908), vol. 2, p. 389.

[2] René Doumic, *Études sur la littérature française*, 1st series (Paris, 1896), p. 216.

[3] See principally 'Joseph de Maistre' (1843) in *Portraits littéraires*: pp. 385–466 in *Œuvres*, ed. Maxime Leroy (Paris, 1949–51), vol. 2; and 'Lettres et opuscules inédits du comte Joseph de Maistre' (2 June 1851): pp. 192–216 in *Causeries du lundi* (Paris, [1926–42]), vol. 4.

future issue. This is a point of view shared alike by Lamennais (who was once his ally) and Victor Hugo, by Sainte-Beuve and Brandes, by James Stephen and Morley and Faguet, who dismiss him as a played-out force. This verdict is supported by his best-known critics in the twentieth century, Laski, Gooch, Omodeo, even his fullest and exceedingly critical modern biographer, Robert Triomphe, who treat him as a queer anachronism, not without influence in his own day, but peripheral and anomalous.[1]

This assessment, intelligible enough in a less troubled world, seems to me altogether inadequate. Maistre may have spoken the language of the past, but the content of what he had to say presaged the future. In comparison with his progressive contemporaries, Constant and Madame de Staël, Jeremy Bentham and James Mill, not to speak of radical extremists and Utopians, he is in certain respects ultra-modern, born not after but before his time. If his ideas did not have wider influence (and apart from ultramontane Roman Catholics and the Savoyard aristocracy among whom Cavour grew up there are not many traces of it), the reason is that the soil was, in his own lifetime, unreceptive. His doctrine, and still more his attitude of mind, had to wait a century before they came (as come they all too fatally did) into their own. This thesis may at first seem as absurd a paradox as any for which Maistre used to be derided; clearly it needs evidence to render it even plausible. This study is an endeavour to provide support for it.

[1] But this opinion is not shared by his Canadian biographer Richard Lebrun, nor by Émile Cioran, nor, indeed, by myself. I wish I could be so dismissive: but the darkest events of our century do not bear this out. See Richard A. Lebrun, *Joseph de Maistre: An Intellectual Militant* (Kingston and Montreal, 1988); E. M. Cioran, *Essai sur la pensée réactionnaire: A propos de Joseph de Maistre* ([Montpellier], 1977).

II

The problem uppermost in public consciousness during Maistre's most creative years was a specific form of the general question of how man could best be governed. The French Revolution discredited the great cluster of rationalist solutions which had been urged with the most ardent eloquence during the last decades of the eighteenth century. What, it was asked, had made it fail? The Great Revolution was an event unique in human history, if only because it was perhaps the most persistently anticipated, discussed, deliberately undertaken reversal of an entire form of life in the west since the rise of Christianity. It was well for those whom it had ruined to talk of it as an inexplicable cataclysm, a sudden outbreak of mass depravity or insanity, a violent eruption of divine anger, or a mysterious thunderstorm out of a clear sky which swept away the foundations of the old world. This, no doubt, is how it may genuinely have appeared to the more bigoted or stupid royalist exiles in Lausanne or Coblenz or London. But to the ideologists of the middle class, and to all those men, of whatever class, who had been influenced by the steady propaganda of the radical or liberal intellectuals, it was, at least in its beginning, a long-awaited deliverance, the decisive victory of light over ancient darkness, the beginning of the phase when human beings would at last begin to control their own destinies, made free by the application of reason and science, no longer victims of Nature, called cruel only because she was misunderstood, or of man, oppressive and destructive only when he was morally or intellectually blind or perverted.

But the revolution did not bring about the desired result, and in the last years of the eighteenth century, and the beginning of the nineteenth, it became increasingly clear both to disinterested historical observers, and still more to the victims of the new industrial age in Europe, that the sum of human misery had not been appreciably decreased, although its burden had to some degree been shifted from one set of shoulders to another.

Consequently attempts to analyse this state of affairs, springing partly from a genuine desire to understand it, partly from a craving for attributing responsibility, or, alternatively, for self-justification, were, as might be expected, made from many quarters. The history of these attempts to diagnose the causes of the failure, and to prescribe remedial measures, is in large part the history of political thought in the first half of the nineteenth century. To pursue its ramifications would take us too far. But the main types of explanation, both critical and apologetic, are familiar enough. Liberals put the blame for everything on the Terror, rule by the mob and the fanaticism of its leaders, which overthrew moderation and reason. Human beings had indeed been within sight of liberty, prosperity and justice, but their own unbridled passions (avoidably or unavoidably, in accordance with the optimism or pessimism of the analyst) or erroneous ideas – for example, belief in the compatibility of centralisation and individual freedom – caused them to lose their way before they reached the promised land. The socialists and communists disagreed, and laid stress on the culpable lack of attention to (and consequent impotence in the face of) social and economic factors – above all, the structure of property relations – shown by the makers of the revolution. Gifted innovators like Sismondi and Saint-Simon offered acute and original explanations of the origins, nature and results of social, political and economic conflicts, very different from the *a priori* methods adopted by their rationalist predecessors. The religiously and metaphysically inclined German romantics attributed the débâcle to the sway of the wrong kind of rationalist ideology, with its deeply fallacious interpretation of history, and its mechanistic view of the nature of man and of society. Mystics and illuminists, whose influence was a good deal more powerful and widespread in the last decades of the eighteenth and the beginning of the next century than is commonly supposed, spoke of failure to understand and, still more, to enter into *rapport* with the occult spiritual forces that (far more than material causes or consciously held opinions) govern the destinies of men and nations. Conservatives, both Catholic and Protestant – Burke, Chateaubriand, Mallet du Pan, Johannes Mueller, Haller and their allies – spoke of the unique power and value of the infinitely complex and unanalysable network – Burke's myriad strands of social and spiritual relationships by which the successive generations of mankind were shaped from birth, and to which they owed most of what they possessed and were. These thinkers celebrated the mysterious strength of inherited, traditional development; they likened it to a broad stream, to resist whose current – as advocated by the foolish French *philosophes,* whose minds were addled by abstractions – was certainly futile, and likely to prove suicidal; some among them compared it to a spreading tree, whose roots lost themselves in obscure depths that could not be plumbed, a tree in the shade of whose intertwined branches the great human flock peacefully grazed. Some spoke of the gradually unrolling pattern of the divine plan, whose successive historical phases were but the revelation in time of the timeless whole, eternally present, in all its manifestations, to the mind of the incorporeal Creator. Whatever the image, the moral was always much the same: reason, in the sense of a capacity for abstraction or ingenious calculation, or for classification and analysis of reality into ultimate ingredients, or in the sense of a faculty capable of developing an empirical or a deductive science of man, was a figment of the *philosophes'* imagination. These thinkers – whether they were influenced by Newtonian physics, or accepted the intuitionist and egalitarian doctrines of Rousseau – spoke of 'man' as such, man as nature made him, identical in all human beings, whose basic attributes, capacities, needs, constitution could be uncovered and analysed by rational methods. Some taught that civilisation constituted a development of this natural man, some that it perverted him; but they agreed that it was on the satisfaction of his requirements that all progress, moral, political, social, intellectual, depended.

Maistre, like Burke, rejected the very notion of the reality of this creature:

The Constitution of 1795, just like its predecessors [he wrote], was made for *man*. But there is no such thing as *man* in the world. In the course of my life I have seen Frenchmen, Italians, Russians etc.; I know, too, thanks to Montesquieu, *that one can be a Persian*. But as for *man*, I declare that I have never met him in my life; if he exists, he is unknown to me.[1]

A science founded on the notion of this figment was impotent before the great cosmic process. Efforts to explain it, still more to alter or deflect it, according to formulas provided by scientific specialists, were merely grotesque, and could be dismissed with a smile of pity or amusement, did they not cause so much unnecessary suffering and, at their worst, rivers of blood – the punishment of history or nature or nature's God upon human folly and presumption.

Historians usually include Maistre among the conservatives. We are told that he and Bonald represent the extreme form of Catholic reaction: traditionalist, monarchist, obscurantist, rigidly tied to a medieval scholastic tradition, hostile to everything that was new and living in post-revolutionary Europe, vainly seeking to restore an ancient pre-nationalist, pre-democratic, largely imaginary medieval theocracy. There is much truth in this as a description of Bonald, who fits the stereotyped image of the ultramontane theocrat at almost every point. Bonald was a man of clear mind and narrow vision, which became narrower and more intense in the course of his long life. An officer and a gentleman in the best and worst senses of these words, Bonald genuinely tried to apply intellectual, moral and political canons derived from Aquinas to the affairs of his own day. He did it with a heavy, mechanical inflexibility, and an obstinate and sometimes complacent blindness to the implications of his age. He taught that natural sciences were tissues of coherent falsehoods, that the desire for individual liberty was a form of original sin, and that all possession of absolute secular

[1] I 74.

power, whether by monarchs or popular assemblies, was founded upon blasphemous rejection of divine authority, whose sole representative was the Roman Church. Thus the usurpation of power by the people was but the obverse and the direct consequence of the original, wicked usurpation of it by kings and their ministers. Competition – the panacea of the liberals – was to Bonald a mutinous denial of divine discipline, just as the search for knowledge outside the sacred groves of orthodox theology was merely a chaotic quest for violent sensations on the part of a corrupt and dissipated generation. Like the papalists in the great medieval controversy, he maintained that the only form of government appropriate to man was the ancient European hierarchy of estates and corporations, social textures hallowed by tradition and faith, with ultimate secular as well as spiritual authority in the hands of the Vicar of Christ, and monarchs as his devout and obedient agents. All this was recorded in ponderous, sombre, remorselessly monotonous prose, with the result that, while Bonald's ideas have entered the general corpus of Catholic political theory and have certainly influenced action, his works, and to some extent his personality, seem today, outside the world of clerical specialists, to be deservedly forgotten or ignored.

Maistre greatly admired Bonald, whom he never met, corresponded with him, and claimed to be his spiritual twin – a claim that has been taken far too seriously by all his biographers, even by the impeccable Faguet. We are told that while Bonald was a Frenchman, Maistre was a Savoyard; Bonald a nobleman of ancient family, Maistre the son of a recently ennobled lawyer; Bonald a soldier and a courtier, Maistre principally a jurist and a diplomat; Maistre a philosophical critic and an exceptionally brilliant writer, Bonald more pedantic and uncompromisingly theological; Maistre a warmer supporter of the royal power, more experienced as a negotiator, and a man of affairs, Bonald more deeply learned, more severely didactic, remoter from the lively aristocratic drawing-rooms in which the brilliant and vivacious Maistre was so welcome and so greatly admired. But these are relatively trivial differences. The two men are represented as indissolubly united, two leaders of a single movement, the double-headed eagle of the Catholic Restoration. This is the impression which several generations of historians, critics and biographers, largely repeating and echoing each other, have conspired to give; but it seems to me misleading. Bonald was an orthodox political medievalist, a pillar of the Restoration, formidable and rock-like, but already somewhat obsolescent in his own time – the dull, unimaginative, erudite, relentlessly dogmatic authority of the Reaction. Napoleon correctly perceived that this bulwark against all critical thought, however overtly hostile to his rule, in fact contributed to its stability, and therefore offered him a seat in the Academy and invited him to act as tutor to his son. Maistre was a personality and a thinker of a different cast. His light was no less dry, his intellectual core was equally hard and icy, but his ideas – both positive, of the world as he found it to be and wished it to become, and negative, directed to the destruction of other schools of thought and feeling – were bolder, more interesting, more original, more violent, indeed more sinister than any dreamt of within Bonald's narrow legitimist horizon. For Maistre understood, as Bonald gave no sign of doing, that the old world was dying, and he perceived, as Bonald could never have done, the terrifying contours of the new order which was coming in its place. Maistre's version of it – for all that it is not framed in the language of prophecy – profoundly shocked his contemporaries. But prophetic it was, and judgements which seemed perversely paradoxical in his day are almost platitudes in ours. To his contemporaries, perhaps to himself, he seemed to be gazing calmly into the classical and feudal past, but what he saw even more clearly proved to be a blood-freezing vision of the future. Therein lie his interest and his importance.

III

Joseph de Maistre was born in 1753 in Chambéry, the eldest of ten children of the President of the Senate, granted his title as the highest judicial official of the dukedom of Savoy, then part of the kingdom of Sardinia. His family came from Nice, and all his life he felt towards France that admiration which is at times found among those who live on the outer rim or just beyond the border of a country to which they are attached by ties of blood or sentiment, and of which they cherish a lifelong romanticised vision. All his life Maistre was a loyal subject of the rulers of his country, but he truly loved only France, which he called (after Grotius) 'the fairest kingdom after the Kingdom of Heaven'.[1] Destiny meant him to be born in France, he wrote on one occasion, but, having lost her way in the Alps, dropped him in Chambéry.[2] He received the normal education of a young Savoyard of good family: he went to a Jesuit school, and became a member of a lay order, one of whose duties it was to succour criminals, and in particular to attend executions and give last aid and comfort to their victims. Perhaps it was because of this that the imagery of the scaffold fills his thoughts. He flirted mildly with constitutionalism and Freemasonry (for which he retained an admiration, even while in later years he obediently condemned it) and, following in his father's footsteps, became a Senator of Savoy in 1788.

Maistre's sympathy for the very mild Freemasons of Savoy left a mark on his outlook. In particular he was influenced by the works of the late-eighteenth-century mystic Louis-Claude de Saint-Martin and his predecessor Martinès de Pasqually. He deeply approved of Saint-Martin's call for beneficence, for pursuit of a virtuous life, his resistance to scepticism, material- ism, the truths of natural science; from him he may have derived

---

[1] I 18.

[2] *Correspondance diplomatique de Joseph de Maistre 1811–1817*, ed. Albert Blanc (Paris, 1860) (hereafter *Correspondance diplomatique*), vol. 1, p. 197.

his lifelong ecumenism – his yearning for Christian unity, his condemnation of the 'stupid indifference that we call *tolerance*'.[1] Martinist, too, was his love of tracing esoteric doctrines in the Bible, occult hints and intimations, visionary interpretations, his interest in Swedenborg, his stress on the mysterious ways in which God moves his wonders to perform, on the cunning of providence in turning the unintended consequences of human activity into factors in the fulfilment of the divine plan, unsuspected by its hopelessly purblind beneficiaries. During his youth the church, at any rate in Savoy, did not object to Masonic tendencies among the faithful – if only because in France, under the leadership of Willermoz, they were a weapon against such enemies as the materialism and anti-clerical liberalism of the Enlightenment. Maistre's early Masonic sympathies duly became a permanent source of suspicion (which pursued him all his life) on the part of the more bigoted supporters of the church and the royal court, even though his devotion to both remained unswerving. But this only began later: during his early years the House of Savoy was, in comparison with the kings of France, mildly progressive. Feudalism had been abolished at the beginning of the eighteenth century; the king's rule was paternalistic but moderately enlightened, the peasants were not crushed by the burden of taxation, nor were the merchants and manufacturers as greatly hampered by the ancient privileges of the nobility and the church as in the principalities of Germany or Italy. The government of Turin was conservative but not arbitrary; there was little extremist feeling, either reactionary or radical; the country was then – as later – governed by a cautious bureaucracy, anxious to preserve peace and avoid complications with its neighbours. When the Terror broke out in Paris it was greeted with incredulous horror; the attitude towards the Jacobins was

---

[1] 'Mémoire au duc de Brunswick', p. 106 in Jean Rebotton (ed.), *Écrits maçonniques de Joseph de Maistre et de quelques-uns de ses amis francs-maçons* (Geneva, 1983).

not unlike that to be found in conservative circles in Switzerland towards the French Commune in 1871, or indeed towards the French resistance during the Second World War, when the frightened *bien pensant* circles in Geneva and Lausanne sympathised with Marshal Pétain. Similarly the reputable, liberally inclined aristocracy of the court shied away in horror from the cataclysm unchained in France. When the militant French Republic duly invaded and annexed Savoy, the king was forced to flee first to Turin, then for some years to Rome, and, after Napoleon had put pressure on the Pope, to his capital of Cagliari in Sardinia. Maistre, who had at first approved of the acts of the States-General in Paris, soon changed his mind and left for Lausanne; from there he went on to Venice and Sardinia, where he lived the typical life of an impoverished royalist émigré, in the service of his master, the king of Sardinia, who became the pensioner of England and of Russia. Maistre's radical temper and his views, always too strongly held and expressed, made him an uncomfortable member of that conservative, provincial, apprehensive little court. He had had some inkling of this when his friend Costa warned him against the publication of a work he composed in 1793 (*Lettres d'un royaliste savoisien à ses compatriotes*): 'anything too vigorously thought, which contains too much energy, sells poorly in this country'.[1] There was probably some relief when he was sent to St Petersburg early in the next century as the official representative of the kingdom of Sardinia.

The revolution, not surprisingly, had the effect on Maistre's strong and tenacious mind of causing him to re-examine the foundations of his faith and outlook. His at best marginal liberalism disappeared without a trace. He emerged a ferocious critic of every form of constitutionalism and liberalism, an ultramontane legitimist, a believer in the divinity of authority

---

[1] Cited by Maistre in a letter to Vignet des Étoles of 16 July 1793 in the Maistre family archives. See Lebrun, op. cit. (p. 96 above, note 1), p. 123, note 68.

and power, and of course an unyielding adversary of all that the *lumières* of the eighteenth century had stood for – rationalism, individualism, liberal compromise and secular enlightenment. His world had been shattered by the satanic forces of atheistical reason: and could be rebuilt only by cutting off all the heads of the hydra of the revolution in all its multiple disguises. Two worlds had met in mortal combat. He had chosen his side and meant to give no quarter.

IV

The central spring of Maistre's entire intellectual activity, from the *Considérations sur la France*, published anonymously in Switzerland in 1797, a powerful, brilliantly written polemical treatise which contains a great many of his most original and influential theses, to the posthumous *Soirées de Saint-Pétersbourg* and the *Examen de la philosophie de Bacon*, was his reaction to what seemed to him the shallowest view of life ever held by influential thinkers. What angered him most was the bland, naturalistic optimism whose validity the fashionable philosophers of the age, particularly in France, seemed to take wholly for granted. True knowledge, it was held in enlightened circles, could be obtained only by the method of the natural sciences, although, no doubt, the notion of what a natural science was, and what it could do, was in the mid-eighteenth century somewhat different from what it grew to be in the two centuries that followed. Only the use of the faculty of reason aided by the growth of knowledge founded on sense perception – not mystical inner light or uncritical acceptance of tradition, dogmatic rules, or the voice of supernatural authority, whether vouchsafed by direct revelation or recorded in sacred texts – only that would provide final answers to the great problems which had occupied men since the beginning of history. There were, of course, sharp disagreements, both between schools of thought and between individual thinkers. Locke believed in intuitive truths in religion and ethics, while Hume did not; Holbach was an atheist, like most of his friends, and was castigated for this by Voltaire. Turgot (whom Maistre once admired) believed in inevitable progress; Mendelssohn did not, but defended the doctrine of the immortality of the soul, which Condorcet rejected. Voltaire believed that books had a dominant influence on social behaviour, whereas Montesquieu believed that it was climate, soil and other environmental factors that created unalterable differences in national character and social and political institutions. Helvétius thought that education and legislation could by themselves wholly alter, and indeed perfect, the character of both individuals and communities; and was duly attacked for this by Diderot. Rousseau spoke of reason and feeling but, unlike Hume and Diderot, suspected the arts and detested the sciences, laid stress on the education of the will, denounced intellectuals and experts and, in direct opposition to Helvétius and Condorcet, held out small hopes for humanity's future. Hume and Adam Smith regarded the sense of obligation as an empirically examinable sentiment, while Kant founded his moral philosophy on the sharpest possible denial of this thesis; Jefferson and Paine considered the existence of natural rights to be self-evident, while Bentham thought this nonsense on stilts, and called the Declaration of the Rights of Man and Citizen bawling on paper.

But sharp as the genuine differences between these thinkers were, there were certain beliefs which they held in common. They believed in varying measure that men were, by nature, rational and sociable; or at least understood their own and others' best interests when they were not being bamboozled by knaves or misled by fools; that, if only they were taught to see them, they would follow the rules of conduct discoverable by the use of the ordinary human understanding; that there existed laws which govern nature, both animate and inanimate, and that these laws, whether empirically discoverable or not, were equally evident whether one looked within oneself or at the world outside. They believed that the discovery of such laws, and knowledge of them, if it were spread widely enough, would of itself tend to promote a stable harmony both between individuals and associations, and within the individual himself. Most of them believed in the maximum degree of individual freedom and the minimum of government – at least after men had been suitably re-educated. They thought that education and legislation founded upon the 'precepts of nature' could right almost every wrong; that nature was but reason in action, and its workings therefore were in principle deducible from a set of ultimate truths like the theorems of geometry, and latterly of physics, chemistry and biology. They believed that all good and desirable things were necessarily compatible, and more than this – that all values were interconnected by a network of indestructible, logically interlocking relationships. The more empirically-minded among them were sure that a science of human nature could be developed no less than a science of inanimate things, and that ethical and political questions, provided that they were genuine, could in principle be answered with no less certainty than those of mathematics and astronomy. A life founded upon these answers would be free, secure, happy, virtuous and wise. In short they saw no reason why the millennium should not be reached by the use of faculties and the practice of methods which had for over a century, in the sphere of the sciences of nature, led to triumphs more magnificent than any hitherto attained in the history of human thought.

All this Maistre set himself to destroy. In place of the *a priori* formulas of this idealised conception of basic human nature, he appealed to the empirical facts of history, zoology and common observation. In place of the ideals of progress, liberty and human perfectibility, he preached salvation by faith and tradition. He dwelt on the incurably bad and corrupt nature of man, and consequently the unavoidable need for authority, hierarchy, obedience and subjection. In place of science he preached the primacy of instinct, Christian wisdom, prejudice (which is but the fruit of the experience of generations), blind faith; in place of optimism, pessimism; in place of eternal harmony and eternal peace, the necessity – the divine necessity – of conflict and suffering, sin and retribution, bloodshed and war. In place of the ideals of peace and social equality, founded on the common interests and the natural goodness of man, he asserted the inherent inequality and violent conflict of aims and interests as being the normal condition of fallen man and the nations to which he belonged.

Maistre denied any meaning to such abstractions as nature and natural right; he formulated a doctrine of language which contradicted all that Condillac or Monboddo had said on this topic. He breathed new life into the discredited doctrine of the Divine Right of Kings, he defended the importance of mystery and darkness – and above all of unreason – as the basis of social and political life. With remarkable brilliance and effectiveness, he denounced all forms of clarity and rational organisation. Temperamentally he resembled his enemies, the Jacobins; like them he was a total believer, a violent hater, a *jusqu'au boutiste* in all things. What distinguished the extremists of 1792 was the completeness of their rejection of the old order: they denounced not merely its vices but its virtues; they wished to leave nothing standing, to destroy the whole evil system, root and branch, in order to build something entirely new, with no concessions, not the smallest debt to the world upon whose ruins the new order was to be raised. Maistre was the polar opposite of this. He attacked eighteenth-century rationalism with the intolerance and the passion, the power and the gusto, of the great revolutionaries themselves. He understood them better than the moderates, and he had some fellow-feeling for some of their qualities; but what was to them a beatific vision was to him a nightmare. He wished to raze 'the heavenly city of the eighteenth-century philosophers'[1] to the ground, not leaving stone on stone.

The methods which he used, as well as the truths which he preached, although he claimed to have derived them largely from Thomas à Kempis or Thomas Aquinas, from Bossuet or

---

[1] The title of a book (New Haven, 1932) by Carl L. Becker.

Bourdaloue, in fact did not owe a great deal to these great pillars of the Roman Church; they have more in common with the anti-rationalistic approach of Augustine or the teachers of Maistre's youth – the illuminism of Willermoz and the followers of Pasqually and Saint-Martin. Maistre was at one with the fathers of German irrationalism and fideism; as well as with those in France who, like Charles Maurras, Maurice Barrès and their followers, acclaimed the values and authority of the Roman establishment without in some cases being believing Christians; with all those who continue to regard the Enlightenment as a personal enemy; and with those who defend transcendent principles whose very meaning would in their view be obscured and misrepresented by any assumption that they could occur on the same level as the sciences and common sense, and so be open to, or need, defence against intellectual or moral criticism.

V

Holbach and Rousseau were complete adversaries, but both spoke of nature with piety, as being in some not too metaphorical a sense harmonious, benevolent and liberating. Rousseau believed that she disclosed her harmony and beauty to the untutored hearts of uncorrupted men, Holbach was convinced that she did so to the educated senses and minds, unclouded by prejudice and superstition, of those who employ rational methods of enquiry to uncover her secrets. Maistre on the contrary accepted the ancient view that men before the Flood were wise; but they sinned and were destroyed; and now their degenerate descendants can find truth not by the harmonious development of their faculties, not in philosophy or physics, but in revelation vouchsafed to the saints and doctors of the Church of Rome, supported only too clearly by observation. We are told to study nature. Let us do so. What are the findings of such impeccable studies as history and zoology? The spectacle of harmonious self-fulfilment of the optimistic rationalist, the

Marquis de Condorcet? The very opposite: that nature turns out to be red in tooth and claw. In the *Soirées de Saint-Pétersbourg* he tells us that

> In the whole vast dome of living nature there reigns an open violence, a kind of prescriptive fury which arms all the creatures to their common doom: as soon as you leave the inanimate kingdom you find the decree of violent death inscribed on the very frontiers of life. You feel it already in the vegetable kingdom: from the great catalpa to the humblest herb, how many plants *die* and how many are *killed*; but, from the moment you enter the animal kingdom, this law is suddenly in the most dreadful evidence. A power, a violence, at once hidden and palpable . . . has in each species appointed a certain number of animals to devour the others: thus there are insects of prey, reptiles of prey, birds of prey, fishes of prey, quadrupeds of prey. There is no instant of time when one creature is not being devoured by another. Over all these numerous races of animals man is placed, and his destructive hand spares nothing that lives. He kills to obtain food and he kills to clothe himself; he kills to adorn himself; he kills in order to attack and he kills to defend himself; he kills to instruct himself and he kills to amuse himself; he kills to kill. Proud and terrible king, he wants everything and nothing resists him . . . from the lamb he tears its guts and makes his harp resound . . . from the wolf his most deadly tooth to polish his pretty works of art; from the elephant his tusks to make a toy for his child – his table is covered with corpses . . . And who [in this general carnage] will exterminate him who exterminates all the others? Himself. It is man who is charged with the slaughter of man . . . So is accomplished . . . the great law of the violent destruction of living creatures. The whole earth, perpetually steeped in blood, is nothing but a vast altar upon which all that is living must be sacrificed without end, without measure, without pause, until the consummation of things, until evil is extinct, until the death of death.[1]

---

[1] The original text of this passage, only part of which is translated above, is worth giving in full, showing Maistre as it does at his most characteristic, picturesque and violent: 'Dans le vaste domaine de la nature vivante, il règne une violence manifeste, une espèce de rage prescrite qui arme tous les êtres *in*

This is Maistre's famous, terrible vision of life. His violent preoccupation with blood and death belongs to a world different from the rich and tranquil England of Burke's imagination, from the slow, mature wisdom of the landed gentry, the deep peace of the country houses great and small, the eternal society

mutua funera: dès que vous sortez du règne insensible, vous trouvez le décret de la mort violente écrit sur les frontières mêmes de la vie. Déjà, dans le règne végétal, on commence à sentir la loi: depuis l'immense catalpa jusqu'à la plus humble graminée, combien de plantes *meurent*, et combien sont *tuées*! mais, dès que vous entrez dans le règne animal, la loi prend tout à coup une épouvantable évidence. Une force, à la fois cachée et palpable, se montre continuellement occupée à mettre à découvert le principe de la vie par des moyens violents. Dans chaque grande division de l'espèce animal, elle a choisi un certain nombre d'animaux qu'elle a chargés de dévorer les autres: ainsi, il y a des insectes de proie, des reptiles de proie, des oiseaux de proie, des poissons de proie, et des quadrupèdes de proie. Il n'y a pas un instant de la durée où l'être vivant ne soit dévoré par un autre. Au-dessus de ces nombreuses races d'animaux est placé l'homme, dont la main destructrice n'épargne rien de ce qui vit; il tue pour se nourrir, il tue pour se vêtir, il tue pour se parer, il tue pour attaquer, il tue pour se défendre, il tue pour s'instruire, il tue pour s'amuser, il tue pour tuer: roi superbe et terrible, il a besoin de tout, et rien ne lui résiste. Il sait combien la tête du requin ou du cachalot lui fournira de barriques d'huile; son épingle déliée pique sur le carton des musées l'élégant papillon qu'il a saisi au vol sur le sommet du Mont-Blanc ou du Chimboraço; il empaille le crocodile, il embaume le colibri; à son ordre, le serpent à sonnettes vient mourir dans la liqueur conservatrice qui doit le montrer intact aux yeux d'une longue suite d'observateurs. Le cheval qui porte son maître à la chasse du tigre se pavane sous la peau de ce même animal: l'homme demande tout à la fois, à l'agneau ses entrailles pour faire résonner une harpe, à la baleine ses fanons pour soutenir le corset de la jeune vierge, au loup sa dent la plus meurtrière pour polir les ouvrages légers de l'art, à l'éléphant ses défenses pour façonner le jouet d'un enfant: ses tables sont couvertes de cadavres. Le philosophe peut même découvrir comment le carnage permanent est prévu et ordonné dans le grand tout. Mais cette loi s'arrêtera-t-elle à l'homme? non, sans doute. Cependant quel être exterminera celui qui les extermine tous? Lui. C'est l'homme qui est chargé d'égorger l'homme. Mais comment pourra-t-il accomplir la loi, lui qui est un être moral et miséricordieux; lui qui est né pour aimer; lui qui pleure sur les autres comme sur lui-même, qui trouve du plaisir à pleurer, et qui finit par inventer des fictions pour se faire pleurer; lui enfin à qui il a été déclaré *qu'on redemandera jusqu'à la dernière goutte du sang qu'il aurait versé injustement* (Gen., IX, 5.)? c'est la guerre qui accomplira le *décret*.

founded on the social contract between the quick and the dead and those yet unborn, secure from the turbulence and the miseries of those less fortunately situated. It is equally remote from the private spiritual worlds of the mystics and illuminists whose lives and teachings touched Maistre in his youth. This is neither quietism nor conservatism, neither blind faith in the status quo, nor merely the obscurantism of the priesthoods. It has an affinity with the paranoiac world of modern Fascism, which it is startling to find so early in the nineteenth century. The only contemporary who in any degree echoes it is Görres in his later diatribes.

N'entendez-vous pas la *terre* qui crie et demande du sang? Le sang des animaux ne lui suffit pas, ni même celui des coupables versé par le glaive des lois. Si la justice humaine les frappait tous, il n'y aurait point de guerre; mais elle ne saurait en atteindre qu'un petit nombre, et souvent même elle les épargne, sans se douter que sa féroce humanité contribue à nécessiter la guerre, si, dans le même temps surtout, un autre aveuglement, non moins stupide et non moins funeste, travaillait à éteindre l'expiation dans le monde. La *terre* n'a pas crié en vain; la guerre s'allume. L'homme, saisi tout à coup d'une fureur *divine*, étrangère à la haine et à la colère, s'avance sur le champ de bataille sans savoir ce qu'il veut ni même ce qu'il fait. Qu'est-ce donc que cette horrible énigme? Rien n'est plus contraire à sa nature, et rien ne lui répugne moins: il fait avec enthousiasme ce qu'il a en horreur. N'avez-vous jamais remarqué que, sur le champ de mort, l'homme ne désobéit jamais? il pourra bien massacrer Nerva ou Henri IV; mais le plus abominable tyran, le plus insolent boucher de chair humaine n'entendra jamais là: *Nous ne voulons plus vous servir.* Une révolte sur le champ de bataille, un accord pour s'embrasser en reniant un tyran, est un phénomène qui ne se présente pas à ma mémoire. Rien ne résiste, rien ne peut résister à la force qui traîne l'homme au combat; innocent meurtrier, instrument passif d'une main redoutable, *il se plonge tête baissée dans l'abîme qu'il a creusé lui-même; il donne, il reçoit la mort sans se douter que c'est lui qui a fait la mort* (*Infixæ sunt gentes in interitu, quem fecerunt* (Ps. IX, [15].)).

'Ainsi s'accomplit sans cesse, depuis le ciron jusqu'à l'homme, la grande loi de la destruction violente des êtres vivants. La terre entière, continuellement imbibée de sang, n'est qu'un autel immense où tout ce qui vit doit être immolé sans fin, sans mesure, sans relâche, jusqu'à la consommation des choses, jusqu'à l'extinction du mal, jusqu'à la mort de la mort (*Car le dernier ennemi qui doit être détruit, c'est la mort.* (S. Paul aux Cor., 1, 15, 26.)).' V 22–5.

Yet life is not for Maistre a meaningless slaughter, not what the Spanish thinker Unamuno called the 'abattoir of the late Count Joseph de Maistre'.[1] For although the issue of the battle is uncertain, although victory cannot be planned, and cannot be gained by mere ingenuity, or by the kind of knowledge that scientists or lawyers claim to possess, yet the invisible hosts, in the end, fight on one side rather than the other, and the ultimate outcome is not in doubt. The divine element is something not altogether unlike the spirit of world history or of humanity, or of the universe, in terms of which the German romantics of the turn of the century – Schelling, the brothers Schlegel – tended to describe and explain the world, a supernatural agency which acts at one and the same time as the power to create and to understand – the maker and interpreter of all there is.

In ironical language which at times resembles Tacitus and at other times Tolstoy, Maistre, no less than the German romantics (and after them the French anti-positivists Ravaisson and Bergson), declared that the method of the natural sciences is fatal to true understanding. To classify, abstract, generalise, reduce to uniformities, deduce, calculate and summarise in rigid, timeless formulas is to mistake appearances for reality, describe the surface and leave the depths untouched, break up the living whole by artificial analysis, and misunderstand the processes both of history and of the human soul by applying to them categories which at best can be useful only in dealing with chemistry or mathematics. In order truly to understand the way things happen a different attitude is required, one that the German metaphysician Schelling, and before him Hamann, found in the inspiration of the divinely inspired poet or prophet – the condition which, being at one with the creative processes of nature itself, causes the seer, in his struggle to fulfil his own

---

[1] '[el] matadero del difunto conde José de Maistre'. Miguel de Unamuno, *La agonía del cristianismo*: p. 308 in *Obras completas*, ed. Manuel García Blanco (Madrid, 1966–), vol. 7.

or his society's ends, to perceive them as an element in the goal towards which the universe – conceived almost as an animate organism – is striving. Maistre sought the answer in revealed religion, and in history, as the embodiment of the inner pattern which at best we see darkly and intermittently, by placing ourselves in the great framework of the tradition of our society, of its modes of feeling and action and thought – in which alone is truth.

Perhaps Burke would not altogether have disagreed with this: not at any rate as much as the German romantic thinkers who recoiled from politics and celebrated the poetry and wisdom of ancient 'folkways', or the genius of artists and thinkers endowed with uncommon powers of creation and divination. Every government founded upon settled law is founded on a usurpation of the prerogative of the divine lawgiver. Hence all constitutions are bad as such. This would have been too much even for Burke; and in any case both the English traditionalists and the German romantics looked on mankind without contempt or pessimism, whereas Maistre, at any rate in the works of his maturity, is consumed by the sense of original sin, the wickedness and worthlessness of the self-destructive stupidity of men left to themselves. Again and again he dwells on the fact that suffering alone can keep human beings free from all falling into the bottomless abyss of anarchy and the destruction of all values. On one side ignorance, wilfulness, idiocy; on the other, as the remedy, blood, pain, punishment – these are the concepts which haunt Maistre's dark world. The people – the mass of mankind – is a child, a lunatic, an absentee owner, who most of all needs a guardian, a faithful mentor, a spiritual director to control both his private life and the use of his possessions. Nothing that is worth while can be performed by men who are incurably corrupt and feeble, unless they are protected from the temptations to dissipate their strength and wealth upon futile ends, unless they are disciplined into doing their appointed task by the perpetual vigilance of their guardians. These in their turn must sacrifice their lives to the maintenance of the fixed and rigid hierarchy which is the true order of nature, with the Vicar of Christ at their head, stretching in symmetrical rows from the highest to the humblest members of the great pyramid of mankind.

It is not for nothing that Maistre thought that he saw, at the beginning of every true road which leads to knowledge and salvation, the great figure of Plato, pointing the way. He looked to the Society of Jesus to act as the élite of Platonic Guardians and save the states of Europe from the fashionable and fatal aberrations of his time. But the central figure in it all, the keystone of the arch on which the whole of society depends, is a far more frightening figure than king or priest or general: it is the Executioner. The most celebrated passage of the *Soirées* is devoted to him.

> Who is this inexplicable being, who, when there are so many agreeable, lucrative, honest and even honourable professions to choose among, in which a man can exercise his skill or his powers, has chosen that of torturing or killing his own kind? This head, this heart, are they made like our own? Is there not something in them that is peculiar, and alien to our nature? Myself, I have no doubt about this. He is made like us externally. He is born like all of us. But he is an extraordinary being, and it needs a special decree to bring him into existence as a member of the human family – a *fiat* of the creative power. He is created like a law unto himself.
>
> Consider what he is in the opinion of mankind, and try to conceive, if you can, how he can manage to ignore or defy this opinion. Hardly has he been assigned to his proper dwelling-place, hardly has he taken possession of it, when others remove their homes elsewhere whence they can no longer see him. In the midst of this desolation, in this sort of vacuum formed round him, he lives alone with his mate and his young, who acquaint him with the sound of the human voice: without them he would hear nothing but groans . . . The gloomy signal is given; an abject servitor of justice knocks on his door to tell him that he is wanted; he goes; he arrives in a public square covered by a dense, trembling mob. A poisoner, a parricide, a man who has committed sacrilege is tossed to him: he seizes him, stretches him, ties him to a

horizontal cross, he raises his arm; there is a horrible silence; there is no sound but that of bones cracking under the bars, and the shrieks of the victim. He unties him. He puts him on the wheel; the shattered limbs are entangled in the spokes; the head hangs down; the hair stands up, and the mouth gaping open like a furnace from time to time emits only a few bloodstained words to beg for death. He has finished. His heart is beating, but it is with joy: he congratulates himself, he says in his heart 'Nobody quarters as well as I.' He steps down. He holds out his bloodstained hand, the justice throws him – from a distance – a few pieces of gold, which he catches through a double row of human beings standing back in horror. He sits down to table, and he eats. Then he goes to bed and sleeps. And on the next day, when he wakes, he thinks of something totally different from what he did the day before. Is he a man? Yes. God receives him in his shrines, and allows him to pray. He is not a criminal. Nevertheless no tongue dares declare that he is virtuous, that he is an honest man, that he is estimable. No moral praise seems appropriate to him, for everyone else is assumed to have relations with human beings: he has none. And yet all greatness, all power, all subordination rest on the executioner. He is the terror and the bond of human association. Remove this mysterious agent from the world, and in an instant order yields to chaos: thrones fall, society disappears. God, who has created sovereignty, has also made punishment; he has fixed the earth upon these two poles: 'for Jehovah is master of the twin poles and upon them he maketh turn the world' . . . ([1 Samuel] 2: 8). [1]

[1] This, the most widely known text by Maistre, is for this reason worth giving in the original: 'Qu'est-ce donc que cet être inexplicable qui a préféré à tous les métiers agréables, lucratifs, honnêtes et même honorables qui se présentent en foule à la force ou à la dextérité humaine, celui de tourmenter et de mettre à mort ses semblables? Cette tête, ce cœur sont-ils faits comme les nôtres? ne contiennent-ils rien de particulier et d'étranger à notre nature? Pour moi, je n'en sais pas douter. Il est fait comme nous extérieurement; il naît comme nous; mais c'est un être extraordinaire, et pour qu'il existe dans la famille humaine il faut un décret particulier, un FIAT de la puissance créatrice. Il est créé comme un monde. Voyez ce qu'il est dans l'opinion des hommes, et comprenez, si vous pouvez, comment il peut ignorer cette opinion ou l'affronter! A peine l'autorité a-t-elle désigné sa demeure, à peine en a-t-il pris possession, que les autres habitations reculent jusqu'à ce qu'elles ne voient plus la sienne. C'est au milieu de cette solitude, et de cette espèce

This is not a mere sadistic meditation about crime and punishment, but the expression of a genuine conviction, coherent with all the rest of Maistre's passionate but lucid thought, that men can only be saved by being hemmed in by the terror of authority. They must be reminded at every instant of their lives of the frightening mystery that lies at the heart of creation; must be purged by perpetual suffering, must be humbled by being made conscious of their stupidity, malice and helplessness at every turn. War, torture, suffering are the inescapable human lot; men must bear them as best they can. Their appointed

---

de vide formé autour de lui qu'il vit seul avec sa femelle et ses petits, qui lui font connaître la voix de l'homme: sans eux il n'en connaîtrait que les gémissements . . . Un signal lugubre est donné; un ministre abject de la justice vient frapper à sa porte et l'avertir qu'on a besoin de lui: il part; il arrive sur une place publique couverte d'une foule pressée et palpitante. On lui jette un empoisonneur, un parricide, un sacrilège: il le saisit, il l'étend, il le lie sur une croix horizontale, il lève le bras: alors il se fait un silence horrible, et l'on n'entend plus que le cri des os qui éclatent sous la barre, et les hurlements de la victime. Il la détache; il la porte sur une roue: les membres fracassés s'enlacent dans les rayons; la tête pend; les cheveux se hérissent, et la bouche, ouverte comme une fournaise, n'envoie plus par intervalle qu'un petit nombre de paroles sanglantes qui appellent la mort. Il a fini: le cœur lui bat, mais c'est de joie; il s'applaudit, il dit dans son cœur: *Nul ne roue mieux que moi.* Il descend: il tend sa main souillée de sang, et la justice y jette de loin quelques pièces d'or qu'il emporte à travers une double haie d'hommes écartés par l'horreur. Il se met à table, et il mange; au lit ensuite, et il dort. Et le lendemain, en s'éveillant, il songe à tout autre chose qu'à ce qu'il a fait la veille. Est-ce un homme? Oui: Dieu le reçoit dans ses temples et lui permet de prier. Il n'est pas criminel; cependant aucune langue ne consent à dire, par exemple, *qu'il est vertueux, qu'il est honnête homme, qu'il est estimable*, etc. Nul éloge moral ne peut lui convenir; car tous supposent des rapports avec les hommes, et il n'en a point.

'Et cependant toute grandeur, toute puissance, toute subordination repose sur l'exécuteur: il est l'horreur et le lien de l'association humaine. Ôtez du monde cet agent incompréhensible; dans l'instant même l'ordre fait place au chaos, les trônes s'abîment et la société disparaît. Dieu qui est l'auteur de la souveraineté, l'est donc aussi du châtiment: il a jeté notre terre sur ces deux pôles: *car Jéhovah est le maître des deux pôles, et sur eux il fait tourner le monde* (*Domini enim sunt cardines terræ, et posuit super eos orbem.* (Cant. Annæ, I, Reg., II, 8.)).' IV 32–3.

masters must do the duty laid upon them by their maker (who has made nature a hierarchical order) by the ruthless imposition of the rules – not sparing themselves – and equally ruthless extermination of the enemy.

And who is the enemy? All those who throw dust in the eyes of the people or seek to subvert the appointed order. Maistre calls them 'la secte'.[1] They are the disturbers and subverters. To the Protestants and Jansenists he now adds deists and atheists, Freemasons and Jews, scientists and democrats, Jacobins, liberals, utilitarians, anti-clericals, egalitarians, perfectibilians, materialists, idealists, lawyers, journalists, secular reformers, and intellectuals of every breed; all those who appeal to abstract principles, who put faith in individual reason or the individual conscience; believers in individual liberty or the rational organisation of society, reformers and revolutionaries: these are the enemy of the settled order and must be rooted out at all costs. This is 'la secte', and it never sleeps, it is forever boring from within.

This is a catalogue which we have heard a good deal since. It assembles for the first time, and with precision, the list of the enemies of the great counter-revolutionary movement that culminated in Fascism. Maistre attempts to turn against the new and satanic order which had made the fatal revolution, first in America, then in Europe, all the violence and fanaticism which he believed them to have unloosed upon the world.

All intellectuals are bad, but the most dangerous are the natural scientists. Maistre tells a Russian nobleman in one of his treatises that Frederick the Great was right when he said that scientists were a great danger to the state: 'The Romans had the rare good sense to buy in Greece, for money, the talents which they lacked; and to despise those who purveyed them. They said, and they smiled when they said it, "The *starveling Greek* will do anything to please you."[2] If they had chosen to imitate

---

[1] e.g. I 407, VIII 91, 222, 223, 268, 283, 311–12, 336, 345, 512–13.

[2] In a footnote he quotes Juvenal's 'Graeculus esuriens in caelum jusseris, ibit' (*Satire* 3. 78), misascribing it to Martial.

such creatures they would have made themselves ridiculous. Because they disdained them, they were great.'[1] So too among the ancients, the Jews and the Spartans attained to true greatness because they did not contaminate themselves with the scientific spirit. 'Too much, even of literature, is dangerous, and the natural sciences are still more worthless to the statesman. The ineptitude shown by scientists when it comes to dealing with people or understanding them or leading them is something known to everybody.'[2] The scientific outlook finds fault in all authority; it leads to the 'disease' of atheism.

> One of the inevitable drawbacks of science in every country, and every place, is to extinguish that love of action which is the true vocation of man; to fill him with sovereign pride, pervert him from himself and the ideas which are proper to him, to make him the enemy of all subordination, a rebel against every law and every institution, a born champion of every innovation . . . The first among the sciences is that of statesmanship. That cannot be learnt in academies. No great minister, from Suger to Richelieu, ever occupied himself with physics or mathematics. The genius of the natural sciences makes impossible that other kind of genius, which is a talent unto itself.[3]

So much for the conviction of the believer in the possibility of leading a happy, harmonious, productive life, under the secure guidance of what in the eighteenth century was often referred to as 'Mother Nature' or 'Dame Nature' – all this springs from the self-deception of shallow minds unable to face reality.

Peace is one thing and reality another. 'What inconceivable magic is it', Maistre asks, 'which makes a man always ready at the first beat of the drum . . . to go without resisting, often even with a kind of eagerness (which also has a peculiar character of its own), in order to blow to pieces on the field of battle his brother who has done him no wrong, and who on his side

---

[1] VIII 299.
[2] VIII 305.
[3] VIII 297–8.

advances to subject him to the same fate if he can?'[1] Men who shed tears if they have to kill a chicken kill on the battlefield without a qualm. They do so purely for the common good, repressing their human feeling as a painful, altruistic duty. Executioners kill a very few guilty men, parricides, forgers and the like. Soldiers kill thousands of guiltless men, indiscriminately, blindly, with wild enthusiasm. Supposing an innocent visitor from another planet were to ask which of these two groups was shunned and despised on earth and which was acclaimed, admired, rewarded, what should we answer? 'Explain to me why the most honourable thing in the world – in the opinion of the entire human race without exception – is the right innocently to shed innocent blood.'[2] What has shown this more vividly than the evil, corrupt, vicious republic of the Jacobins? That satanic kingdom, Milton's Pandemonium?

Yet man is born to love. He is compassionate, just and good. He sheds tears for others and such tears give him pleasure. He invents stories to make him weep. Whence then this furious desire for wars and slaughter? Why does man plunge into the abyss, embracing with passion that which inspires him with such loathing? Why do men who revolt over such trivial issues as attempts to change the calendar allow themselves to be sent like obedient animals to kill and be killed? Peter the Great could send thousands of soldiers to die in defeat after defeat; but when he wanted to shave off his boyars' beards he almost faced a rebellion. If self-interest is what men pursue, why do they not form a league of peoples and attain to that universal peace which they profess that they so ardently yearn for? There is only one valid answer: men's desire to immolate themselves is as fundamental as their desire for self-preservation or happiness. War is the terrible and eternal law of the world. Indefensible on the rational plane, it is nevertheless mysteriously and irresistibly attractive. At the level of reasoned utilitarianism, war is indeed

[1] V 3–4.
[2] V 10.

all it is thought to be, mad and destructive. If nevertheless it has governed human history, this only shows the inadequacy of rationalist explanations, in particular of examining war as if it were a deliberately planned or explicable, or justifiable, phenomenon. Wars will not cease, however hateful, because wars are not a human invention: they are divinely instituted.

Education may alter the level of knowledge and of the overt opinions of men, but there is a deeper level at which it is impotent. This Maistre calls the invisible world, in which the inscrutable, because supernatural, element in the individual (as in societies) plays its irresistible part. Reason, so exalted in the eighteenth century, is in reality the feeblest of instruments, a 'flickering light'[1] weak in theory and practice, incapable alike of altering the behaviour of men or explaining its causes. Whatever is rational collapses because it is rational, man-made: only the irrational can last. Rational criticism will erode whatever is susceptible to it: only what is insulated against it, by being inherently mysterious and inexplicable, can survive. What man makes, man will mar: only the superhuman endures.

History abounds in examples of this truth. What is more absurd than hereditary monarchy?[2] Why should wise and virtuous kings be expected to be succeeded by equally good descendants? Freedom to choose the monarch – elective monarchy – is surely more reasonable. Yet the unhappy state of Poland is evidence enough of the unfortunate consequences to which this leads: while the totally irrational institution of hereditary kingship is one of the most stable of all human institutions. Democratic republics are certainly more rational than monarchy: yet even at its most splendid in Periclean Athens, how long did democracy survive? And at what ultimate cost? Whereas sixty-six kings, some bad, some good, but on the average adequate enough, have governed the great French kingdom well enough for fifteen hundred years. Again, what could prima facie

[1] I 111.
[2] V 116.

be more irrational than marriage and the family? Why should two beings remain joined to each other even though their tastes and views of life come to differ? Why should so obstinate a pretence survive? Yet the unbroken union of two beings, and the mysterious bond of the family, persist, despite their insult to abstract reason.

In an effort to refute the view that history is reason in action, if by reason is meant the operation of anything resembling the normal working of the discursive human intellect, Maistre multiplies examples of the self-defeating nature of rational institutions. The rational man seeks to maximise his pleasures, minimise his pain. But society is not an instrument for this at all. It rests on something much more elemental, on perpetual self-sacrifice, on the human tendency to immolate oneself to the family or the city, or the church or the state, with no thought of pleasure or of profit, on the craving to offer oneself upon the altar of social solidarity, to suffer and die in order to preserve the continuity of hallowed forms of life. Not until a good deal later in the nineteenth century do we again find such violent emphasis on irrational goals, romantic conduct unrelated to self-interest or pleasure, acts springing from the passion for self-surrender and self-annihilation.

An action in Maistre's universe is ineffective precisely in proportion as it is directed to the achievement of day-to-day interests, and derives from calculating, utilitarian tendencies which compose the outer surface of human character; and it is effective, memorable, in tune with the universe precisely to the degree to which it springs from unexplained and unexplainable depths, and not from reason, nor from individual will – the heroic individual, to whom Byron and Carlyle pay homage, the contemner of danger who defies the storm, is to Maistre just as blind in his self-reliance as the foolish scientist or social planner or captain of industry. What is best and strongest is often violent, irrational, gratuitous, and therefore necessarily misrepresented, and made to seem absurd, only by being falsely ascribed to intelligible motives. Human action in his sense is justified only when it derives from that tendency in human beings which is directed neither to happiness nor to comfort, nor to neat, logically coherent patterns of life, nor to self-assertion and self-aggrandisement, but to the fulfilment of an unfathomable divine purpose which men cannot, and should not try to, fathom – and which they deny at their peril. This may often lead to actions involving pain and slaughter, which in terms of the rules of sensible, normal, middle-class morality may well be regarded as arrogant and unjust, but which nevertheless derive from the dark unanalysable centre of all authority. This is the poetry of the world, not its prose, the source of all faith and all energy, whereby alone man is free, capable of choice, of creation and destruction, superior to the causally determined, scientifically explicable, mechanical movements of matter, or of natures lower than his, ignorant of good and evil.

Like all serious political thinkers, Maistre has before his mind a view of the nature of man. This view is deeply, but not wholly, Augustinian. Man is weak and very wicked, but he is not fully determined by causes. He is free, and an immortal soul. Two principles struggle for supremacy within him: he is both a *theomorph* – made in the image of his maker, a spark of the divine spirit – and a *theomach*, a sinner, a rebel against God. His freedom is very limited: he belongs to a cosmic stream which he cannot escape. He cannot indeed create, but he can modify. He can choose between good and evil, God and the Devil, and he is responsible for his choices. Alone in all creation he struggles: for knowledge, for self-expression, for salvation. Condorcet compared human society with that of bees and beavers. But no bee, no beaver, wants to know more than its ancestors; birds, fishes, mammals remain fixed in their monotonous, repetitive cycles. Man alone knows he is degraded. It is 'the proof of his greatness and his wretchedness, of his sublime rights and his unbelievable degradation'.[1] He is a 'monstrous centaur',[2] living at once in

---

[1] IV 66.
[2] IV 67.

the world of grace and that of nature, a potential angel and soiled with vice. 'He does not know what he wants; he wants what he does not want; he does not want what he wants; he *wants to want*; he sees within himself something which is not himself, and which is stronger than himself. The wise man resists and cries *"Who will deliver me?"* The fool gives in and calls his weakness happiness.'[1]

Men – moral beings – must submit freely to authority: but they must submit. For they are too corrupt, too feeble to govern themselves; and without government they collapse into anarchy and are lost. No man, and no society, can govern itself; such an expression is meaningless: all government comes from some unquestioned coercive authority. Lawlessness can only be stopped by something from which there is no appeal. It may be custom, or conscience, or a papal tiara, or a dagger, but it is always a *something*. Aristotle is plainly right, some men are slaves by nature;[2] to say they should not be is unintelligible. Rousseau says that man is born free, but is everywhere in chains. 'What does he mean? . . . This mad pronouncement, *Man is born free*, is the opposite of the truth.'[3] Men are too wicked to be let out of the chains immediately they are born: born in sin, they are made tolerable only by society, only by the state, which repress the aberrations of untrammelled individual judgement. Like Burke, by whom he was influenced, and perhaps like Rousseau (on some interpretations), Maistre believes that societies have a general soul, a true moral unity, by which they are shaped. But he goes further:

> Government [he declares] is a true religion. It has its dogmas, its mysteries, its priests. To submit it to the discussion of each individual is to destroy it. It is given life only by the reason of the

---

[1] IV 67–8.
[2] II 338, VIII 280.
[3] II 338. Faguet, paraphrasing Maistre, uses a brilliant epigram apparently of his own devising: 'Dire: les moutons sont nés carnivores, et partout ils mangent de l'herbe, serait aussi juste.' op. cit. (p. 94 above, note 1), p. 41.

nation, that is by a political faith, of which it is a *symbol*. Man's first need is that his growing reason be put under the double yoke [of church and state]. It should be annihilated, it should lose itself in the reason of the nation, so that it is transformed from its individual existence into another – communal – being, as a river that falls into the ocean does indeed persist in the midst of the waters, but without name or personal identity.[1]

Such a state cannot be created by, or on the basis of, a written constitutioń: a constitution may be obeyed, but it cannot be worshipped. And without worship – without superstition even, which is 'un ouvrage avancé',[2] a forward position, of religion – nothing can stand. What this religion demands is not conditional obedience – the commercial contract of Locke and the Protestants – but the dissolution of the individual in the state. Men must give – not merely lend – themselves. Society is not a bank, a limited-liability company formed by individuals who look on one another with suspicious eyes – fearful of being taken in, duped, exploited. All individual resistance in the name of imaginary rights or needs will atomise the social and the metaphysical tissue, which alone has the power of life.

This is not authoritarianism in the sense advocated by Bossuet or even Bonald. We have left far behind us the symmetrical Aristotelian constructions of Thomas Aquinas or Suárez and are fast approaching the worlds of the German ultra-nationalists, of the enemies of the Enlightenment, of Nietzsche, Sorel and Pareto, D. H. Lawrence and Knut Hamsun, Maurras, d'Annunzio, of *Blut und Boden*, far beyond traditional authoritarianism. The façade of Maistre's system may be classical, but behind it there is something terrifyingly modern, and violently opposed to sweetness and light. Nor is the tone remotely that of the eighteenth century, not even of the most violent and hysterical voices who mark its highest point of revolt – like Sade or Saint-Just – nor yet is it that of the frozen

---

[1] I 376.
[2] V 197.

reactionaries who immured themselves against the champions of freedom or revolution within the thick walls of medieval dogma. The doctrine of violence at the heart of things, the belief in the power of dark forces, the glorification of chains as alone capable of curbing man's self-destructive instincts, and using them for his salvation, the appeal to blind faith against reason, the belief that only what is mysterious can survive, that to explain is always to explain away, the doctrine of blood and self-immolation, of the national soul and the streams flowing into one vast sea, of the absurdity of liberal individualism, and above all of the subversive influence of uncontrolled critical intellectuals – surely we have heard this note since. In practice if not in theory (at times offered in a transparently false scientific guise), Maistre's deeply pessimistic vision is the heart of the totalitarianisms, of both left and right, of our terrible century.

VI

The burden of Maistre's philosophy is a full-scale attack on reason as preached by the eighteenth-century *philosophes*, and it owes a debt both to the new sense of nationhood that arose, at any rate in France, as a result of the revolutionary wars, and to Burke and his denunciation of the French Revolution and of timeless, universal rights and values, and his stress on the concrete, the binding force of custom and tradition. Maistre holds up English empiricism, in particular the views of Bacon[1] and Locke, to scorn, but pays reluctant homage to English public life, which is to him, as to so many western Catholic theorists, a provincial culture cut off from the universal truths of

[1] The burden of the treatise which he devoted to refuting Bacon is that he had not the metaphysical power to understand the non-empirical elements of the sciences which he heralded; that at most he was the barometer of climatic changes, not their creator, not so much the 'passionate lover of the sciences' as their 'amorous eunuch' (VI 533–4). There may be some justice in this, although it is unlikely that Maistre intended or realised it.

Rome, but much the best that can be achieved without possessing the true faith, the nearest approximation in secular terms to the full spiritual ideal of which the English imagination has always regrettably fallen short. English society is admirable because it rests on acceptance of a way of life, and does not perpetually seek to re-examine its own foundations.[1] Whoever questions an institution or a way of life demands an answer. The answer, supported by rational argument, will itself be liable to further questions of the same type. And every answer will tend to be perpetually open to doubt and to disbelief.

Once such scepticism is permitted the human spirit becomes restless, since it sees no final solution to its questioning. Once the foundations are called into question, nothing permanent can be established. Doubt and change, disintegrating corrosion from within and without, render life too precarious. To explain as Holbach and Condorcet explained is to explain away and leave nothing standing. Individuals are tormented by doubts which cannot be settled, institutions are subverted and are replaced by other forms of life, equally doomed to destruction. There is no resting-place anywhere, no order, no possibility of a tranquil, harmonious and satisfying life.

Whatever is solid must be protected from such assaults. Hobbes certainly understood the nature of sovereignty, making the rule of the Leviathan free from all obligations, absolute, and unquestionable. But Hobbes's state, like those of Grotius or Luther, is a man-made construction, unprotected from the perennial questions which atheists and utilitarians have put in every generation: Why live thus and not otherwise? Why should one obey this authority rather than some other, or none? Once the intellect is permitted to raise these disturbing issues there is no holding it; once the first move has been made there is no help, the rot has set in for good.

There is little doubt that Maistre was in some degree influenced by Burke's views. Every opponent of the French

[1] I 246–7.

Revolution drew weapons from that great armoury. He was not a disciple of the great Irish counter-revolutionary writer even though he speaks well of him. He has no truck with Burke's cautious conservatism, or his praise of the Act of Settlement, whereby the usurper William of Orange robbed the devout Catholic, James II, of his legitimate rights; nor is Burke's advocacy of compromise and adjustment, or his talk of a social contract, even though it is a contract between the living and the dead and the unborn, to his taste. Burke is not theocratic, not absolutist, not addicted to extremes like the ultramontane Maistre, yet Burke's denunciation of abstract ideas, of timeless and universal political truths detached from historical development, detached from the processes of organic growth which make men and societies, his total opposition to the liberation, advocated by such as Rousseau, of human beings from the artificial and removable shell of tradition, social texture, the inner life of communities and states, the impalpable strands which hold societies together and give them their character and strength – all this Maistre shared with him, and perhaps to some extent derived from him. He quotes him with relish, but the influence of Jesuit ideas remained far more powerful.

Maistre declares in language which at times rises to classical dignity and beauty – what Sainte-Beuve spoke of as his 'incomparable eloquence'[1] – that rationalistic or empirical explanation is in effect a cloak for sin; for at the heart of the universe there is a mystery, impenetrably dark. The authority of all the great living forces of social life, of the strong and rich and great over the weak and poor and small, the right to exact obedience which belongs to conquerors and priests, to the heads of family and church and state alike, flows from this occult source, whose very power consists in its opaqueness to the exploration of reason. 'One can say quite briefly: kings order you, and you must march.'[2] Such authority is absolute because there is no method

[1] 'Joseph de Maistre' (see p. 95 above, note 3), p. 422.
[2] V 2.

whereby it can be questioned, and omnipotent because there is no way in which it can be resisted. Religion is superior to reason not because it returns more convincing answers than reason, but because it returns no answer at all. It does not persuade or argue, it commands. Faith is truly faith only when it is blind; once it looks for justification it is done for. Everything in the universe that is strong, permanent and effective is beyond and, in a sense, against reason. Hereditary monarchy, war, marriage last precisely because they cannot be defended, and therefore cannot be refuted out of existence. Irrationality carries its own guarantee of survival in a way reason could never hope to do. All Maistre's monstrous paradoxes are a development of this, in its day, exceedingly novel thesis.

Maistre's doctrine has obvious resemblances to the attacks on rationalism and scepticism of earlier defenders of religion (for example by the illuminist sects and his favourite modern mystic, Saint-Martin), but it differs from them not merely by its violence, but by making a virtue of what had earlier been allowed as possible weaknesses, or at any rate difficulties, in the theocratic conception of life. It is a return to the bold, absolute irrationalism of the early church from the qualified rationalism of St Thomas and the great sixteenth-century theologians from whom he professes to derive inspiration. Maistre does speak of divine reason, and he speaks about providence, by which everything is ultimately shaped in its own unfathomable way. But divine reason for him is unlike anything appealed to by deists in the eighteenth century – reason implanted by God in man and the source of the epoch-making triumphs of Galileo and Newton – an instrument for the creation of rational happiness according to the plans made by benevolent despots or wise sovereign assemblies. Maistre's notion of divine reason is of an activity that is transcendent, and therefore hidden from the human eye. It cannot be deduced from any knowledge obtainable by simple human means; glimpses of it may be vouchsafed to those who have steeped themselves in God's revealed world, and so may learn from nature and history as determined by divine providence, even though they may not understand its ways or purposes. They feel secure because they have faith. They do not question because they have wisdom enough to understand the folly of applying human categories to divine power. Above all they do not look for general theories which will explain everything. For nothing is more fatal to true wisdom than scientifically established general principles.

Maistre held very penetrating and remarkably modern views on the dangers (largely ignored by the French *lumières*) of general principles and their application. Both in theory and in practice he was exceptionally sensitive to differences of context, of subject-matter, of historical circumstances and situations, of levels of thought, to the nuances which words and expressions acquire in different usages, to the varieties and non-equivalences of thought and language. Every discipline for him has its own logic, and he says again and again that to apply to theology canons valid in natural science, or to history concepts that apply in formal logic, must lead to absurdities. To each province its own mode of belief, its own methods of proof. A universal logic, like a universal language, empties the symbols used of all that accumulated wealth of meaning created by the continuous process of slow precipitation by which the mere passage of time enriches an old language, endowing it with all the fine, mysterious properties of an ancient, enduring institution. To analyse the precise associations and connotations of the words we use is not possible, to throw them away is suicidal lunacy. Each age has its own vision; to explain, still more to judge, the past in terms of our own contemporary values will make, and often has made, nonsense of history.

Maistre speaks of this in language reminiscent of Burke, Herder and Chateaubriand. 'The action of Christianity has been divine and for this reason has moved slowly, for all legitimate operations, of whatever kind, always proceed by insensible steps. Whenever one encounters noise, turmoil, haste', wilful efforts to overturn, to blow up, 'one may be sure that it is crime

or madness that is at work. *Non in commotione Dominus.*[1]
Everything grows, nothing good or permanent has been accomplished overnight. All improvisation carries the seeds of its own swift decay, and it is always the attempt to transform things by the wave of the magic wand – to change them abruptly and violently – that is the central crime of revolutions. Every country and nation and association has its own traditions, not exportable abroad. The Spaniards, for example, are making a grave mistake in trying to adopt the British constitution, the Greeks in thinking that they can become a national state overnight. Some of Maistre's prophecies have proved comically false: it was clear, he declared, that no such city as Washington would ever be built; or if it was, it never would be called Washington; and even if it had this name, it would never become the seat of the Congress.[2]

Abstraction is fatal in the physical no less than in the social world. Maistre mocks at the all-providing, all-explaining entity dignified under the name of Nature by the Encyclopedists. 'Who on earth is this woman?'[3] Nature, so far from being the beneficent provider of all good things, the source of all life and knowledge and happiness, is to him an eternal mystery; cruel in her methods, the scene of brutality, pain and chaos; serving God's inscrutable purpose, but seldom a source of comfort or enlightenment.

---

[1] VIII 282.
[2] I 88. He was equally mistaken about the future of the Greek kingdom, and by his sombre and, as it turned out, baseless warnings merely incurred the reputation of an obstructive busybody in the eyes of his fellow exile in St Petersburg, the Greek patriot Alexander Hypsilanti, about whose intentions he was kept informed by an ambitious phanariot lady, Roxandra Stourdza, later Countess of Edling and Sainte-Beuve's correspondent, to whom Maistre wrote letters of social gossip and fatherly advice. The correspondence ceased when Maistre's own position in St Petersburg began to be politically insecure, and the Countess decided that what had been a useful friendship was beginning to become a political liability.
[3] IV 132–3.

The eighteenth century is full of paeans to the simple virtues of the noble savage. Savages are, Maistre informs us, not noble, but sub-human, cruel, dissolute and brutal. Anyone who has lived among them can testify that they are the refuse of mankind. So far from being uncorrupted prototypes, early exemplars of natural taste and natural morality, from which civilisation has perverted the nations of the west, they are rejected models, casualties, failures of God's creative process. The Christian missionaries sent among these creatures have spoken about them with too much kindness. Because these good priests could not bring themselves to attribute to any of God's creatures the squalor and vices in which they are in fact sunk, it does not follow that these sorry cases of arrested development are models for us to follow. What is it that Rousseau and his like are calling upon us to do? He echoes the famous words of Montesquieu: 'The savage cuts down the tree to eat its fruit; he unharnesses the ox given him by missionaries and cooks its flesh with the wood of his cart. After three centuries all he wants of us is powder to kill others, fire-water to kill himself. Thievish, cruel, dissolute, he nevertheless differs from us. We at least have to overcome our nature; the savage follows his; crime is his natural taste, he feels no remorse.'[1] Maistre then makes his readers' flesh creep with a catalogue of the typical pleasures of a savage's life: parricide, eviscerating his mate, scalping, cannibalism, wild debauchery. What is the purpose of savages in creation? To be a caution to us. To show us how deep man can fall. The language of savage tribes has not the primitive strength and beauty of a beginning, only the confusion and ugliness of decay. It is the 'debris of ancient languages in ruins'.[2]

As for Rousseau's State of Nature, in which savages are said to exist, and the so-called Rights of Man which they are thought to recognise, and in whose name France and Europe have been

---

[1] IV 84–5.
[2] IV 63.

plunged into cruel massacres, what are these rights? Inherent in what men? No metaphysical, magic eye will detect abstract entities called rights that are not derived from some specific human or divine authority. Just as there is no lady called Nature, so there is no creature called Man. And yet revolutions are made, nameless atrocities are committed in the name of this chimera.

Four or five centuries earlier [Maistre wrote in his memoir on Russia] the Pope would have excommunicated the handful of importunate lawyers, and they would have gone to Rome to obtain absolution. The great Lords on their side would have restrained a few mutinous tenants[1] in their lands, and everything would have been kept in order. In our day, the two anchors of society – religion and slavery – having failed us at one and the same moment, the ship was carried away by the storm, and was wrecked.[2]

It was only when the authority of the Roman Church had become firmly established that slavery could be – and was – abolished.

Rationalism leads to atheism, individualism, anarchy. The social fabric holds together only because men recognise their natural superiors, they obey because they feel a sense of natural authority which no rationalist philosophy can reason away. There can be no society without a state; no state without sovereignty, the ultimate court of appeal; no sovereignty without infallibility; no infallibility without God. The Pope is God's representative on Earth, all legitimate authority is derived from him.

This is Maistre's political theory and a dominant influence on reactionary, obscurantist and, in the end, Fascist ideas in the years that followed, and a source of discomfort to conventional

---

[1] 'censitaires'.
[2] VIII 283ʹ–4.

conservatives and churchmen. More immediately it inspired much ultramontane, anti-state authoritarianism in France, and anti-political, theocratic movements in Spain and Russia as well as France. His concept of divine authority is not only deeply anti-democratic but wholly opposed to individual liberty, social and economic equality and the political implications of human fraternity. Well might he have echoed the remark attributed to Metternich: 'If I had a brother, I would have called him cousin.' Liberal Catholicism would have seemed to Maistre absurd, and indeed self-contradictory – the seeds of this tendency in his old papalist ally, Lamennais, worried him in the last years of his life. Brandes justly observes that, for liberals, Maistre represents the richest flowering of everything that they exist to oppose, and this not because he was a reactionary in the sense of living in the past, or lingering on as an obsolete relic of a superseded civilisation, but on the contrary because he understood his own age all too well, and actively resisted its liberal tendencies with all the latest intellectual weapons of his time.

The most dangerous enemy of the human race – the destroyer whose aim and function it is to sap the foundation on which all societies rest – is the Protestant, the man who lifts his hand against the universal church. Bayle, Voltaire, Condorcet are but feeble, secular disciples of the great subverters – Luther, Calvin and their followers. Protestantism is the revolt of individual reason or faith, conscience against blind obedience, which is the sole base of all authority: hence it is *au fond* political rebellion. No bishop, no king. Catholics, Maistre declares, in his *Reflections on Protestantism*, have never rebelled against sovereigns, only Protestants have done so.[1] This surprising assertion is supported by the monstrous sophistry that since, after Constantine, state and church were one, acts of insubordination by Catholics – for example, assassination of heretical rulers by Catholic zealots – are acts of revolt not against true authority

[1] VIII 67.

but against usurpers. The Spanish Inquisition was a method of preserving not merely the true faith, but the minimum degree of security and stability without which no society can survive. The Inquisition, in his view, has been much misrepresented.[1] In most instances it was an instrument of mild, beneficent re-education which brought many souls to repentance and return to the true faith. It served to save Spain from the destructive religious conflicts of France, England, Germany, and so protected the national unity of that pious kingdom. (This went too far. Maistre's apologia, which would have pleased Philip II, found little echo even among the most zealous champions of the policies of the church.) Successful defiance of clerical authority was responsible for the bloodshed and chaos brought upon Germany by the Thirty Years War. No land can rebel against the church and achieve greatness. Hence the Revocation of the Edict of Nantes was justified by patriotic considerations alone. 'In a superior age, everything is so. The ministers, the magistrates of Louis XIV were as great in their sphere as his generals, his painters, his gardeners were in theirs . . . what our miserable time calls superstition, fanaticism, intolerance and so forth was a necessary ingredient of the greatness of France.'[2] Calvinism was the most dangerous of the enemies of this greatness: it was undermined in France until it could be toppled; when it fell, not a dog barked. As for those who say that by this act France lost gifted craftsmen who emigrated and enriched other lands by their skills, let those who are moved by such shopkeepers' (*boutiquières*) considerations 'look elsewhere for answers than in my books'.[3]

Jansenists were not much better: Louis XIV levelled Port-Royal to the ground, he let a cart roll over it, and 'made good corn grow where only bad books had grown before'.[4] As for

[1] See *Lettres à un gentilhomme russe sur l'inquisition espagnole*. III 283–401.
[2] VIII 81.
[3] VIII 82.
[4] III 184.

Pascal, Maistre decides that he owed nothing to Port-Royal. Heresy must be extirpated; half-measures will always recoil upon those who do not go far enough. 'Louis XIV stamped on Protestantism, and he died in his bed, full of years, in a blaze of glory. Louis XVI caressed it, and died on the scaffold.'[1] 'No institution is firm or lasting if it rests on man's strength alone. History and reason combine to show that the roots of all great institutions are to be found outside this world . . . Sovereignties, in particular, possess strength, unity, stability only to the degree to which they are sanctified [*divinisées*] by religion.'[2]

Maistre had a unique grasp of the values against which he fought. No criterion, he observed, is so fallible as impiety. One must look at what it hates, what puts it in a rage, what it attacks always, everywhere, and with fury – that will be the truth. In the phrase used of him by Anatole France, he was 'l'adversaire de tout son siècle'.[3] Such activity is not reactionary but counter-revolutionary, not passive but active, not a vain attempt to reproduce the past but a formidable and effective effort to enslave the future to a vision of the past which is never purely fanciful, but, on the contrary, deeply grounded in a grimly realistic interpretation of contemporary events.

Maistre was not a romantic pessimist in the sense in which Chateaubriand or Byron or Büchner or Leopardi were so. The world order was for him neither chaotic nor unjust but, to the eye of faith, what it must and should be. Against those who in every age asked why the just went without bread while the wicked prospered, he replied that this rested on a childish misunderstanding of what divine laws were. 'Rien ne marche au hasard . . . tout a sa règle.'[4] If there is a law, it cannot brook exceptions; if a good man falls on evil days we cannot expect God to alter the laws without which all would be chaos, for the

---

[1] VIII 82.

[2] VIII 94.

[3] Anatole France, *Le Génie latin* (Paris, 1913), p. 242.

[4] IX 78; cf. III 394.

benefit of a private individual. If a man has the gout, he is unlucky, but he is not thereby led to doubt the existence of laws of nature; on the contrary, medical science, to which he applies, itself presupposes them. If a just man suffers disasters, that equally provides no reason for scepticism about the existence of good government in the universe. The existence of laws cannot prevent individual misfortunes; no laws can be so operated as to fit individual cases, for in that case they would cease to be laws. There is a definite sum of sin in the world, and it is expiated by a proportionate total amount of suffering; that is the divine principle. But there is nothing which says that human justice or rational equity must govern divine action: that each individual sinner must himself be punished, at any rate in this world. So long as evil enters the world, somewhere blood will flow; the blood of the guiltless as well as of the guilty is providence's way of redeeming sinful mankind. The innocent will be massacred, if need be vicariously for others, until the balance is adjusted. This is Maistre's theodicy: the explanation of Robespierre's Terror, the justification of all inescapable evil in the world.

Maistre's celebrated theory of sacrifices is founded on this theorem, according to which responsibility is not individual but collective. We are all parts of one another in sin and suffering: hence the sins of the fathers are inevitably visited upon the children, however individually innocent, for who else is there for them to be visited upon? Wicked acts cannot be left for ever unexpiated, even in this world, any more than a disequilibrium can continue to exist indefinitely in the physical world. Maistre 'saw only two elements in history,' Lamennais sadly observed in later life: 'on one side crime, on the other punishment. He was endowed with a generous and noble soul, and his books are all as if written on the scaffold.'[1]

---

[1] Letter of 8 October 1834 to the Comtesse de Senfft: Félicité de Lamennais, *Correspondance générale*, ed. Louis le Guillou (Paris, 1971–81), vol. 6, letter 2338, p. 307.

VII

Protestantism had disrupted the unity of mankind, and created chaos, misery and social disintegration. The eighteenth-century philosophers recommended as a remedy against this *malaise* the regulation of human lives according to a rational plan. But plans founder, precisely because they are rational, because they are plans. War is one of the most apparently planned of human activities. Yet no one who has seen a battle can maintain that it is the orders issued by generals that decide what happens. Neither the general nor his subordinates can possibly tell what is going on; the noise of guns, the chaos, the shrieks of the wounded and the dying, the mutilated bodies – 'five or six kinds of intoxication'[1] – the violence and the disorder are too great. Victories are attributed to the clever dispositions of generals only by those who do not understand the factors of which life is composed. Who wins a victory? Those who are filled with the inexplicable sense of their own superiority; neither troops nor generals can adequately tell what the proportion of casualties may be between them and their enemies. 'It is imagination that loses battles.'[2] Victory is a moral and psychological rather than a physical event, due to a mysterious act of faith; not a successful consequence of carefully laid plans, or of feeble human wills.

Maistre's observations on how battles are fought and won, contained in the celebrated Seventh Conversation in the *Soirées*, constitute probably the best and most vivid formulation of his perpetually recurring theme of the inevitable chaos of the battlefield and the irrelevance of the alleged dispositions of commanders, which later played so great a part in Stendhal's description in *The Charterhouse of Parma* of Fabrice on the battlefield of Waterloo; and plainly had a dominant influence on the doctrine of human action developed by Tolstoy (who is known to have read Maistre) in *War and Peace*. And indeed it is

[1] V 34.
[2] V 33.

Maistre's, as it is Tolstoy's, doctrine of life in general. Life is not a Zoroastrian struggle between light and darkness, as represented by democrats and rationalists, for whom the church is darkness, or conversely by the pious authoritarians, for whom it lies in the wicked forces of atheism; but the blind confusion of a permanent battlefield in which men fight because they cannot do otherwise, under the mysterious decree by which God conducts the universe. Nor does the outcome depend on reason or strength or even virtue, but on the role for which a particular man or nation has been cast in the universal inscrutable drama of historical existence; and of the part assigned to us in this drama we can at best grasp only some tiny fraction. It is idle folly to pretend to understand the whole, still more demented to imagine that we can alter it by superior wisdom. Believe, and do what the Lord, through his representative on earth, commands.

'Let us not lose ourselves in systems!'[1] He is particularly opposed to systems which appear to be based on any method claiming some connection with the natural sciences. The very language of science to Maistre is something degraded; and he notes, prophetically enough, that the degradation of language is always the surest sign of the degradation of a people.[2] Maistre's interest in and ideas about language are characteristically bold and penetrating and, even in their excesses, foreshadow twentieth-century thought. His thesis is that, like all ancient and stable institutions, like kingship, like marriage, like worship, language is a mystery of divine origin. There are those who think that language is a deliberate human invention, a technique created to facilitate communication. According to such theorists thoughts can be thought without symbols: first we think, then we find suitable symbols to express our thoughts, like gloves to fit a hand. This doctrine, held by ordinary men and somewhat uncritically by a good many philosophers until our own times, both Maistre and particularly

---

[1] VIII 294.
[2] IV 63.

Bonald firmly deny. To think is to use symbols, to use an articulated vocabulary. Thoughts are words although unspoken; 'la pensée et la parole', Maistre declared, 'ne sont que deux magnifiques synonymes'.[1] The origins of words – the commonest of all symbols – *are* the origins of thought. There cannot be a moment when man invented the first language, for to invent one must think, and thinking is employing symbols, that is, language. The use of words in general cannot have been invented artificially any more than the 'use' of thoughts, with which it is identical. And the uninvented is for Maistre the mysterious, the divine.

One may, reasonably enough reject the notion of the necessarily divine origin of all that is not artefact, and yet concede the profound originality of the identification of thought and language as a natural phenomenon, the object of such natural sciences as biology and social psychology. The seed of this crucial notion may perhaps be found in that celebrated simile of Plato's *Theaetetus* which Maistre quotes and in which language is spoken of as 'the discourse of the soul with herself'.[2] But if so, it fell on stony ground. Hobbes appears to have rediscovered this truth for himself; and it lies near the heart of Vico's system, with which we are told that Maistre was acquainted.[3]

Maistre enjoys himself a great deal at the expense of eighteenth-century speculations about the origins of language. Rousseau, he declares, is puzzled about how men first began to use words, but the omniscient Condillac knows the answer to this and to all other questions: language clearly came about as a result of the division of labour. Thus one generation of men said BA, another added BE; Assyrians invented the nominative, and the Medes invented the genitive.[4] Such irony was appropriate

---

[1] IV 119.

[2] ibid.

[3] See Elio Gianturco, *Joseph de Maistre and Giambattista Vico: Italian Roots of Maistre's Political Culture* (Columbia University Ph.D. thesis) (Washington, 1937).

[4] IV 88.

enough in the face of the militant lack of historical sense of some among the more fanatical *philosophes*; the rest of Maistre's theory had no similar justification. Since words are the repository of the thought and feeling and view of themselves and of the external world of our ancestors, they embody also their conscious and unconscious wisdom, derived from God to form experience. Hence ancient and traditional texts, especially those contained in sacred books which express the immemorial wisdom of the race, modified and enriched by the impact of events, are so many valuable quarries whence expert knowledge, zeal and patience may extract much hidden gold. Medieval philosophy was scoffed at for its search for hidden meanings and its far-fetched methods of interpretation of sacred texts; but to Maistre, for whom, as for Vico and the German romantics, language is not a human invention, it is a delving for hidden knowledge, a kind of psychoanalysis of the collective unconscious of mankind, or at any rate of Christendom. Only in darkness are great, concealed treasures to be found. Hence the clarification demanded by the Encyclopedists is for him tantamount to causing all that may be profound and fertile in words to evaporate; it annihilates their virtue and dehydrates them of significance. One might, of course, make a similar case for astrology and alchemy, but that would not have frightened Maistre; he was not interested in the methods of natural science: he was interested in the visionary Swedenborg and mystical explanations of natural phenomena; and would have agreed no less readily than his contemporary William Blake that more recondite wisdom was to be found in the occult sciences than in manuals of modern chemistry or physics. Moreover the political value of sacred books can scarcely be exaggerated.[1]

Since thought *is* language, and enshrines the oldest historical

---

[1] 'Comment la Turquie est-elle gouvernée? Par l'Alcoran . . . sans lui le trone ottoman disparaîtrait en un clin d'œil. Comment la Chine est-elle gouvernée? Par les maximes, par les lois, par la religion de Confucius, dont l'esprit est le véritable souverain qui gouverne depuis deux mille cinq cents ans . . .'. VIII 290.

memories of a people or a church, to reform linguistic usage is to attempt to destroy the force and influence of all that is most sacred, wise and authoritative. Of course Condorcet would want to have a universal language, to make communication easier between the enlightened men of all nations, for such a language could be 'purified' of the accumulated superstitions and prejudices of the ages, and would then cease to breed the illusions that today, in Condorcet's view, pass under the name of theology and metaphysics. But, Maistre asks, what are these prejudices and superstitions? We can by now anticipate his answer: they are those very convictions whose origins are shrouded in mystery, whose force cannot be rationally explained; they are those old beliefs and conceptions which have stood the test of time and experience, and enshrine the mature wisdom of the ages; to throw them aside is to remain without a rudder in the turbulent element where every false step means death. And the best, because least modern, most richly laden of languages is the language of the church and of the great Roman state, the best government known to man. The language of the Romans and of the Middle Ages is to be welcomed precisely for the reasons for which Bentham rejected and denounced it, because it is *not* clear, not easily susceptible to scientific use, because the words themselves carry within them the impalpable authority of the immemorial past, the darkness and the suffering of human history, by which alone salvation may be bought. Latin will of itself go far to guarantee right-mindedness; the Latin vocabulary with its specific limitations, its resistance to modernity, is essential to this: Orwell's 1984 merely echoes the crucial thesis that control of language is essential to control of lives, even though the means chosen by his élite, whose aims are somewhat different from Maistre's, is a language not traditional, but artificial, specially constructed – in fact the object of Maistre's attack.

Maistre, consistently with this, defends the Jesuits as the only dependable educators, using Latin as the vehicle of the truth, embodied in the medieval morality, and attacks Speransky and the group of advisers with whom Tsar Alexander I had meditated a kind of New Deal for the Russian Empire. He pushed this attitude very far; for him irrationality was almost valuable in itself, since he approved of everything impervious to the disintegrating processes of reason. Rational faith is much too vulnerable. A good dialectician can knock holes in any structure which rests on so feeble a foundation. What reason makes, reason can mar. Hence Maistre's appeals to Aquinas are very unconvincing. A pupil of the Jesuits, he could hardly do otherwise; but the truth he saw lay outside the Thomist ken, namely that that alone is ultimately impregnable to which the methods of rational argument are wholly and in principle inappropriate and irrelevant. There is again a certain parallel with Tolstoy, whose ironical attitude to faith in scientific experts and to the liberal belief in progress, and more specifically to such believers in the power of human will and human intellect as Speransky, Napoleon and the learned German military strategists (as, indeed, later to the entire Russian intelligentsia), is very similar to that of the Sardinian agent at St Petersburg.

Maistre uses very similar arguments to demolish the, to him, equally absurd theory of the social contract as the basis of society. Contracts, he correctly maintains, presuppose promises, and the means of enforcing them; but a promise is an act which is only intelligible, can only be conceived, within an elaborate network of already existing conscious social conventions. And the machinery of enforcement presupposes the existence of a developed social structure; to have reached the stage of a contract there must not only already exist a society living by rules and conventions, but one which has reached a very considerable degree of order and complexity. To isolated savages in a 'state of nature' social conventions, including promises, contracts, enforceable laws and so forth, can mean nothing at all. Hence to suppose that societies are created by contracts, and not the other way round, is not only a historical but a logical absurdity. But then only Protestants can ever have supposed that society was an artificial association like a bank or a business.[1]

Society, Maistre declares in more than one passionate outburst, bearing plain marks of Burke's influence, is not an elaborately constructed, artificial association based on calculation of self-interest or happiness, but rests at least as much on the uncreated, original, overpowering human yearning for sacrifice, the impulse to immolate oneself on a sacred altar without hope of return. Armies obey orders and go to their death; it would be grotesque to suppose them animated by thoughts of personal advantage; and as discipline is to armies, so in a very different degree is all obedience to organised power – an activity traditional, mysterious, irresistible, against which there is no appeal.

It is only since the Renaissance, Maistre informs us, that this truth has been obscured and denied. Luther and Calvin, Bacon and Hobbes, Locke and Grotius, influenced in their turn by the ancient heresies of Wyclif and Hus, have propagated this great error, according to which all power and authority depend on something so feeble and arbitrary as an artificial convention. The great French Revolution has demonstrated the falsity of their short-sighted optimism, for it was the punishment of God upon those who entertained such theories and ideas. Society is not an association for mutual profit, it is a *maison correctionelle*, almost a penal settlement. It is not, indeed, governed by reason, but then democracy, which is certainly more rational than despotism, breeds misery everywhere except where, as among the admirable English, being unwritten and merely 'felt', it is a real source of power, that is, can enforce the very contracts on

[1] Cf. Vico on Spinoza's notion of the state: 'a society of hucksters'. *The New Science of Giambattista Vico*, trans. Thomas Goddard Bergin and Max Harold Fisch, revised ed. (New York, 1968), para. 335 (p. 98). And Bonald: 'as if society consisted only of the walls of our houses or the ramparts of our towns; as if there were not, wherever a human being is born, a father, a mother, a child, a language, heaven, earth, God and society'. [L. G. A.] de Bonald, *Du divorce* . . ., 2nd ed. (Paris, 1805), p. 13.

which shallow thinkers who ignore both facts and logic purport to found it.

What matters is not reason but power. Wherever there is a vacuum, power must sooner or later enter and create a new order out of revolutionary chaos. The Jacobins and Napoleon may be criminals, tyrants, but they wield power, they represent authority, they exact obedience, above all they punish and thereby restrain the centrifugal tendencies of weak and fallible men. Consequently they are a thousand times preferable to the critical intellectuals, the destructive pedlars of ideas who pulverise the social structure and destroy every vital process until some force, however illegal, rises up in response to the claims of history to sweep them out of its way.

All power is from God. Maistre's interpretation of the celebrated Pauline text is very literal. All force commands respect. All weakness is to be despised, no matter where it is found, even in the acts of an anointed monarch of 'the fairest kingdom after the Kingdom of Heaven'[1] – Louis XVI of France. The Jacobins were scoundrels and murderers, but the Terror re-established authority, preserved and extended the frontiers of France, and therefore counts higher in the scale of ultimate values than the liberals and idealists of the Gironde who let power slip from their feeble grasp. It is certain that legitimate authority alone will stand up to chance and change. Mere conquest, not sanctioned by the eternal laws of the true church, is robbery: 'it is no more permitted to steal towns or provinces than watches or snuff-boxes',[2] and this is no less true of the makers of the frontiers of 1815 than of Frederick the Great or Napoleon.[3] Maistre condemns naked militarism again and

---

[1] See p. 103 above, note 1.

[2] IX 77.

[3] Maistre's attitude to Napoleon was curiously and characteristically ambivalent. On the one hand Napoleon is a vulgar upstart and a brutal destroyer of ancient values, the persecutor of both the Pope and legitimate monarchs, the blasphemous perpetrator of a coronation that was a horrible travesty of a sacred rite, a moral outcast, the enemy of mankind. On the other hand his clear grasp of the realities of power, his open contempt for

again: 'Every time something is perfected in the sphere of the art of war, that is a misfortune pure and simple.'[1] Military government (even in his own Savoy) he calls *la bâtonocratie*,[2] the rule of the big stick, and it is 'the horror of the age'.[3] 'I have always detested, do now and shall all my life detest military

---

democrats, liberals and intellectuals, and the other members of the hateful *secte*, but above all the contrast between the stupidity and weakness of the Bourbons and the military and administrative genius of a man who once again lifted France to a pinnacle of glory, could not but appeal powerfully to the apostle of realism and authority. Maistre, official representative though he was of a victim of the French emperor, and subjected to daily humiliation by the mere presence of a French ambassador in St Petersburg (which automatically precluded official recognition of his own proper diplomatic status), longed to meet Napoleon. Napoleon for his part was impressed by the brilliance of Maistre's writings, which he was said to find politically sympathetic. Maistre found his situation immensely tantalising. He wrote to the court at Cagliari, setting out his case. Napoleon was, it was true, a usurper; but was he more of one than William of Orange, whose dynasty was recognised by all the crowned heads of Europe? Napoleon was a callous murderer, but had he killed as many innocent victims as Elizabeth of England? All power was, after all, from God, both legitimate and illegitimate; and Bonaparte had protected and enlarged the frontiers of the great kingdom of France, which he could not have achieved had he not in some sense been an instrument of providence. These casuistries merely scandalised the Sardinian officials. King Victor Emanuel was deeply shocked, and severely forbade his minister to have any truck with the Corsican monster. Maistre was profoundly disappointed. But he prized loyalty above all virtues; the less worthy the embodiment of the legitimate royal power, the greater obedience was due to it, so that the principle of unquestioning obedience owed by the subject to his sovereign might shine forth the more clearly. His diplomatic rejoinders grew more acid and ironical in tone. He had been accused of making a 'surprising' request (XI 104–5). He assured his royal master that he would at all times obey all his orders to the letter; but not to cause him surprise – that he could not promise. He never met Napoleon.

[1] Letter of 24 April/4 May 1816 to the Count de Vallaise (the Sardinian foreign minister): *Correspondance diplomatique*, vol. 2, p. 205.

[2] IX 59.

[3] Letter of 22 July/3 August 1804 to the Chevalier Rossi (the Sardinian secretary of state), in the Turin state archive: cited by J. Mandoul, *Joseph de Maistre et la politique de la maison de Savoie* (Paris, 1899), p. 311.

government.'[1] He detests it because it is arbitrary, and weakens
the authority of kings and ancient institutions, and leads to
revolutions and the subversion of traditional Christian values.[2]
Yet there are moments when chaos threatens: the worst government is preferable to anarchy; indeed only the most ruthless
despotism can check the disintegration of society. In this he is
at one with Machiavelli and Hobbes and all the defenders of
authority as such.

Revolution – the worst of evils – is itself a divine process, sent
to punish wickedness and regenerate our fallen nature by
suffering (we are reminded of the theological interpretation of
the defeat of France by Pétain and his supporters in 1940), as
mysterious as all other great historical forces, so that 'it is not
men who direct the revolution, it is the revolution that uses
them'.[3] It may indeed make use of the vilest instruments –
Robespierre's 'infernal genius alone could perform this prodigy
[the victory of France over the Coalition] . . . This monster of
strength, drunk with blood and success, this terrifying
phenomenon . . . was at once a terrible punishment sent upon
French men and the sole means of saving France.'[4] He excited
them to a pitch of violence, he hardened their hearts, he drove
them wild with the blood of the scaffolds until they fought like
madmen and crushed everyone. Yet without the revolution

---

[1] IX 58; and again 'Blessed a thousandfold be those princes who allow us
to forget a little the art of war', VII 134; and on the military regimes of the
later Roman Empire: they were 'a permanent plague', I 511. On this whole
subject see François Vermale's *Notes sur Joseph de Maistre inconnu* (Chambéry,
1921), and in particular chapter 3, 'Joseph de Maistre contre le militarisme
piémontais', pp. 47–61, esp. pp. 48–9. Yet he declared that if the monarch
decreed a military dictatorship, he would, however reluctantly, accept it.

[2] This sharp contrast between war and militarism was echoed by
Proudhon (in language almost identical with Maistre's) in his *La Guerre et la
paix*. It is possible that Tolstoy, who read Maistre's writings while writing
his own *War and Peace*, consciously or unconsciously owes this very paradox,
which plays a part in his own masterpiece, not merely to Proudhon (as one at
least of his critics, Boris Eikhenbaum, supposes), but to Maistre himself.

[3] I 7.
[4] I 18.

(which men like Robespierre are deluded enough to think that they can make, whereas it is clear that it is not they who have made the revolution, but the revolution that made them) he would have remained the mediocrity that he had been before.

Men who seize power do not know how they come to do so; their influence is more of a mystery to them than to others: circumstances which the great man can neither foresee nor direct have done everything for him, and without his help – this is 'the secret force that plays with human plans',[1] providence, Hegel's cunning of reason. But man is vain and imagines that his own will can break through the inexorable laws by which God governs the world. He tires of repeating again and again that it is this delusion on the part of weak, deceived creatures, swollen with self-conceit, that is at the root of the belief in democracy. A false sense of one's own wisdom and power, blind refusal to recognise the superiority either of other men or of institutions, leads to the ridiculous mosaic of declarations of the rights of men and claptrap about liberty. 'Whoever says that man is born to freedom utters a sentence which has no meaning.'[2] Man is what he is and was, what he does and did; to say that man is not what he *should* be is an offence to sanity. We must listen to history, which is 'experimental politics', that is, the only reliable teacher of this subject: 'She will never tell us the opposite of the truth.'[3] One genuine experiment blows up a hundred volumes of abstract speculation.[4]

Yet notions of popular liberty and democracy rest on just such groundless abstractions, supported neither by empirical experience nor by divine revelation. If men decline to recognise authority where it legitimately belongs – in the church and the 'divinisé' monarchy – they will fall under the yoke of the tyranny of the people, which is the worst of all. Those who create revolts in the name of freedom end by becoming tyrants,

[1] I 118.
[2] I 426.
[3] VIII 294; cf. I 266, I 426, II 339, VII 540.
[4] I 426.

said Bonald (quoting Bossuet and echoed by Dostoevsky half a century later); and Maistre merely adds that the inevitable consequence of faith in the principles of Rousseau is a situation in which the people is told by its masters '"*You believe that you don't want this law, but we assure you that you do. If you dare reject it, we shall shoot you down in order to punish you for not wanting what you do want*" and they then do so.'[1] No clearer formula for what has rightly been called 'totalitarian democracy' has surely ever been uttered. Maistre says sardonically that if a good many scientists perished on the guillotine, they had only themselves to blame.[2] The ideas in whose name they were killed were their own; and, like all mutiny against authority, bound to destroy their authors.

Maistre's violent hatred of free traffic in ideas, and his contempt for all intellectuals, are not mere conservatism, nor the orthodoxy and loyalty to church and state in which he was brought up, but something at once much older and much newer – something which at once echoes the fanatical voices of the Inquisition, and sounds what is perhaps the earliest note of the militant anti-rational Fascism of modern times.

VIII

Some of Maistre's acutest pages are reserved for Russia, in which he spent fifteen of the most creative years of his life.[3] Alexander I used him for a time as a confidential adviser, and Maistre furnished him with observations and advice he clearly meant to apply beyond Russia herself, to the whole of contemporary Europe. He became celebrated for his political epigrams, which proved much to the taste of Alexander and his advisers,

[1] I 107.
[2] I 9.
[3] *Quatre chapitres sur la Russie*, from which the quotations that follow are taken, is a collection of *obiter dicta* by Maistre which contains remarks of remarkable insight and prophetic power, but is today almost entirely forgotten.

especially after the Emperor's liberal phase was over. Such maxims as 'Man in general, if reduced to himself, is too wicked to be free'[1] or 'Everywhere the few lead the many, for without a more or less powerful aristocracy public authority is not sufficient for this end'[2] must have found great favour in the aristocratic *salons* of St Petersburg, and he is mentioned with approval in contemporary Russian memoirs.[3]

Maistre's observations on Russia are exceedingly pungent. The greatest danger comes from the encouragement of liberalism and the sciences so fatally promoted by Alexander's enlightened advisers. In a letter to Prince Alexander Golitsyn, the secular director of the Orthodox Church, he points to three main sources of danger to the stability of the Russian state: the spirit of sceptical enquiry stimulated by the teaching of the natural sciences; protestantism, which declared that all men are born free and equal, and that all power rests in the people, which foments resistance to authority as a natural right; and, finally, demands for the immediate liberation of the serfs. No sovereign, he declares, has enough strength to govern several million human beings unless he is aided either by religion or slavery.[4] Before Christianity, society reposed on slavery. After

[1] VIII 279 (cf. II 339).

[2] VIII 280 (cf. II 339).

[3] For example by Vigel' and Zhikharev: F. F. Vigel', *Zapiski* (Moscow, 1928), vol. 1, p. 275 (cf. vol. 2, p. 52); S. P. Zhikharev, *Zapiski sovremennika* (Moscow, 1934), vol. 2, pp. 112–13. On the other hand Leo Tolstoy, who certainly used both Maistre's own writings and the memoirs of his contemporaries when he was working on the historical background of *War and Peace*, paints an ironical portrait of him. Disguised as 'le Vicomte de Mortemart', a typical aristocratic French émigré at his best in a St Petersburg *salon*, he tells a silly anecdote about Napoleon, the Duc d'Enghien and the actress Mlle Georges to a group of fashionable ladies at a glittering evening party in the Russian capital. Later, referred to merely as 'un homme de beaucoup de mérite', he appears at another party in conversation with Prince Vasily about Kutuzov. He is mentioned by name later in the novel. *War and Peace*, book 1, part 1, chapters 1, 3; book 3, part 2, chapter 6; book 4, part 3, chapter 19. In the translation by Louise and Aylmer Maude, edited by Henry Gifford (Oxford, 1983), the references are vol. 1, pp. 5, 13; vol. 2, pp. 771–3, 1159.

[4] VIII 288.

it on religious authority – control by priests – hence slavery could be abolished. But in Russia, because of its Byzantine beginnings, the Tartar rule and the schism from Rome, the church lacks authority; hence slavery exists in Russia because it is needed, because the emperor could not rule without it.[1] Calvinism would undermine the Russian state; natural science has not yet (in Russia, which is combustible enough) lit the flame of that incendiary pride which has already consumed part of the world, and will finish it off altogether if nothing stops it.[2] The end of the educator is to impart the knowledge that God created men for society, which cannot exist without government, which in its turn requires obedience, fidelity, a sense of duty on the part of subjects. He embodied his advice in a number of specific recommendations:[3] correct abuses but delay the liberation of the serfs as long as possible; be careful about ennobling commoners – this is in the spirit of the historian Karamzin in his influential *Note on Old and New Russia*, which was suspicious of Speransky and his reforming zeal; encourage the wealthy landed gentry and personal merit, but not commerce; restrain science; promote the principles of the Roman and Greek character; protect Roman Catholicism, and use Jesuit teachers wherever possible; avoid giving posts to foreigners, who are capable of anything; if foreign teachers are to be employed at all, let them at least be Roman Catholics. This was very well received by the anti-western conservatives. Count Uvarov, Curator of the St Petersburg school district, proved an apt pupil, and in 1811 eliminated philosophy, political economy, aesthetics, commercial studies from the schools in his care, and later, as Minister of Education, proclaimed the notorious triple formula – Orthodoxy, Autocracy, Nationality – which expressed the same principles applied to universities and the entire educational system. This programme was in

[1] VIII 284.
[2] VIII 285.
[3] VIII 355–9.

effect rigorously followed in Russia for half a century – from the middle years of the reign of Alexander I to the reforms of Alexander II in the 1860s. It was viewed with deep nostalgia by the famous High Procurator of the Holy Synod (that is, the church) in the 80s and 90s.

If Russia grants liberty to its inhabitants, it is lost. Here are his words:

> If one could lock a Russian desire in a fortress it would blow it up. There is no one who *wants* as passionately as a Russian wants . . . Observe the Russian merchant even of the lower class, and you will see how intelligent and alert he is about his interests; watch him executing the most dangerous enterprises, particularly on the field of battle, and you will see how daring he can be. If it occurs to us to give liberty to something like thirty-six million men of this kind, and we do it – one can never insist upon this enough – in an instant a general conflagration will break out, by which Russia will be consumed.[1]

And again:

> These serfs, as they receive their freedom, will find themselves among instructors who are more than suspect, and priests without power and without repute. Thus exposed, without preparation, they will infallibly and suddenly pass from superstition to atheism, from passive obedience to unbridled activity. Liberty will have upon all those temperaments the effect of heady wine upon a man entirely unused to it. The mere spectacle of this freedom will demoralise even those who have no part in it . . . To this you must add the indifference, the incapacity or the ambition of a few noblemen, criminal activities from abroad, the manœuvres of the hateful sect which never sleeps and so on, and so on, plus a few Pugachevs[2] of the University, and the state will, in all probability, quite literally, *break* in half, like a wooden beam which is too long and sags in the middle.[3]

---

[1] VIII 288–9.
[2] Emelyan Ivanovich Pugachev was the leader of a peasant and Cossack rebellion crushed in the reign of Catherine the Great.
[3] VIII 291–2.

Again:

> what an inexplicable delusion, whereby a great nation has reached a
> point where it imagines it can go against a law of the universe. The
> Russians want everything in a day. There is no middle way. One
> must creep slowly towards the goals of science, one cannot fly
> there! The Russians have conceived two equally unfortunate ideas.
> The first is to put literature and science at the head of everything,
> and the second is to amalgamate into one whole the teaching of all
> the sciences. [1]

And in the same strain:

> What will happen in Russia if modern doctrines penetrate to the
> people, and the temporal power has only itself to lean upon? On the
> very eve of the universal catastrophe, Voltaire had said 'Books did
> it all.' Let us repeat while we are still in the bosom of happy Russia,
> still on her feet, 'Books did it all'; let us beware of books! A great
> political step in this country would be to retard the reign of
> science, and use the authority of the church as a powerful ally of the
> sovereign, until such time as science may safely be allowed to
> penetrate society. [2]

And again:

> If the Russians, who have a certain tendency to do everything for
> fun (I do not say make fun of everything), play with this serpent
> too, no people will be more cruelly bitten. [3]

The only hope lies in preserving the privileges of the church
and the nobility, and keeping merchants and the lower classes in
their place. Above all one must not favour 'the propagation of
science among the lowest classes of the people; one must
prevent, without seeming to do so, any enterprise of this kind

[1] VIII 300.
[2] VIII 344.
[3] VIII 354.

which might be conceived by ignorant or subversive zealots'.[1]
Also, one must

> exercise more rigorous supervision over immigrants from the west,
> particularly over Germans and Protestants, who come to this
> country to instruct the youth in all kinds of subjects. One can be
> very sure that of every hundred foreigners of this kind who make
> their way into Russia, at least ninety-nine are the most undesirable
> acquisitions for the state, for those who have property, a family,
> morals and a reputation stay at home.[2]

Indeed Maistre was almost the first western writer openly to
advocate the policy of the deliberate retardation of the liberal
arts and sciences, the virtual suppression of some of the central
cultural values which transformed western thought and conduct
from the Renaissance to our day. But it was the twentieth
century that was destined to see the richest flowering and the
most ruthless application of this sinister doctrine. It has perhaps been the most characteristic and gloomiest spiritual
phenomenon of our time and is far from over yet.

IX

As a sharp realistic observer of his own times, Maistre is
equalled only by Tocqueville. We have seen how prophetically
he analysed Russian conditions. Similarly, at a period when his
fellow legitimists looked on the Great Revolution as a passing
phase whose results could be annulled, a momentary aberration
of the human spirit after which things might be made to flow
much as before, Maistre declared that one might as well try to
bottle all the water in the Lake of Geneva as attempt to restore
the pre-revolutionary order.[3] Nothing could weaken France so
much as a Royalist counter-revolution aided by foreign powers,

---

[1] VIII 357.
[2] VIII 358–9.
[3] IX 58.

which would lead to the dismemberment of that wonderful kingdom. It was the glorious revolutionary armies that preserved France.

Following one of his spiritual mentors, the Savoyard bishop Thiollaz, he predicted the restoration of the Bourbons, but added that the dynasty would not last, since all authority was founded on faith, and they had conspicuously lost all genuine belief in themselves and their destiny. And in any case some reforms had to be introduced. Charles II of England was not, fortunately for that country, Charles I. By contrast, the emperors Alexander and Napoleon genuinely fascinated him; he could scarcely be expected to admire the House of Savoy, which he served so faithfully, and he made it clear, sometimes too clear, that his loyalty was not to persons but to the institution of royalty itself. He took a great deal of sardonic pleasure in rubbing into the provincial, easily frightened Sardinian court unpalatable truths about the progress of events in Europe. His dispatches were written in the courteous style of conventional diplomacy, but even so could not wholly conceal the mixture of loyalty and contempt which he felt for his addressees.

This political realism as well as the deliberate sharpness with which it was expressed made him, all his life, suspect at Cagliari and Turin as a dangerous extremist, a kind of royalist Jacobin.[1] He was certainly the biggest fish which that petty, nervous, pompous, infinitely cautious little court had ever captured. He was a man of recognised genius, widely admired, by far the most famous Savoyard of his time. It was impossible not to employ him, but he was best kept at a distance, in St Petersburg, where his disquieting observations evidently delighted the unaccountable Alexander.

The best years of his life were spent in St Petersburg, and the portraits which his biographers have left us are largely based on the impressions of his friends and acquaintances of this period. They convey the image of a devoted and tenderly affectionate

---

[1] See p. 146 above, note 3.

father, a loyal, delightful and sensitive friend; and indeed his private correspondence bears this out. He addressed amusing letters, full of solicitude, irony and gossip, to noble Russian ladies, whom he converted to his own faith, much too successfully for the Tsar's taste.[1]

All the testimony which Maistre's well-known Russian

[1] The best known of his converts was Mme Svétchine, whose famous Paris *salon* in the 1830s and 40s became the centre of ultramontane Catholicism. But there were others, better known in their own day in St Petersburg society, who became members of Maistre's *cénacle,* among them Countess Edling (née Stourdza, the celebrated phanariot *intrigante*), beautiful Tolstoy, the Princes A. and M. Golitsyn, Prince Gagarin, who later became a Jesuit in Paris and wrote memoirs (indeed it is his reminiscences and those of Mme Svétchine that shed most light on Maistre's spiritual influence upon the Petersburg nobility), and, not least, the beautiful wife of Admiral Chichagov, who was converted to Rome, greatly to the displeasure of her family. Leo Tolstoy's very unsympathetic account in *War and Peace* of the Countess Hélène's relations with the Jesuits is probably founded on the activities of Maistre's circle. Illuminism had made great inroads in Russian court circles – the emperor himself was a conspicuous convert to it under the influence of Prince Golitsyn and later of Madame von Krüdener. Maistre, who had had associations with Masonic lodges in his youth, admired Saint-Martin's devotional works. He looked on their author as an ally – a fellow-traveller with the church (much as some Catholics in this century viewed Bergson) who melted materialism, preserved men from the Protestant ice which freezes the human heart, acted as a bridge towards the true church from Calvinistic aridity and 'accustom[ed] men to dogma and spiritual ideas' (VIII 330), and worked for the unity of Christendom. He understood the Petersburg atmosphere well, and did what he could to excite sympathy for the Catholic cause; in particular he exerted himself to protect the French Jesuits, whose Order had been dissolved by the Pope and who had fled to Russia from the revolution, and, in fact, procured permission for them to establish a Jesuit college on Russian soil. The Russian Orthodox Church had become increasingly suspicious of these activities. Indeed it may be his over-zealous activity both as a champion of this order, to which all his life he remained deeply devoted, and as a fisher of well-born souls, that caused Alexander, with his customary brusqueness, and without apparent cause (but in all probability urged to do so by the head of the Orthodox Church), to ask for Maistre's sudden, to him deeply distressing, recall in 1817. He returned to Turin by way of Paris, and died four years later, a holder of a high sinecure in Piedmont, his masterpiece, *Les Soirées de Saint-Pétersbourg,* still unpublished.

friends have left to the sweetness of his character, his mordant irony and his high spirits in conditions of exile and material indigence further supports this verdict. His moral and political world is the exact opposite: it is full of sin, cruelty and suffering, and only able to survive through the violent repression exercised by the chosen instruments of power, who wield absolute and crushing authority, and carry on an unceasing war against every tendency to free enquiry or the pursuit of life or liberty or happiness by any secular path. His world is much more realistic and more ferocious than that of the romantics. Half a century had to pass before this same unmistakable note is heard in Nietzsche or Drumont or Belloc, or the French *intégralistes* of the *Action française*, or, in a still more debased form, in the spokesmen of the totalitarian regimes of our own times; yet Maistre himself felt that he was the last defender of a civilisation that was perishing. It was encircled by enemies and must be defended with a most merciless ferocity. Even his attitude to such apparently theoretical subjects as the nature of language or the progress of chemistry takes on a fierce polemical glow.[1] When one is engaged in a desperate defence of one's world and its values, nothing can be given away, any breach in the walls might be fatal, every point must be defended to the death.

X

Five years after Maistre's death the leaders of the Saint-Simonian School declared that the task of the future consisted in the reconciliation of the ideas of Maistre with those of Voltaire. At first this seems absurd. Voltaire stands for individual liberty and Maistre for chains; Voltaire cried for more light, Maistre for

---

[1] Faguet thinks that this is due merely to the desire to contradict any view held by the other side – in this case the views of Condillac or Condorcet and their friends. It may be so: whatever Maistre's motive, it is a formidable, brilliantly conducted counter-offensive.

more darkness. Voltaire hated the Roman Church so violently that he denied it even a minimum of virtue. Maistre liked even its vices, and regarded Voltaire as the Devil incarnate. His celebrated pages on Voltaire in the *Soirées*[1] – which rise to a climax of hatred as he describes his enemy's grimace, his perpetual hideous leering grin, as a kind of horrible *rictus* – come from the heart. Yet there is a curious and, as time would show, frightening truth in this Saint-Simonian observation, as in so much of the doctrine of that confused but strikingly prophetic movement. Modern totalitarian systems do, in their acts if not in their style of rhetoric, combine the outlooks of Voltaire and Maistre; they have inherited, particularly, the qualities which the two have in common. For, polar opposites as they are, they both belong to the tough-minded tradition in classical French thought. Their ideas may have strictly contradicted one another, but the quality of mind is often exceedingly similar (as later critics have indeed remarked, without, as a rule, investigating what this quality is, and what its influence has produced). Neither Voltaire nor his enemy is guilty of any degree of softness, vagueness or self-indulgence of either intellect or feeling, nor do they tolerate it in others. They stand for the dry light against the flickering flame, they are implacably opposed to all that is turbid, misty, gushing, impressionistic – to the eloquence of Rousseau, Chateaubriand, Hugo, Michelet, Bergson, Péguy. They are ruthlessly deflationary writers, contemptuous, sardonic, genuinely heartless and, at times, genuinely cynical. Beside their icy, smooth, clear surface Stendhal's prose is romantic, and Flaubert's writings are an imperfectly drained marsh. Marx, Tolstoy, Sorel, Lenin are – in the cast of their minds (not their ideas) – their true successors. The tendency to cast a glance upon the social scene so chilly as to cause a sudden shock, to deflate and dehydrate, to use ruthless political and historical analysis as a deliberate technique of

---

[1] IV 205–10; at VI 458–9 he compares him to a precious cargo infected by the plague.

shock treatment, has entered into modern political techniques to a marked degree.

If the capacity for the uncompromising exposure of sentimental and confused processes of thought, for which Voltaire was so largely responsible, be combined with Maistre's historicism, his political pragmatism, his equally low estimate of human capacity and goodness, and his belief that the essence of life is the craving for suffering and sacrifice and surrender; if to this is added Maistre's considered belief that government is impossible without perpetual repression of the weak and confused majority by a minority of dedicated rulers, hardened against all temptation to indulge in humanitarian experiments; then we begin to approach the strong strain of nihilism in all modern totalitarianism. Voltaire can be made to strip away all liberal delusions, and Maistre to provide the nostrum by which the bleak, bare world which results is to be administered. Voltaire, it is true, defended neither despotism nor deception, whereas Maistre preached the need for both. 'The principle of the sovereignty of the people', he says (echoing Plato and Machiavelli, Hobbes and Montesquieu), 'is so dangerous that even if it were true, it would be necessary to conceal it.'[1] This is echoed by the famous remark attributed to Rivarol that equality is wonderful, but why tell the people? The Saint-Simonians were not perhaps being so paradoxical after all; and their founder's admiration for Maistre, which seemed so odd to the liberals and socialists whom Saint-Simon inspired, is founded on a genuine affinity. The content of Orwell's celebrated nightmare (as well as the actual systems which inspired it) is directly related to the visions of both Maistre and Saint-Simon. It owes something also to the deep political cynicism to be found in Voltaire, to which the words of that incomparable writer gave a far wider influence than the work of truly great original thinkers like Machiavelli or Hobbes.

[1] IX 494.

XI

An eminent philosopher once remarked that, in order truly to understand the central doctrines of an original thinker, it is necessary, in the first place, to grasp the particular vision of the universe which lies at the heart of his thought, rather than attend to the logic of his arguments. For the arguments, however cogent and intellectually impressive, are, as a rule, only the outworks – the defensive weapons against real and possible objections on the part of actual and potential critics and opponents. They illuminate neither the psychological process by which the thinker in question came to his conclusion, nor even the essential, let alone the sole, means of conveying and justifying the central conception which those whom the thinker seeks to convince must grasp, if they are to understand and accept the ideas that are being put forward.

As a generalisation this plainly goes too far; however they may have arrived at their positions, such thinkers as Kant or Mill or Russell, for example, seek to convince us by rational arguments, and Kant at any rate by nothing else. They make it plain that, if such arguments are exposed by counter-arguments as fallacious, or their conclusions are refuted by common experience, they are prepared to regard themselves as mistaken. But the generalisation does hold of many thinkers of a more metaphysical type – Plato, Berkeley, Hegel, Marx, not to speak of more deliberately romantic or poetical or religious writers, whose influence has extended both for better and for worse far beyond the confines of academic circles. They may use arguments – indeed they often do – but it is not by these, whether valid or invalid, that they stand or fall or are justly estimated. For their essential purpose is to expound an all-embracing conception of the world and man's place and experience within it, they seek not so much to convince as to convert, to transform the vision of those whom they seek to address, so that they see the facts 'in a new light', 'from a new angle', in terms of a new pattern in which what had earlier seemed to be a casual amalgam of elements is presented as a systematic, interrelated unity. Logical reasoning may help to weaken existing doctrines, or refute specific beliefs, but it is an ancillary weapon, not the principal means of conquest: that is the new model itself, which casts its own emotional or intellectual or spiritual spell upon those who are converted.

It used to be said of Maistre, principally by his admirers in the nineteenth century, that he used the weapon of reason to defeat reason, of logic to prove the inadequacy of logic. But this is not so. Maistre is a dogmatic thinker whose ultimate principles and premises nothing can shake, and whose considerable ingenuity and intellectual power are devoted to making the facts fit his preconceived notions, not to developing concepts which fit newly discovered, or newly visualised, facts. He is like a lawyer arguing to a brief: the conclusion is foregone – he knows that he must arrive at it somehow, for he is convinced of the truth, no matter what he may learn or encounter. The problem is only how to convince the doubting reader, how to dismiss awkward or plainly contrary evidence. James Stephen is right in saying that his principal mode of argument is to beg the question.[1] He starts from unquestioned principles, and is then determined to carry his theories through, no matter what the evidence. Any theory can, in fact, be triumphantly vindicated, given a sufficient number of *ad hoc* hypotheses (like the epicycles of Ptolemaic astronomy) to account for apparent exceptions, and any doctrine can be 'saved', although it will of course become progressively useless as the number of cases it would seem to apply to grows less with each extra *ad hoc* hypothesis superimposed to meet some logical obstacle.

For his fundamental beliefs – in innate ideas planted in us by God; in spiritual truths of which rational or empirical formulations are a mere, at times distorting, veil; in ancient wisdom,

---

[1] Sir James Fitzjames Stephen, *Horae Sabbaticae*, third series (London, 1892), p. 254.

possessed by men before the Flood, of which we now have merely unconnected fragments; in intuitive certainty about good and evil, right and wrong; in all the undemonstrated and indemonstrable dogmas of his church at its most unyielding – for all this Maistre offers no serious argument. It is clear that he would not consider any empirical experience, anything that common sense or science would regard as evidence, as in principle capable of upsetting these truths. The proposition that if two beliefs contradict one another, or are each contradicted by apparently unanswerable objections, yet are laid down by faith, or by authority, then both must be believed and are in principle reconcilable, even though we cannot see how they are so because of the feebleness of our intellect – this proposition is not argued, but simply asserted. Similarly the notion that if reason conflicts with common sense it must be treated like a poisoner, and expelled with curses upon its head, is not compatible with any degree of respect for rational thought, the appeal is to authority not experience, it is pure dogma used as a polemical battering-ram.

So, for example, Maistre maintains that all suffering, whether it falls on the heads of the guilty or the innocent, must be expiation of sin committed by someone at some time. Why is this so? Because pain must have a purpose, and since its only purpose is penal, there must, somewhere in the universe, exist a sum of transgression sufficient to cause a corresponding sum of suffering to occur; else the existence of evil could not be explained or justified, and the universe would lack moral government. But this is unthinkable: that the world is governed by a moral purpose is self-evident. [1]

He boldly asserts that no constitution is the result of deliberation; that the rights of individuals or peoples are best unwritten, or if they are written down must be merely the transcription of unwritten rights which have existed for all time, and are metaphysically intuited, for whoever lives by a text is weakened

---

[1] IV 22–8.

by it. What then of written constitutions? In Maistre's last years (even at the time of the writing of his essay on constitutions) the American Constitution was functioning vigorously and successfully; but that is only because it is based on England's unwritten constitution.[1] But this is not true of France, or the Code Napoléon, or the new Spanish Constitution: Maistre knows that they must fail. He needs no argument. He knows, as Burke knew, what is lasting and what is transient, what is destined to exist for ever, and what is the brittle work of human hands. 'Institutions . . . are strong and durable to the extent that they are conceived of as divine.'[2] Man creates nothing. He can plant a tree, but not make it. He can modify but not create. The French Constitution of 1795 is a mere 'academic exercise';[3] 'a constitution which is made for all nations is made for none'.[4] It must grow out of the particular circumstances and character of a nation, at a particular time, at a particular place. Men fight for abstract principles – 'children killing each other to build a huge house of cards'.[5] 'Republican institutions' – the product of the rickety structures of human deliberation – 'have no roots; they are just *placed* on the ground, whereas what came before [monarchy and church] was *planted*.'[6]

> A man must have lost his senses to believe that God has commissioned academies to tell us what He is and what is our duty to Him. It belongs to prelates, nobles, great officers of state . . . to teach nations what is good and bad . . . others have no right to argue about matters of this sort . . . Those who speak or write in such a way as to rob a people of its natural dogma should be hanged like burglars.[7]

[1] I 87.
[2] I 56.
[3] I 74.
[4] ibid.
[5] I 78.
[6] I 127.
[7] V 108.

And whence do prelates, nobles, great officers of state derive their authority? From the sovereign: in the secular state from the king; but ultimately from the source of all spiritual authority, the Pope. Liberty is the gift of kings: a nation cannot give itself liberty, rights and all liberties must have been conceded by the sovereign at some date. Basic rights are not conceded: they exist because they exist, born in the mists of the past, of inscrutable divine origin.[1] The rights of the sovereigns themselves have no date, for they are eternal. Sovereignty must be indivisible, for if it is distributed there is no centre of authority, and all things fall to pieces. Earthly sovereigns and legislators can act only in the name of God, and all they can do is to reassemble or reorganise already existing rights, duties, liberties, privileges, which have existed since the day of the creation.

All this seems dead medieval dogma, and Maistre believed in it precisely because it was so. When he meets with apparent exceptions he has a short way of dealing with them: he notes that someone might point out that the British constitution, for instance, seems to rest securely on the division of powers (the empirical study of actual governments did not enter his sphere of interest: on this point he simply repeats the famous misjudgement of Montesquieu). How is one to explain this? The answer is that the British constitution is a marvel; it is divine. For no human minds could have formed an order out of elements so chaotic. If letters cast out of a window were to form a poem would not that be an argument for the working of a force more than human? The very absurdities and conflicts of British laws and customs are evidence of divine power guiding the faltering hands of men. For there can be no doubt that the British constitution would have collapsed long ago had it been of merely human origin. This is an argument in a circle with a vengeance.

Someone might at this point object, as against the

[1] I 68.

proposition that whatever is written is a feeble instrument as against what is unwritten, that the Jews have after all survived successfully by belief in the text of the Old Testament. Maistre is ready for this too: the Bible has preserved the Jews precisely because it is divine; otherwise they would of course have collapsed long ago. Yet elsewhere he forgets the unique status of the Old Testament, and speaks of the fact that what has preserved social stability in Asia or Africa is not mere brute force, but the immense political authority of the Koran, of Confucius, or of other sacred texts of conspicuously non-divine origin, embodying propositions clearly not compatible with the revealed truths of the scriptural Testaments, either Old or New. Thus he not merely begs the question, argues in circles, but does not bother to be consistent. But then if reason is a poisoner to be avoided at all costs, this is all to the good.

It is not in rational argument, not even in ingenious casuistry, that the strength of Maistre lies. His language may at times wear the mask of reason, but it is irrationalist and dogmatic through and through. Nor is the conviction that some of his theses undoubtedly carry due only to the fact that his style is vigorous, brilliant, original and amusing. 'They both [Maistre and Newman] write as well-bred men talk,' said James Stephen.[1] The declamation is often dazzling. Maistre is the most readable of all French publicists in the nineteenth century, but that is not what constitutes his strength. His genius consists in the depth and accuracy of his insight into the darker, less regarded, but decisive factors in social and political behaviour.

Maistre was an original thinker, swimming against the current of his time, determined to explode the most sacrosanct platitudes and pious formulas of his liberal contemporaries. They stressed the power of reason; he pointed out, perhaps too gleefully, the persistence and extent of irrational instinct, the power of faith, the force of blind tradition, the wilful ignorance about their human material of the progressives – the idealistic

[1] op. cit. (p. 162 above, note 1), p. 306.

social scientists, the bold political and economic planners, the passionate believers in technocracy. While all around him there was talk of the human pursuit of happiness, he underlined, again with much exaggeration and perverse delight, but with some truth, that the desire to immolate oneself, to suffer, to prostrate oneself before authority, indeed before superior power, no matter whence it comes, and the desire to dominate, to exert authority, to pursue power for its own sake – that these were forces historically at least as strong as the desire for peace, prosperity, liberty, justice, happiness, equality.

His realism takes violent, rabid, obsessed, savagely limited forms, but it is realism nevertheless. The acute sense of what could or what could not be undone, which made him say as early as 1796 that once the revolutionary movement had done its work, France as a monarchy could be saved only by the Jacobins, that efforts to restore the old order were blind folly, that the Bourbons, even if restored, could not last, never deserted him. Blindly dogmatic in matters of theology (and theory generally), in practice he was a clear-eyed pragmatist, and knew this. It is in this mood that he insists that religion need not be true, or rather that its truth simply consists of the fact that it fulfils our aspirations. 'If our conjectures are plausible . . . if above all they are comforting and able to make us better, what more can one ask? If they are not true, they are good; or rather, since they are good does that not make them true?'[1]

No one who has lived through the first half of the twentieth century, and, indeed, after that, can doubt that Maistre's political psychology, for all its paradoxes and the occasional descents into sheer counter-revolutionary absurdity, has proved, if only by revealing, and stressing, destructive tendencies – what the German romantics called the dark, nocturnal side of things – which humane and optimistic persons tend not to want to see, at times a better guide to human conduct than the faith of believers in reason; or at any rate can provide a

[1] I 40.

sharp, by no means useless, antidote to their often over-simple, superficial and, more than once, disastrous remedies.

XII

It is not perhaps surprising that so bold and articulate a figure provoked very sharp reactions on the part of his critics throughout his century, as, indeed, he has in our own day. He excited at various periods curiosity, disgust, adulation and blind hatred. Certainly few men have had comments so inept made about them by their commentators. Because he was a good father and husband and a good friend, F.-A. de Lescure says that this 'aigle de l'intelligence fut débonnaire comme l'agneau, candide comme la colombe'.[1] Even the bishops who have paid him tribute have stopped short of this. Because he spoke of the divinity of war, he seems to J. Dessaint to be a Darwinian before Darwin.[2] Because he upsets accepted views, he is compared to the heretical Protestant theologian David Friedrich Strauss; because he conceded the importance of nationalism, he is a precursor of the Italian Risorgimento, of President Wilson, and of the doctrine of self-determination;[3] and because he is

---

[1] [F.-A.] de Lescure, *Le Comte Joseph de Maistre et sa famille 1753–1852: Études et portraits politiques et littéraires* (Paris, 1892), p. 6.

[2] J. Dessaint, 'Le Centenaire de Joseph de Maistre', *La Revue de Paris*, 1 July 1921, pp. 139–52: see p. 143.

[3] On the efforts to represent Maistre as a precursor of the Italian Risorgimento see Albert Blanc, who edited his diplomatic correspondence (see p. 103 above, note 2), and J. Mandoul in his book already cited (p. 147 above, note 3) – and later even so perceptive a scholar as Adolfo Omodeo (*Un reazionario: Il conte J. de Maistre* (Bari, 1939)) – who treat him almost as one of the liberal Italian patriots, to be classed, if not with Mazzini, then with Rosmini and Gioberti. But this seems unfounded. Maistre was anti-Gallican, and defended the secular authority of the Pope; hence he could, at a pinch, be aligned on the side of those who looked to the Vatican to unify Italy and end the division into secular, foreign-dominated, princely states or republics. And he did somewhere remark that nothing was more grievous for politically conscious men than to have to submit to foreign

among the first to use the term 'société des nations',[1] he was a prophet of the League of Nations, although he only used the term to deride this as a typical rationalist absurdity.[2]

The reminiscences of those who met him paint a portrait of a man of great charm, alternating between shafts of brilliant wit and fierce philippics, always found fascinating by his audience, particularly in St Petersburg, where he was much in demand in aristocratic circles, liable to put paradoxical questions, and prone not to listen to the answers much, a wonderful stylist – Lamartine called him the heir to Diderot[3] – equally admired by the great critic Sainte-Beuve, unique in his kind. The best account of him is indeed that of Sainte-Beuve, who speaks of him as an austere, sober, but passionate lonely thinker, furious for truth, brimming with ideas, with scarcely anyone in St Petersburg or anywhere else to address them to, or discuss them with, and hence liable to write for himself alone and, if only for that reason, push things too far with his 'ultra-vérités',[4] always on the attack, striking at the strongest suit of his opponents, eager to draw fire, aiming to kill. Consequently he was often offensive: one of Sainte-Beuve's best examples is Maistre's riposte to Madame de Staël, who lectured him on the merits of the Church of England. 'Yes,' he

---

domination – no nation wished to obey another, hence the honour paid to the liberators of nations. But it is a far cry from this unexceptionable platitude to the elevation of Maistre into a prophet of the Risorgimento. So far as he committed himself to any species of patriotic emotion Maistre remained, to the end of his days, a fervent admirer of France, which 'exerce sur l'Europe une véritable magistrature' (I 8), and a staunch supporter of its royal dynasty: King Bomba, in whose veins flowed the blood of that great house, would certainly have meant more to him than idealistic revolutionaries; liberalism and democracy he hated and despised; and revolution was certainly the worst of all fates that could befall social order.

[1] V 13.

[2] Some, though not all, of these curiosities have been collected by Constantin Ostrogorsky in his *Joseph de Maistre und seine Lehre von der höchsten Macht und ihren Trägern* (Helsingfors, 1932).

[3] A. de Lamartine, *Cours familier de littérature*, vol. 8 (Paris, 1859), p. 44.

[4] 'Joseph de Maistre' (see p. 95 above, note 3), p. 427.

said, '. . . it is like an orang-utan among the apes'[1] – his typical description of the other Protestant denominations. Sainte-Beuve calls him *un grand et puissant esprit* under whose charm he remained all his life. In appearance he was dignified, handsome, and described by a Sicilian visitor as 'la neve in testa ed il fuoco in bocca'[2] (with snow upon his head and fire in his mouth).

Maistre, like Hegel, was aware that he was living at a time of the passing away of a long epoch of human civilisation. 'Je meurs avec l'Europe, je suis en bonne compagnie,'[3] he wrote in 1819. Léon Bloy saw his writings as a funeral oration over the civilised Europe of his day, and of ours.[4] Nevertheless it is not as the last voice of a dying culture, as the last of the Romans (as he saw himself), that he is of interest today. His works and his personality are significant not as an end but as a beginning. They matter because he was the first theorist in the great and powerful tradition which culminated in Charles Maurras, a precursor of Fascists, and of those Catholic anti-Dreyfusards and supporters of the Vichy regime who were sometimes described as being Catholics before they were Christians. Maurras may have been prepared to collaborate with Hitler's regime for some of the same reasons as those that attracted Maistre to Napoleon (whom he vainly attempted to meet) and made him respect his arch-enemy, Robespierre, far more than the moderates whom they destroyed, or the knock-kneed regiment of *bien pensant* mediocrities who formed his sovereign's entourage in Cagliari.

In Maistre's scale of values power comes almost highest, because power is the divine principle which governs the world, the source of all life and action, the paramount factor in the development of mankind; and whoever knows how to wield it, above all to make decisions, acquires the right to obedience, and

[1] ibid., p. 429.
[2] ibid., p. 455.
[3] XIV 183.
[4] Léon Bloy, 'Le Christ au dépotoir', *Le Pal* No 4 (2 April 1885): p. 83 in *Œuvres de Léon Bloy*, ed. Joseph Bollery and Jacques Petit ([Paris], 1964–75), vol. 4.

is by that token the instrument chosen by providence or history, at that particular moment, to work its mysterious purposes. The concentration of power in a single source, the very essence of the despotic rule of Robespierre and his henchmen against which moderates like Constant and Guizot reacted so passionately, is to Maistre infinitely preferable to its dispersion according to man-made rules. But, of course, to locate power where it should truly and securely lie – in ancient, established, socially created institutions, not made by the hand of man, and not in democratically chosen or self-appointed individuals – that is political and moral insight and wisdom. All usurpation must fail in the end, because it flouts the divine laws of the universe; power resides only in him who is the instrument of such laws. To resist them is to pit the fallible resources of a single intellect against the cosmic stream, and this is always childishness and folly, and more than this – criminal folly, directed against the human future. What this future is, only a realistic appraisal of history and men's natures in their great variety can tell you. For all his theoretical apriorism Maistre preached the doctrine that events must be studied empirically, and with due regard to changing historical conditions – each situation in its proper context – if we are to understand the working of the divine will.

This historicism, and indeed interest in the varieties of power over human beings, and in the processes of the formation of societies and their spiritual and cultural components, which Herder and Hegel and the German romantics were preaching in far darker language, and Saint-Simon in a more abstract fashion, is today so much part of our historical outlook that we have forgotten how little time has passed since the day when these notions were not platitudes but paradoxes. Maistre is our contemporary, too, in denouncing the impotence of abstract ideas and deductive methods which, though he may not say so, dominated pious Catholic apologists no less than their opponents. No one has done more than he to discredit the attempt to explain how things happen, and to lay down what we are to do, by deduction from such general notions as the nature of man, the nature of rights, the nature of virtue, the nature of the physical world, and so on – a deductive procedure whereby we can derive in the conclusion only what we import into the premises, without noticing or admitting that this is all that we are doing.

Maistre is rightly called reactionary, yet he attacked uncritically accepted concepts more fiercely and effectively than many a self-styled progressive. His method is far closer to modern empiricism than, say, those of the scientifically-minded Comte or Spencer, or for that matter those of liberal historians of the nineteenth century. Again, Maistre was among the earliest thinkers to perceive the very great social and philosophical importance of such 'natural' institutions as linguistic habits, modes of speech, prejudices and national idiosyncrasies in moulding the character and beliefs of men. Vico had spoken of language, images, mythology as offering an insight into the growth of men and institutions obtainable nowhere else. Herder and the German philologists studied them as issuing out of the deepest aspirations and most typical characteristics of their nation; the fathers of political romanticism, in particular Hamann, Herder, Fichte, thought of them as free and spontaneous forms of self-expression fulfilling the true demands of human nature, in contrast with the rigid despotism of the centralised French state, which crushed the natural inclinations of its subjects. Maistre stresses not these amiable and, in part, imaginary attributes of the 'Volksseele', acclaimed by enthusiastic champions of the life and growth of societies, but on the contrary the stability, permanence, impregnability, authority of the dark mass of half-conscious memories and traditions and loyalties, together with the even darker forces below the level of consciousness, and above all the power of institutions, regarded as supernatural, in the exacting of collective obedience. He lays great emphasis on the fact that absolute rule succeeds best when even to question its roots is terrifying. He feared and detested science because it shed too much light, and so dissolved the mystery which alone resisted sceptical enquiry. Keen as his eye was, even he could scarcely have foreseen that a day would come when the technical resources of science would be combined with those not of reason but of unreason, that liberalism would be faced with two enemies instead of one – the despotism of rational scientific organisation on one side, and the forces of anti-rational mystical bigotry on the other – and that these two forces, celebrated by the followers of Voltaire and those of Maistre respectively, would join hands in that very alliance which Saint-Simon had prophesied with such fervent and mistaken optimism.

Maistre, like Pareto, believed in élites, but without Pareto's cynical indifference to the choice of particular scales of moral values – to wit, that adopted by the élite, and the very different one preached by it to the masses; even if he thought that too much light was not good for the majority of mankind. Like Georges Sorel he believed in the necessity of a social mythology and in the inevitability of wars, both national and social, but unlike him he did not allow that the leaders of the victorious class themselves must see through the myths by the adherence to which alone the masses can and should be led to victory. Like Nietzsche he detested equality, and thought the notion of universal liberty an absurd and dangerous chimera, but he did not revolt against the historical process, or wish to break the frame within which humanity had thus far made its painful way. He was not taken in by the social and political shibboleths of his time, and saw the nature of political power as clearly, and stated it in terms as naked, as Machiavelli and Hobbes, or Bismarck and Lenin in their day. For this reason, Catholic leaders in the nineteenth century, both priests and laymen, who paid him much formal homage as a strong and pious doctrinaire, nevertheless felt disquiet at the mention of his name, as if the weapons he had forged, in good faith, for defensive purposes were too dangerous – bombs which might explode unexpectedly in the hands of those who held them.

Maistre saw society as an inextricable network of weak,

sinful, helpless human beings, torn by contradictory desires, driven hither and thither by forces too violent for their control, too destructive to be justified by any comfortable rationalist formula. All achievement was painful, and likely to fail, and could be accomplished, if at all, only under the guidance of a hierarchy of beings of great wisdom and strong will, who, being the repositories of the forces of history (which to him is almost God's word made flesh), laid down their lives in performing their task of organisation, repression, and preservation of the divinely ordained order; by this act of sacrifice achieving communion with the divine order, whose law is a self-immolation which defies explanation and brings with it no reward in this world. The social structure which he advocated derived from Plato's Guardians in the *Republic* and the Nocturnal Council in the *Laws* at least as much as from Christian tradition; it has affinities with the sermon of the Grand Inquisitor in Dostoevsky's famous parable. His vision may be detestable to those who truly value human freedom, resting as it does on a dogmatic rejection of a light by which most men still live, or wish to live; yet in the course of constructing his great thesis Maistre boldly, more than once, and often for the first time, revealed (and violently exaggerated) central truths, unpalatable to his contemporaries, indignantly denied by his successors, and recognised only in our own day – not, indeed, because of our more perfect insight or greater self-knowledge or honesty, but because an order which Maistre regarded as the only remedy against the dissolution of the social fabric came into being, in our own time, in its most hideous form. In this way totalitarian society, which Maistre, in the guise of historical analysis, had visualised, became actual; and thereby, at inestimable cost in human suffering, has vindicated the depth and brilliance of a remarkable, and terrifying, prophet of our day.

EUROPEAN UNITY
AND ITS VICISSITUDES

I

IT IS by now a melancholy commonplace that no century has seen so much remorseless and continued slaughter of human beings by one another as our own. Compared with it, even the wars of religion and the Napoleonic campaigns seem local and humane. I am not qualified to undertake a general examination of the causes of hatred and strife in our time. I should like to direct attention to only one aspect of this situation. We live in an age in which political ideas, conceived by fanatical thinkers, some of them very little regarded in their own day, have had a more violently revolutionary influence on human lives than at any time since the seventeenth century. I should like to discuss one group of such ideas, by which our own lives have been profoundly affected both for good and evil.

Our ideas about the ends of life are, in one essential respect, unlike, and indeed opposed to, those of our forefathers, at least those prevalent before the second half of the eighteenth century. According to these the world was a single, intelligible whole. It consisted of certain stable ingredients, material and spiritual; if they were not stable they were not real. All men possessed certain unchanging characteristics in common, called human nature. And although there existed obvious differences between individuals, cultures, nations, the similarities between them were more extensive and important. The most important common characteristic was considered to be the possession of a faculty called reason, which enabled its possessor to perceive the truth, both theoretical and practical. The truth, it was assumed, was equally visible to all rational minds everywhere. This common nature made it not only necessary, but also reasonable, for human beings to attempt to communicate with each other, and to try to persuade one another of the truth of what they believed; and, in extreme cases, to inflict compulsion upon others, on the assumption (made, for example, by Sarastro in the great fable of the age of reason, Mozart's *Magic Flute*) that if men obeyed orders (or were, if all else failed, forced to obey) they would, as a result of this, perceive the validity of what their educators or legislators or masters themselves knew to be true; they would follow this, and be wise and good and happy. In the twentieth century this claim to universality, whether of reason or any other principle, is no longer taken for granted; what Walter Lippmann had called the public philosophy has ceased to be the automatic presupposition of politics or social life, and this has vastly transformed our lives.

This is most obvious in the case of Fascism. The Fascists and National Socialists did not expect inferior classes, or races, or individuals to understand or sympathise with their own goals; their inferiority was innate, ineradicable, since it was due to blood, or race, or some other irremovable characteristic; any attempt on the part of such creatures to pretend to equality with their masters, or even to comprehension of their ideals, was regarded as arrogant and presumptuous. Caliban was considered incapable of lifting his face to the sky and catching even a glimpse of, let alone sharing, the ideals of Prospero. The business of slaves is to obey; what gives their masters their right to trample on them is precisely the alleged fact – which Aristotle asserted – that some men are slaves by nature, and have not enough human quality to give orders themselves, or understand why they are being forced to do what they do.

If Fascism is the extreme expression of this attitude, all nationalism is infected by it to some degree. Nationalism is not consciousness of the reality of national character, nor pride in it. It is a belief in the unique mission of a nation, as being intrinsically superior to the goals or attributes of whatever is outside it; so that if there is a conflict between my nation and other men, I am obliged to fight for my nation no matter at what cost to other men; and if the others resist, that is no more than one would expect from beings brought up in an inferior culture, educated by, or born of, inferior persons, who cannot *ex hypothesi* understand the ideals that animate my nation and me. My gods are in conflict with those of others, my values with those of strangers, and there exists no higher authority – certainly no absolute and universal tribunal – by which the claims of these rival divinities can be adjudicated. That is why war, between nations or individuals, must be the only solution.

We think, for the most part, in words. But all words belong to specific languages, the products of specific cultures. As there is no universal human language, so there exists no universal human law or authority, else these laws, this authority, would be sovereign over the earth; but this, for nationalists, is neither possible nor desirable; a universal law is not true law: cosmopolitan culture is a sham and a delusion; international law is only called law by a precarious analogy – a hollow courtesy intended to conceal the violent break with the universalism of the past.

This assumption is less obvious in the case of Marxism, which in theory, at least, is internationalist. But Marxism is a nineteenth-century ideology, and has not escaped the all-pervasive separatism of its time. Marxism is founded on reason; that is to say, it claims that its propositions are intelligible, and their truth can be 'demonstrated' to any rational being in possession of the relevant facts. It offers salvation to all men: anyone can, in principle, see the light, and denies it at his own peril.

In practice, however, this is not so. The theory of economic base and ideological superstructure on which Marxist sociology is founded teaches that the ideas in men's heads are conditioned by the position occupied by them, or by their economic class, in the productive system. This fact may be disguised from individual persons by all kinds of self-delusions and rationalisations, but 'scientific' analysis will always reveal that the vast majority of any given class believe only that which favours the interests of that class – interests which the social scientists can determine by objective historical analysis – whatever reasons they may choose, however sincerely, to give for their beliefs; and conversely they disbelieve, reject, misunderstand, distort, try to escape from, ideas belief in which would weaken the position of their class.

All men are to be found, as it were, on one of two moving stairs; I belong to a class which, owing to its relationship to the forces of production, is either moving upwards towards triumph, or downwards towards ruin. In either case my beliefs and outlook – the legal, moral, social, intellectual, religious, aesthetic ideas – in which I feel at home, will reflect the interests of the class to which I belong. If I belong to a class moving towards victory, I shall hold a realistic set of beliefs, for I am not afraid of what I see; I am moving with the tide, knowledge of the truth can only give me confidence; if I belong to a doomed class, my inability to gaze upon the fatal facts – for few men are able to recognise that they are destined to perish – will falsify my calculations, and render me deaf and blind to truths too painful for me to face. It follows that it must be useless for members of the rising class to try to convince members of the falling order that the only way in which they can save themselves is by understanding the necessities of history and therefore transferring themselves, if they can, to the steep stair that is moving upwards, from that which runs so easily to destruction. It is useless, because *ex hypothesi* members of a doomed class are conditioned to see everything through a falsifying lens: the plainest symptoms of approaching death will seem to them evidence of health and progress; they suffer from optimistic hallucinations, and must systematically misunderstand the warnings that persons who belong to a different economic class, in their charity, may try to give them; such delusions are themselves the inevitable by-product of clinging to an order which history has condemned. It is idle for the progressives to try to save their reactionary brothers from defeat: the doomed men cannot hear them, and their destruction is certain. All men will not be saved: the proletariat, justly intent upon its own salvation, had best ignore the fate of their oppressors; even if they wish to return good for evil, they cannot save their enemies from 'liquidation'. They are 'expendable' – their destruction can be neither averted nor regretted by a rational being, for it is the price that mankind must pay for the progress of reason itself: the road to the gates of Paradise is necessarily strewn with corpses.

Although it has been reached by a different road, this conclusion is curiously similar to the nationalist or Fascist point of view, and different from the outlook of previous ages. However bitter the hatreds between Christians, Jews and Muslims, or between different sects within these faiths, the argument for the extermination of heretics always rested on the belief that it was in principle possible to convert men to the truth, which was one and universal, that is, visible to all; that only a few individuals were lost beyond redemption, being too blinded and perverted to be saved by anything but the sufferings of death. This rests on the assumption that men, as such, have a common nature, which makes communication in principle always possible and therefore always morally obligatory. It is this assumption that was at first questioned, and then altogether collapsed. The sheep must not try to save the goats – that is irrational and unrealisable.

The division of mankind into two groups – men proper, and some other, lower, order of beings, inferior races, inferior cultures, subhuman creatures, nations or classes condemned by history[1] – is something new in human history. It is a denial of common humanity – a premise upon which all previous humanism, religious and secular, had stood. This new attitude permits

---

[1] Even if it is allowed that individuals can save themselves by a great leap on to the upward-moving stair – as, after all, Marx and Engels themselves and many another bourgeois revolutionary did – this is a step which can be taken only by individuals, but never by entire classes or even large parts of them.

men to look on many millions of their fellow men as not quite human, to slaughter them without a qualm of conscience, without the need to try to save them or warn them. Such conduct is usually ascribed to barbarians or savages – men in a pre-rational frame of mind, characteristic of peoples in the infancy of civilisation. This explanation will no longer do. It is evidently possible to attain to a high degree of scientific knowledge and skill, and indeed, of general culture, and yet destroy others without pity, in the name of a nation, a class, or history itself. If this is childhood, it is the dotage of second childhood in its most repulsive form. How have men reached such a pass?

II

It may be worth considering at least one of the roots of this frightening characteristic of our time. Among the questions that men have asked in every generation are the fundamental questions of how men should live. Questions of this kind are called moral, political, social; they torment every age, and although they take different forms, and receive different answers in accordance with changing circumstances and ideas, yet they possess a certain family resemblance. Some questions persist longer than others; those that arise out of permanent human characteristics are called basic or perennial in every generation. 'How should I live?' 'What should I do?' 'Why should I obey others, and how far?' 'What is freedom, duty, authority?' 'Should I seek happiness, or wisdom, or goodness? And why?' 'Should I realise my own faculties, or sacrifice myself to others?' 'Have I a right to govern myself, or only to be governed well?' 'What are rights? What are laws? Is there a purpose which individuals, or societies, or the entire universe, cannot but seek to fulfil? Or are there no such purposes, only the wills of men determined by the food they eat, and the environments in which they grow?' 'Is there such a thing as the will of the group, the society, the nation, of which the individual world is but a fragment, and in the framework of which alone the will of the individual has any effectiveness or significance?' The state (or church) versus individuals and minorities; the state's will to power or efficiency or order versus the individual's claims to happiness or personal liberty or a moral principle: all these are questions partly of value, partly of fact – of 'ought' and 'should' as much as 'is' – by which men at all recorded times have been beset.

I think that it is true to say that whatever answers were returned to these fundamental questions, they were regarded, at any rate before the middle of the eighteenth century, as in principle capable of being answered. (If a question was such that you did not know even what *kind* of answer could be the correct answer to it, even though you might not yourself know what the answer was, this meant that the question itself was not intelligible to you, that it was, in fact, not a question at all.) Questions of value were regarded as being answerable in the same sense as questions of fact. I may not myself be able to tell you how far Lisbon is from Constantinople, but I know where you could look for the answer. I cannot myself tell what matter is composed of, who governed Ethiopia in the fifth century before Christ, whether the patient will die of this disease or not, but there are experts whom I can consult, who will do their best to discover the truth by using methods recognised as appropriate in our common society. That is what is meant by saying that I know that a true answer must be discoverable in principle, though I may not happen to know it, and nobody may know it.

The same assumption was made about questions of value, questions of the form 'What should one do? What justifies this or that? Is this good or bad, right or wrong, permitted or forbidden?' The history of moral, political, theological thought is a history of violent conflicts between the rival claims of rival experts. Some men looked for the answer in the word of God as contained in his sacred books; others in revelation, or faith, or holy mysteries which we believe although we may not understand; still others in the pronouncements of the appointed interpreters of God – churches and priests – and if the churches did not always return the same answer, no one doubted that one or other of such answers must be true – if not the answer of this denomination, then of that one. Some found the answer in rational metaphysics, or in an infallible intuition of some other kind, such as the verdict of the individual conscience. Others again discovered it in empirical observation, in the scientific laboratory, and in the application of mathematical methods to the data of experience. Wars of extermination were fought over rival claims to the true answers to these crucial questions. The price was, after all, the solution of the deepest and most important questions that any man could ask – about the true way of living; and for the sake of salvation men were ready to die, particularly if they believed that the soul was immortal and would obtain its just reward after the death of the body. But even those who did not believe either in immortality or in God were prepared to suffer and die for the truth, provided they were quite sure that it was the truth; for to find the truth and live according to it was surely the ultimate goal of anyone capable of seeking it. This was the faith of Platonists and Stoics, Christians and Jews, Muslims and deists and atheistic rationalists. Wars for principles and causes, both religious and secular, indeed human life itself, would have seemed meaningless without this deepest of all assumptions.

It was the breaking of this foundation-stone that created the modern outlook. Let me try to put this as simply as I can. It was not merely that the notion of objective truth in morals or politics was shaken by the rise of scepticism or subjectivism or relativism. The consequences of overthrowing the older notion of universal moral truth, true for all men, everywhere, at all times, could have been fitted into the older systems: it could be, and was, said that men's needs and characters are rendered different by climate, or soil, or heredity, or human institutions; one could work out functional formulas which would give to each man, or group, or race what they needed most, and still derive the formulas themselves from a single universal principle common to all men – that the needs were all human needs, rational responses of similar natures to differences or changes in environment or circumstances. Men and their needs could be analysed, classified, and in the light of natural and historical knowledge adjusted to each other, harmonised, so that a society would be created in which as many needs of as many men as possible were given the greatest possible satisfaction by the social and political arrangements. That was the programme of the Enlightenment and, in particular, of utilitarianism. Within the framework of the relativity of needs it was still presupposed that the questions of how men should live, what was to be done, what justice or equality or happiness were, were factual questions which could be settled by observation, if not of the universe as a whole or of the ways of God, then of men's natures, by such new sciences as psychology, anthropology, physiology. In the place of priests or metaphysical sages, the moral experts now were to be scientists, or technical experts. But the test of what was right was still that of objective truth which rational beings could discover for themselves. The change I speak of is something much more radical and upsetting than this.

III

The old view rested upon at least three central presuppositions. First: that all questions of value were answerable objectively. Some said that only rational men could obtain these answers; mystics and irrationalists pointed to other paths. But no one doubted that if the answers were in any sense true, they were true for all men. Second: that the universal truths were in principle accessible to human beings. One school of thinkers held that some men were more capable of discovering these truths than others. These – notably Plato and his followers – tended to believe in a natural order in which the better-endowed were placed higher than the worse, in moral or intellectual, or religious, or technological or racial hierarchies; while their opponents believed that every man could in principle be his own expert – this lies at the heart of much Protestant doctrine and of the views of Rousseau and Kant and secular democracy. Third: it was assumed that true values could not conflict with each other. It was maintained that if the universe was a cosmos and not chaos, if objective answers could be found to the question of how life was to be lived, then there must be some one way of living which was demonstrably the best. For if there were two ways of living, both such that no better ways could be conceived, and they proved incompatible with one another, then the conflict between them – and therefore between their adherents – was not in principle rationally soluble. But if there was no single universal answer, true for all men, at all times, everywhere, it followed that the question was not a genuine question, for all real questions must by definition be capable of a true solution, one and one only, all other solutions being necessarily false.

This can be put in another way. All questions have their answers. The answer must take the form of a true statement of fact. No truth can contradict any other truth – that is a simple, and undoubtedly valid, rule of logic. Consequently the true answers to such questions as 'Should I seek power, or knowledge, or happiness, or to do my duty, or to create beautiful objects?', 'Should I coerce others?', 'Should I seek freedom or peace or salvation?', cannot conflict, for if they did, one truth would be incompatible with another, which is logically impossible. From this it logically follows that since all truths are compatible with one another, or perhaps even entail one another, it must be possible to deduce the perfect pattern of life, compounded of all the true answers to all the agonising questions, and this pattern men should seek to realise. Men may be too weak, too sinful, too ignorant, to discover what this perfect pattern is, or to live by its light when they have discovered it, but unless such a pattern exists their questions cannot be answered, and literally unanswerable questions are *ex hypothesi* not questions at all, they are only will-o'-the-wisps, neuroses, forms of personal or social *malaise*, something which a psychiatrist should cure, not something which a thinker can solve.

One of the consequences of these fundamental assumptions – by which men had lived for more than two thousand years – is that conflict and tragedy are not intrinsic to human life. Tragedy – as opposed to mere disaster – consists in the conflicts of human actions, or characters, or values. If, in principle, all questions are answerable, and all answers are compatible, then such conflicts are in principle always avoidable. The tragic element in life is therefore always due to avoidable human mistakes: perfect beings would not know it; there can be no incongruity, and therefore neither comedy nor tragedy, in a world of saints and angels.

These presuppositions, which had ruled western thought since classical antiquity, were no longer taken for granted in the first quarter of the nineteenth century. By that time a new and immensely influential image began to take possession of the European mind. This is the image of the heroic individual, imposing his will upon nature or society: of man not as the crown of a harmonious cosmos, but as a being 'alienated' from it, and seeking to subdue and dominate it.

Let me give an example of what I mean. In the sixteenth century Calvin and Luther asked theological questions similar to those asked by, say, Loyola or Bellarmine; because their answers were different, they fought bitter wars against each other. Neither side had, or could have had, any respect for the position of the other – on the contrary, the more stubbornly and violently the enemy fought, the more deeply damned he was in the eyes of the true believer, who knew that he, and not the other, possessed the truth; indeed the more deeply your adversary believed in his heresies, the more hateful he must be in the sight of God and man. When the Pope burnt Bruno, or Calvin burnt Servetus, they thought their victims rebels against the light of the truth, the light which all men could in principle see, because the criteria of truth were public, so that any man whose heart and mind and soul had not been perverted could apply them, and attain to the same vision of eternal verities. The criterion was conceived as being at least as universal as any now used by physical scientists, who feel they can depend upon the fact that any other competent scientist, faced with the same data, applying the same tested methods, must reach the same inescapable conclusions.

There is therefore nothing romantic or tragic, nothing that can inspire sympathy, in the fate of a condemned heretic. A heretic is a danger to himself and to the society which he seeks to pervert; his soul should be saved, but there is certainly nothing dignified or worthy of admiration in the violence and stubbornness with which he resists the truth; on the contrary, the more stubborn he is, the more damned and the more odious; and the more quickly forgotten. When Muslims were killed in the Crusades, the notion that it might be right for a Muslim to defend his values, as it was right for the Crusaders to defend theirs, and for precisely the same reasons; the idea that men should be respected for dying for their ideals and principles, no matter how mistaken they may be, because any man who dies for what he believes to be true is *eo ipso* worthier of respect than one who compromises his beliefs, or seeks to save his life at the cost of his principles – this was not a conceivable position in the Middle Ages.[1] One was obliged, of course, to lay down one's life for the truth, but there was nothing noble in dying for a falsehood, even if one mistook it for truth. The notion that the truth is not necessarily one, that values are many, that they may conflict, that there is something sublime in dying for one's own vision of the truth even though it may be condemned by the rest of the world – that, I think, would before the eighteenth century have seemed to be a very eccentric position. There is

[1] Montesquieu's remark that when Montezuma said that the Aztec religion might be best for the Aztecs and the Christian religion best for Spaniards, what he said was not absurd, was regarded as most scandalous both by the church and by the radicals.

nothing that can be called 'my' as against 'your' truth, truths of one age in contrast with those of another; there is only *the* truth. Christians must be charitable: to die for a falsehood, as Muslims did, doubtless moved the better among them to compassion; brave men, men endowed with virtues which could have served a better cause, had to be killed, and it was ignoble to spit upon their corpses, or defile their tombs. Pity was one thing: admiration for fidelity to a false ideal, fidelity as such, was something not intelligible before the period of which I speak.

By, say, 1820 a very different view prevails. Now you will find poets and philosophers, particularly in Germany, saying that the noblest thing a man can do is to serve his own inner ideal, no matter at what cost. This ideal may be confined to the solitary individual to whom it is revealed, it may appear false or absurd to all others, it may be in conflict with the lives and outlook of the society to which he belongs, but he is obliged to fight for it, and, if there is no other way, die for it. But supposing it is false? At this point a radical shift of categories occurs, and one that marks a great revolution of the human spirit. The question of whether an ideal is true or false is no longer thought important, or indeed wholly intelligible. The ideal presents itself in the form of a categorical imperative: serve the inner light within you because it burns within you, for that reason alone. Do what you think right, make what you think beautiful, shape your life in accordance with those ends which are your ultimate purpose, to which everything else in your life is a means, to which all else must be subordinated, that, and no less, is what is asked of you. Imperatives, demands, orders to fulfil tasks are neither true nor false, they are not propositions, they do not describe anything, they do not state facts, they cannot be verified or falsified, they are not discoveries which you may have made and others can check; they are *goals*. The model for ethics and politics has suddenly shifted from analogy with the natural sciences, or theology, or any form of knowledge or description of facts, to something compounded out of the concepts of biological drives and goals and those of artistic creation. Let me explain this more concretely.

IV

When an artist is engaged in creating a work of art, he does not, despite naïve views to the contrary, transcribe from some pre-existent model. Where is the painting before the painter has painted or conceived it? Where is the symphony before the composer has conceived it? Where is the song before the singer has sung it? These questions have no meaning. They are like asking 'Where is the walk before I have walked it?', 'Where is my life before I have lived it?' Life is the living of it, the walk is the walking of it, the song is what I compose or sing when I compose or sing it, not something independent of my activity; creation is not an attempt to copy some already given, fixed, eternal, Platonic pattern. Only craftsmen copy: artists create.

This is the doctrine of art as free creation. I am not concerned with its truth; only with the fact that this notion of goals or ideals, as of something not discovered, but invented, becomes a dominant category of western thought. This entails the conception of the end of life not as something that exists independently and objectively, and which human beings can look for, as for some buried treasure which, whether discovered or not, exists in its own right; but as an activity – having the shape, the quality, the direction, the end of an activity – not something made, but a doing or a making, which has no existence, indeed is not intelligible, apart from the doer, the inventor, the creator whose activity it is. It is this notion that entered and transformed social and political life in Europe, and displaced the older ideal of political action as measured by pre-existent public standards, which were an objective ingredient of the universe, discerned most clearly by the man with the sharp eye – the expert, the sage – in virtue of which indeed he was called wise or expert. The end of a man now is to realise the personal vision within him at whatever cost; his worst crime is to be untrue to this inner goal that is his, and his alone. What the effect of this vision may be on others does not concern him; he must be faithful to his inner light; that is all he knows and all he needs to know. The artist is only more conscious of his calling; so is the philosopher, the educator, the statesman; but it is present in every man.

The figure of the professional sage, the man who has acquired specialised knowledge of a province of reality, and can guide your steps so as not to come into conflict with it, begins to melt away before the person of the romantic hero. The hero need be neither wise, nor inwardly harmonious, nor an effective guide to his generation. He might, like Beethoven (whose image profoundly affected the romantics), be rough, ignorant, poor, wear dirty clothes, be remote from the world, stupid about practical problems, ill-behaved, rude and violent in his relations to other human beings, but he is a sacred being because he is wholly dedicated to an ideal; he can defy the world in a thousand ways, earn hatred and unpopularity, break the rules of society, of politics, of religion, but one thing he may not do, and that is to sell himself to the philistines. If he compromises his inner vision, gives up what he knows to be his calling – the creation of a work of art or science, or living a certain form of life – and gives this up for riches, or popularity, or an established position in society, or comfort, or pleasure, or the attainment of an inner or outer harmony at the price of suppressing doubts or qualms within himself, he has betrayed the light and is damned for ever. It makes no difference whether a man's own inner light shines for others or not; nor whether he serves it successfully; serve it he must, even if he makes himself ridiculous in the process, even if all he does ends in failure. Indeed this sort of failure is considered as being morally infinitely superior to worldly success, even success as an artist – provided only that it is the fruit of the blind and exclusive service of what a man knows to be his mission, of what the inner voices tell him that he must do.[1]

This is the outlook which Fichte and Friedrich Schlegel, and in a sense Byron too, bound upon the imagination of their contemporaries, this is the new *Weltanschauung* of Schiller's *Karl Moor*, of Kleist's heroes, to some degree of Ibsen's strong, solitary, world-defying figures. It is largely a German, or at any rate a Nordic, conception, something that may, perhaps, go back to the mysticism of men like Eckhart or Boehme – that found powerful expression in the theology of the Reformation, and perhaps may be traced even further back, to the wandering Teutonic tribes who carried their own customs from east to west and from north to south, ignoring the universal legal system of the Roman Empire and the Roman Church, and imposing their own tribal *consuetudines* (as the Romans called them) upon the *jus gentium* – the law of nations common to all men, or at any rate to the great majority of them. The custom of the tribe is the expression of its personality, it *is* the tribe, and goes with it on its wanderings, and bends whatever resists it to its will. Fichte's self is an active, creative principle that imposes its personality upon the dead world of nature which resists it – raw material waiting to be shaped – not, as the Stoics or the Thomists, or the French materialist philosophers, or Shaftesbury, or Rousseau, each in their own very different fashion, had taught, something to be followed or imitated or worshipped or obeyed, the wise, all-provident, all-healing agency which men defy at their peril.

Fichte's conception of man as demiurge, imposing his

---

[1] Mozart and Haydn would have been utterly astonished to hear that the merit of their symphonies was unimportant compared with the purity of their motives, because they were sacred vessels, priests dedicated to the service of a jealous god. They looked on themselves as purveyors: carpenters made tables, and if these were well made, they found favour and were bought and their makers became rich and famous. Artists made works of art to satisfy demand. When someone suggested to Mozart, then in dire poverty, that he compose a work and dedicate it to a noble patron, he remarked indignantly that he might have sunk low but not so low as to have to write a work without receiving a commission for it.

sovereign will on dead matter, afterwards so violently drama-
tised by Carlyle and Nietzsche, is at once the expression and the
symptom of this new and revolutionary attitude. The unitary
European world is shattered by it. Each separate entity, the
individual, the group, the culture, the nation, the church –
whatever is an identifiable 'personality' of its own – now pursues
its own independent goals. Independence – capacity to
determine one's own course – becomes as great a virtue as
interdependence once was. Reason unites, but will – self-
determination – divides. If I am a German I seek German
virtues, I write German music, I rediscover ancient German
laws, I cultivate everything within me which makes me as rich,
as expressive, as many-sided, as full a German as it is possible for
me to be. If I am a composer, I seek to make myself as much of a
composer as I can be, to subordinate every aspect of life to the
single sacred goal, to which nothing can be too great a sacrifice.
That is the romantic ideal at its fullest. The old presuppositions have vanished overnight. What is the common
ideal of life? The very notion has lost relevance. Questions of
behaviour have no answers, since they are no longer conceived as
questions. If I ask 'What should I do?', 'What is good or worth
possessing?', 'Are all my values compatible with one another?',
the answer lies not in knowledge conceived as reflective but in
action itself. I look within myself and 'realise myself' in
accordance with the goals that I find within me, the commands
of my own inner voice – a voice which speaks in every man if he
will listen. Are my values compatible with one another?
Perhaps not. Knowledge is an absolute goal; and so perhaps are
peace or happiness: but knowledge of some fatal fact may
destroy my peace or happiness. If this is so, then there is no help:
I am committed to the collision between these incompatible
ideals. Justice and mercy are not compatible, yet I must seek
both; must, because I have no choice: to deny either is to lie, to
sin against the light.

To realise what such values are is at times to recognise that
they are both absolute and irreconcilable. In this way tragedy

enters into life as part of its essence, not as something which can be resolved by rational adjustment: to hope to eliminate it is merely to cheat oneself, to be superficial, to avert one's eye from the truth; and this is to betray one's integrity, the most heinous sin of all – deliberate moral suicide. So too in my relations with others: I have an ideal to which I consecrate my life, you have another; our lives are not intelligible save in terms each of its own inner pattern; if these ideals come into conflict, it is incomparably better that we fight a duel, in which one of us may kill the other or we both die, than that either of us should compromise his beliefs. I respect you far more for fighting for your ideal, which I detest, than for any form of compromise, reconciliation, attempt to evade your responsibility to your true self. This leads to the conception of the noble enemy who is immensely superior to the peaceful, benevolent philistine or the craven friend. All ends are equal; ends are what they are, men pursue what they pursue, and there is no way of establishing objective hierarchies valid for all men and all cultures. The only principle which must be sacredly observed is that each man shall be true to his own goals, even at the cost of destruction, havoc, death. That is the romantic ideal in its fullest, most fanatical form.

The last hundred and fifty years have, in a sense, been a scene of conflict and interplay between the older universal ideal founded upon reason and knowledge, and the new romantic ideal, which derives from the notion of artistic creation and organic craving for self-expression and self-assertion, or for self-immolation, which is an inverted form of the same phenomenon. When one looks on the romantic ideal now, after all the good and evil that it has done, it seems both bright and dark. On the one hand it marks the birth of the new aesthetic ideal, the reverence before integrity as such. Idealism (a word which acquires its modern significance only in the course of this revolution of ideas), which before the eighteenth century was thought a touching, but immature and ludicrous, characteristic and was contrasted unfavourably with practical good sense, acquired in the early nineteenth century an absolute value of its own, which we still respect: to say of a man that he is an idealist is to say that, although his goals may seem to us absurd or even repellent, if his behaviour is disinterested and he is ready to sacrifice himself in the name of a principle and against his obvious material interests, we think him worthy of deep respect. This is a wholly modern attitude, and with it goes the high value placed upon martyrs and minorities as such. The older view venerated martyrs only when they died for what was recognised to be the truth, minorities only when they suffered persecution for the true faith, not, as was the case among the romantics, for any beliefs, any principle at all, provided the motive was good, provided, that is, it was held with sufficient sincerity and depth.

What I am attempting to describe is, in fact, a kind of secularised Christianity, a translation of the Christian outlook into individualistic, moral or aesthetic terms: the attitude, the quality of feeling, are the same, but the reasons for them – and their content – have altered. Christianity contrasted failure in this life with beatitude after death, or (in its Platonic mystical forms) failure in the world of shadows and appearance with eternal joy in the real world of which daily life is but a delusive image. The romantic outlook condemns success as such as both vulgar and immoral; for it is built, as often as not, on a betrayal of one's ideals, on a contemptible arrangement with the enemy. A correspondingly high value is placed upon defiance for its own sake, idealism, sincerity, purity of motive, resistance in the face of all odds, noble failure, which are contrasted with realism, worldly wisdom, calculation, and their rewards – popularity, success, power, happiness, peace bought at morally too high a price. This is the doctrine of heroism and martyrdom, as against that of harmony and wisdom. It is inspiring, audacious, splendid, and sinister too. It is the last aspect that I wish to emphasise.

The moving figure of Beethoven in his garret creating immortal works in poverty and suffering duly yields to that of

Napoleon, whose art is the making of states and peoples. If self-realisation is aimed at as the ultimate goal, then might it not be that the transformation of the world by violence and skill is itself a kind of sublime aesthetic act? Men either possess creative genius, or they do not; those who do not must regard it as their proper destiny, indeed as a high privilege, to be moulded – and broken – by those who do. As the artist blends colours and the composer sounds, so the political demiurge imposes his will upon his own raw material – average, ungifted human beings, largely unconscious of the possibilities dormant within them – and shapes them into a splendid work of art – a state or an army, or some great political, military, religious, juridical structure. This may entail suffering: but like discords in music it is indispensable to the harmony and effect of the whole. The victims of these great creative operations must take comfort, and indeed be exalted, by the consciousness that they are thereby lifted to a height which their own lower natures could never by themselves have achieved. This is the justification of acts which in terms of an older morality might be called brutal interference, imperialism, the crushing and maiming of individual human beings for the glory of a conqueror, or a state, or an ideology, the genius of the race.

From this to extreme nationalism and to Fascism is but a short step. Once the assumption is made that life must be made to resemble a work of art, that the rules that apply to paints or sounds or words also apply to men, that human beings can be looked on as so much 'human material', a plastic medium to be wrought at will by the inspired creator, the notion of individuals as each constituting an independent source of ideals and goals – an end in himself – is overthrown. This frightening conclusion follows from the same assumptions as the romantic virtues – the value placed upon martyrdom, defiance, integrity, dedication to one's own ideals – in the name of which the old universal laws were broken. Tribal customs, something which belongs exclusively to Franks or Lombards, and will not yield before the larger principles which are common to this tribe and other tribes, to this man and this civilisation but to past and future men and civilisations too, come as a violently disruptive force to the west. If values are not found but made, if what is true of the arts (and perhaps only of the arts) applies more widely in the field of human relations, then each inventor must seek to realise his own invention, each visionary impose his own vision, each nation its own goal, each civilisation its own values. Hence the war of all against all, and the end of European unity. Irrational forces are now set above rational, for what cannot be criticised or appealed from seems more compelling than what reason can analyse; the deep, dark sources of art and religion and nationalism, precisely because they are dark and resist detached examination, and vanish under intellectual analysis, are guarded and worshipped as transcendent, inviolable, absolute.

I may be told that, after all, industrialism, which rose with, and as an element in, nationalism, is not a disruptive but an integrating force; trade and industry break down national barriers, unify. But historically this is far from true. Industrialism lifted and armed the nationally conscious middle classes, and set them against the cosmopolitan governing élites in Europe. Nationalism is fed by industrialism, but does not need it for its growth. After 1914, after Hitler and Nasser and the awakening of Africa, after still less anticipated events – the rise of the state of Israel, the revolt in Budapest – what sane observer could still maintain the old thesis that nationalism is a by-product of the rise of capitalism, and declines with its decline? Not the Marxists, at any rate not those in power today: least of all in their practice. Whence then did these ruinous fallacies spring?

V

It is a truism that European history is a kind of dialectic between craving for public order and for individual liberty. The quest for order is a kind of fear before the elements, an attempt to build walls and hedges against the chaos caused by absence of control, against the weakening of traditions, habits, rules of life, in an effort to preserve the banisters that human beings need to prevent them from toppling over into an abyss, to connect them with their past and point a path to the future. When institutions become too set and obstruct growth, order becomes oppression and worship of it self-stultifying; sooner or later it is broken through by the almost physiological desire to live, move, create, by the need for novelty and change. Romanticism was just such an outbreak against a moral and political structure that had become a suffocating straitjacket: in due course this became decayed, and one fine day burst asunder in country after country. Like all revolutions, romanticism revealed new truths, endowed men with insights which they were never wholly to lose again, renovated the ancient establishment, and went too far and led to distortions and excesses, its own tyranny and its own victims. The distortions are all too familiar: our generation has paid for them more heavily, perhaps, than any other human society has ever paid for an aberration of the spirit.

The origins of this revolt are well known. The armies of Richelieu and of Louis XIV had crushed and humiliated a large part of the German population, and stifled the natural development of the new culture of the Protestant renaissance in the north. The Germans, a century later, rebelled against the dead hand of France in the realms of culture, art and philosophy, and avenged themselves by launching the great counter-attack against the Enlightenment. It took the form of glorification of the individual, the national and the historical, against the universal and the timeless; of the exaltation of genius, of the unaccountable, of the leap of the spirit that defies all rules and conventions, of the worship of the individual hero, the giant above and beyond the law, and an assault upon the great impersonal order with its unbreakable laws, and its clear assignment of its own place to every human function and group and class and purpose, which had been characteristic of the classical tradition, and had entered deeply into the texture of the western world, both ecclesiastical and secular. Variety in the place of uniformity; inspiration in the place of tried and tested rules or traditions; the inexhaustible and the unbounded in the place of measure, clarity, logical structure; the inner life and its expression in music; worship of the night and the irrational: that was the contribution of the wild German spirit, which broke like a fresh wind into the airless prison of the French Establishment. This great revolt of the humiliated Germans against the dead and levelling rationalist pedantry of French thought and taste in the mid-eighteenth century had, in its beginnings, a life-giving effect upon art and ideas about art, upon religion, upon personal relationships between human beings, upon individual morality. Then the tidal wave of feeling rose above its banks, and overflowed into the neighbouring provinces of politics and social life with literally devastating results. All forms of going to the bitter end were thought more worthy of man than peaceful negotiation, stopping half-way; extremism, conflict, war were glorified as such.

Few things have played a more fatal part in the history of human thought and action than great imaginative analogies from one sphere, in which a particular principle is applicable and valid, to other provinces, where its effect may be exciting and transforming, but where its consequences may be fallacious in theory and ruinous in practice. It was so with the romantic movement and its nationalist implications. The heroic individual, the free creator, became identified not with the unpolitical artist, but with leaders of men bending others to their indomitable will, or with classes, or races, or movements, or nations that asserted themselves against others, and identified their own liberty with the destruction of all that opposed them. The notion that liberty and power are identical, that to be free is to make free with whatever stands in your path, is an ancient idea which the romantics seized on and wildly exaggerated. Even more typical of romanticism is the insane, egomaniacal self-prostration before one's own true inner essence, one's private feelings, the composition of one's own blood, the shape of one's own skull, the place of one's own birth, as against that which one shares with other people – reason, universal values, a sense of the community of mankind.

The neo-rationalism of Hegel and of Marx, in a sense, tried to oppose the unbridled subjectivism of the romantics, and their self-worship, by an effort to discover objective standards in the inexorable forces of history, or the laws of the evolution of the human spirit or the growth of productive forces and relations. But they were themselves sufficiently infected by romanticism to make progress consist in the defeat and absorption of the rest of society by one victorious section of it. For Hegel, progress and the liberation of the human spirit consist in the triumph of reason as embodied in the state over other forms of human organisation, the victory of the historic nations over the unhistoric, of 'Germanic' culture over the rest, and of Europe over other 'discarded' human cultures, the 'dead' civilisation of China, for example, or the barbarous Slav nations. Without conflict, struggle, strife (so Hegel tells us) progress ceases, stagnation sets in. Similarly for Karl Marx, the proletarians can only become free by suppressing their adversaries with whom they, *ex hypothesi*, can have nothing in common. Progress is self-assertion, the conquest of an area in which the agent can freely develop and create by eliminating (or absorbing) whatever obstructs it, both animate and inanimate. In Hegel it is the nation organised as a state. In Marx it is the class organised as a revolutionary force. In both cases a large number of human beings must be sacrificed and annihilated if the ideal is to triumph. Unity may be the ultimate goal of humanity, but its method of attaining it is war and disintegration. The path may lead to a terrestrial paradise, but it is strewn with the corpses of the enemy, for whom no tear must be shed, since right and wrong, good and bad, success and failure, wisdom and folly, are all in the end determined by the objective ends of history, which has 'condemned' half mankind – unhistoric nations, members of obsolete classes, inferior races – to what Proudhon called 'liquidation', and Trotsky, in an equally picturesque phrase, described as the rubbish heap of history.

Yet there is a central insight given us by romantic humanism – this same untamed German spirit – which we shall not easily forget. Firstly that the maker of values is man himself, and may therefore not be slaughtered in the name of anything higher than himself, for there is nothing higher; this is what Kant meant when he spoke of man as an end in himself, and not a means to an end. Secondly, that institutions are made not only by, but also for, men, and when they no longer serve him they must go. Thirdly that men may not be slaughtered, either in the name of abstract ideas, however lofty, such as progress or freedom or humanity, or of institutions, for none of these have any absolute value in themselves, inasmuch as all that they have has been conferred upon them by men, who alone can make things valuable or sacred; hence attempts to resist or change them are never a rebellion against divine commands to be punished by destruction. Fourthly – and this follows from the rest – that the worst of all sins is to degrade or humiliate human beings for the sake of some Procrustean pattern into which they are to be forced against their wills, a pattern that has some objective authority irrespective of human aspirations.

This conception of man, inherited from the romantic move-ment, remains in us to this day: it is something which, despite all that mankind has lived through, we in Europe have not abandoned. For this reason, when Hegel and Marx prophesied inevitable doom for all those who defied the march of history, their threats came too late. Hegel and Marx, each in his fashion, tried to tell human beings that only one path to liberty and salvation lay before them – that which was offered them by history, which embodied cosmic reason; that those who failed to adapt themselves, or to realise that rationality, interest, duty, power, success were, in the long run, identical with one another and with morality and wisdom, would be destroyed by 'the forces of history', to defy which was suicidal folly. But this line of metaphysical intimidation proved on the whole ineffective.

Too many men were prepared to defend their principles even against the irresistible power with which Marx threatened to annihilate them. The ideals of individual human beings commanded respect and even reverence, even if no guarantees of objective validity could be provided. Fidelity to an ideal, indestructible regard for what a man himself, whatever his reasons, believed to be true, or right, became something in the name of which men were prepared to defy the big battalions, even if these were identified with the mysterious power of history or reality itself. It was no longer possible to persuade men that Don Quixote was not merely foolish and unpractical and obsolete (which no one had denied), but that because he had ignored the historic position of his nation, or race, or class he was defying the forces of progress and was therefore vicious and wicked too. Men stood up, as they had always done, and became martyrs for their beliefs, and were admired for it, at times even by those who destroyed them. They were tortured and died for principles which, so at any rate they believed, were universal and binding on all men, part of the human essence in virtue of which men were rightly called men. They could not break these principles, without feeling that they had forfeited all right to human respect. They could not betray them and face themselves or others. For this reason the appeals to realism made to defeated countries in 1940 by victorious German leaders, who said, reasonably enough, that resistance was useless, that the new order was coming, that this new order would transform the values of all the world, that to resist was not only to be crushed, but to be written off as fools or enemies of the light by later generations, inevitably conditioned by the morality of the victors – this type of argument failed to break the spirit of those who truly believed in universal human values. Some resisted in the name of universal ideals enshrined in churches, or national traditions, or objective knowledge of the truth, others stood up for goals which were none the less sacred because they were individual and private to their possessors.

This dedication to ideals, irrespective of their 'source' – it is sometimes even denied that there is a source to seek – has an affinity with the modern existentialist position, which declares that the attempt to seek guarantees for moral beliefs in some vast, objective metaphysical order is no more than a pathetic attempt on the part of men to look for help outside themselves, to lean on something stronger than themselves, to derive rational justification for their acts by proving that they are ordained by some objective establishment; that they do this because they have not the courage to face the fact that there may exist no such establishment, that their values are what they are, and men commit themselves as they do, for no reason, or rather for the only reason that can, in principle, be given, namely that, being what they are, this particular end – whatever it may be – is what they have chosen, is their ultimate goal; that is what choice entails – and beyond it there is no other, and since a final goal justifies all else it cannot itself need justification. Such existentialists are legitimate descendants of that humanist romanticism which declares that man is independent and is free, that is to say, that the essence of man is not consciousness, nor the invention of tools, but the power of choice. Human history, as a famous Russian thinker once remarked, has no libretto: the actors must improvise their parts. Reality bursts through the patterns in which we try – in our effort to find assurance and comfort – to arrange it. The universe is not a jigsaw puzzle, of which we try to piece together the fragments, in the knowledge that one pattern exists, and one alone, in which they must all fit. We are faced with conflicting values; the dogma that they must somehow, somewhere be reconcilable is a mere pious hope; experience shows that it is false. We must choose, and in choosing one thing lose another, irretrievably perhaps. If we choose individual liberty, this may entail a sacrifice of some form of organization which might have led to greater efficiency. If we choose justice, we may be forced to sacrifice mercy. If we choose knowledge we may sacrifice innocence and happiness. If we choose democracy, we may sacrifice a strength that comes from militarisation or from obedient hierarchies. If we choose equality, we may sacrifice some degree of individual freedom. If we choose to fight for our lives, we may sacrifice many civilised values, much that we have laboured greatly to create. Nevertheless, the glory and dignity of man consist in the fact that it is he who chooses, and is not chosen for, that he can be his own master (even if at times this fills him with fear and a sense of solitude), that he is not compelled to purchase security and tranquïllity at the price of letting himself be fitted into a neat pigeon-hole in a totalitarian structure which contrives to rob him of responsibility, freedom and respect both for himself and others, at one single stroke.

VI

The disintegrating influence of romanticism, both in the comparatively innocuous form of the chaotic rebellion of the free artist of the nineteenth century and in the sinister and destructive form of totalitarianism, seems, in western Europe at least, to have spent itself. The forces that make for stability and reason are beginning to reassert themselves. But nothing ever goes back completely to its starting-point; the progress of humanity appears to be not cyclical, but a painful spiral, and even nations learn from experience. What has emerged from the recent holocausts?[1] Something approaching a new recognition in the west that there are certain universal values which can be called constitutive of human beings as such. Romanticism in its inflamed state – Fascist, National Socialist, and communist too – has produced a deep shock in Europe, less by its doctrines than by the actions of its followers – by trampling on certain values which, when they were brutally thrown aside, proved their vitality, and returned like war cripples to haunt the European conscience.

What are these values? What is their status, and why should

---

[1] [This was written in 1959.]

we accept them? May it not be true, as some existentialist and nihilist extremists have maintained, that there are no human values, still less European values? Men simply commit themselves as they commit themselves, for no reason. I dedicate myself to being a poet, and you to being a hangman: this is my choice and that is yours, and there are no objective standards in terms of which these choices can be graded, whereby my morality is superior or inferior to yours. We choose as we choose, that is all that can be said; and if this leads to conflict and destruction, that is a fact about the world which must be accepted as gravitation is accepted, something which is inherent in the dissimilar natures of dissimilar men, or nations, or cultures. That this is not a valid diagnosis has been made clear if only by the great and widespread sense of horror which the excesses of totalitarianism have caused. For the fact of shock reveals that there does exist a scale of values by which the majority of mankind – and in particular of western Europeans – in fact live, live not merely mechanically and out of habit, but as part of what in their moments of self-awareness constitutes for them the essential nature of man.

What is this nature? Physically it is not too difficult to say: we think that men must possess a certain physical, physiological and nervous structure, certain organs, certain physical senses and psychological properties, capacities for thinking, willing, feeling, and that anyone who lacks too many of these properties should not properly be called a man, but an animal or an inanimate object. But there are also certain moral properties which enter equally deeply into what we conceive of as human nature. If we meet someone who merely disagrees with us about the ends of life, who prefers happiness to self-sacrifice, or knowledge to friendship, we accept them as fellow human beings, because their notion of what is an end, the arguments they bring to defend their ends, and their general behaviour, are within the limits of what we regard as being human. But if we meet someone who cannot see why (to take a famous example) he should not destroy the world in order to relieve a pain in his little finger, or someone who genuinely sees no harm in condemning innocent men, or betraying friends, or torturing children, then we find that we cannot argue with such people, not so much because we are horrified as because we think them in some way inhuman – we call them moral idiots. We sometimes confine them in lunatic asylums. They are as much outside the frontiers of humanity as creatures who lack some of the minimum physical characteristics that constitute human beings. We lean on the fact that the laws and principles to which we appeal, when we make moral and political decisions of a fundamental kind, have, unlike legal enactments, been accepted by the majority of men, during, at any rate, most of recorded history; we regard them as incapable of being abrogated; we know of no court, no authority, which could, by means of some recognised process, allow men to bear false witness, or torture freely, or slaughter fellow men for pleasure; we cannot conceive of getting these universal principles or rules repealed or altered; in other words, we treat them not as something that we, or our forefathers, freely chose to adopt, but rather as presuppositions of being human at all, of living in a common world with others, of recognising them, and being ourselves recognised, as persons. Because these rules were flouted, we have been forced to become conscious of them.

This is a kind of return to the ancient notion of natural law, but, for some of us, in empiricist dress – no longer necessarily based on theological or metaphysical foundations. Hence to speak of our values as objective and universal is not to say that there exists some objective code, imposed upon us from without, unbreakable by us because not made by us; it is to say that we cannot help accepting these basic principles because we are human, as we cannot help (if we are normal) seeking warmth rather than cold, truth rather than falsehood, to be recognised by others for what we are rather than to be ignored or misunderstood. When these principles are basic, and have been long and widely recognised, we tend to think of them as universal ethical laws, and we assume that when human beings pretend that they for the liberty of others, to allow justice or fairness to be exercised.

Antigone is faced with a dilemma to which Sophocles implies one solution, Sartre offers the opposite, while Hegel proposes 'sublimation' on to some higher level – poor comfort to those who are agonised by dilemmas of this kind. Spontaneity, a marvellous human quality, is not compatible with capacity for organised planning, for the nice calculation of what and how much and where – on which the welfare of society may largely depend. We are all aware of the agonising alternatives in the recent past. Should a man resist a monstrous tyranny at all costs, at the expense of the lives of his parents or his children? Should children be tortured to extract information about dangerous traitors or criminals?

These collisions of values are of the essence of what they are and what we are. If we are told that these contradictions will be solved in some perfect world in which all good things can be harmonised in principle, then we must answer, to those who say this, that the meanings they attach to the names which for us denote the conflicting values are not ours. We must say that the world in which what we see as incompatible values are not in conflict is a world altogether beyond our ken; that principles which are harmonised in this other world are not the principles with which, in our daily lives, we are acquainted; if they are transformed, it is into conceptions not known to us on earth. But it is on earth that we live, and it is here that we must believe and act.

The notion of the perfect whole, the ultimate solution, in which all good things coexist, seems to me to be not merely unattainable – that is a truism – but conceptually incoherent; I do not know what is meant by a harmony of this kind. Some among the Great Goods cannot live together. That is a conceptual truth. We are doomed to choose, and every choice may entail an irreparable loss. Happy are those who live under a discipline which they accept without question, who freely obey the orders of leaders, spiritual or temporal, whose word is fully accepted as unbreakable law; or those who have, by their own methods, arrived at clear and unshakeable convictions about what to do and what to be that brook no possible doubt. I can only say that those who rest on such comfortable beds of dogma are victims of forms of self-induced myopia, blinkers that may make for contentment, but not for understanding of what it is to be human.

V

So much for the theoretical objection, a fatal one, it seems to me, to the notion of the perfect state as the proper goal of our endeavours. But there is in addition a more practical socio-psychological obstacle to this, an obstacle that may be put to those whose simple faith, by which humanity has been nourished for so long, is resistant to philosophical arguments of any kind. It is true that some problems can be solved, some ills cured, in both the individual and social life. We can save men from hunger or misery or injustice, we can rescue men from slavery or imprisonment, and do good – all men have a basic sense of good and evil, no matter what cultures they belong to; but any study of society shows that every solution creates a new situation which breeds its own new needs and problems, new demands. The children have obtained what their parents and grandparents longed for – greater freedom, greater material welfare, a juster society; but the old ills are forgotten, and the children face new problems, brought about by the very solutions of the old ones, and these, even if they can in turn be solved, generate new situations, and with them new requirements -- and so on, for ever – and unpredictably.

We cannot legislate for the unknown consequences of consequences of consequences. Marxists tell us that once the fight is won and true history has begun, the new problems that may arise will generate their own solutions, which can be peacefully realised by the united powers of harmonious, classless society.

This seems to me a piece of metaphysical optimism for which there is no evidence in historical experience. In a society in which the same goals are universally accepted, problems can be only of means, all soluble by technological methods. That is a society in which the inner life of man, the moral and spiritual and aesthetic imagination, no longer speaks at all. Is it for this that men and women should be destroyed or societies enslaved? Utopias have their value – nothing so wonderfully expands the imaginative horizons of human potentialities – but as guides to conduct they can prove literally fatal. Heraclitus was right, things cannot stand still.

So I conclude that the very notion of a final solution is not only impracticable but, if I am right, and some values cannot but clash, incoherent also. The possibility of a final solution – even if we forget the terrible sense that these words acquired in Hitler's day – turns out to be an illusion; and a very dangerous one. For if one really believes that such a solution is possible, then surely no cost would be too high to obtain it: to make mankind just and happy and creative and harmonious for ever – what could be too high a price to pay for that? To make such an omelette, there is surely no limit to the number of eggs that should be broken – that was the faith of Lenin, of Trotsky, of Mao, for all I know of Pol Pot. Since I know the only true path to the ultimate solution of the problems of society, I know which way to drive the human caravan; and since you are ignorant of what I know, you cannot be allowed to have liberty of choice even within the narrowest limits, if the goal is to be reached. You declare that a given policy will make you happier, or freer, or give you room to breathe; but I know that you are mistaken, I know what you need, what all men need; and if there is resistance based on ignorance or malevolence, then it must be broken and hundreds of thousands may have to perish to make millions happy for all time. What choice have we, who have the knowledge, but to be willing to sacrifice them all?

Some armed prophets seek to save mankind, and some only their own race because of its superior attributes, but whichever the motive, the millions slaughtered in wars or revolutions – gas chambers, gulag, genocide, all the monstrosities for which our century will be remembered – are the price men must pay for the felicity of future generations. If your desire to save mankind is serious, you must harden your heart, and not reckon the cost.

The answer to this was given more than a century ago by the Russian radical Alexander Herzen. In his essay *From the Other Shore*, which is in effect an obituary notice of the revolutions of 1848, he said that a new form of human sacrifice had arisen in his time – of living human beings on the altars of abstractions – nation, church, party, class, progress, the forces of history – these have all been invoked in his day and in ours: if these demand the slaughter of living human beings, they must be satisfied. These are his words:

> If progress is the goal, for whom are we working? Who is this Moloch who, as the toilers approach him, instead of rewarding them, draws back; and as a consolation to the exhausted and doomed multitudes, shouting 'morituri te salutant', can only give the . . . mocking answer that after their death all will be beautiful on earth. Do you truly wish to condemn the human beings alive today to the sad role . . . of wretched galley slaves who, up to their knees in mud, drag a barge . . . with . . . 'progress in the future' upon its flag? . . . a goal which is infinitely remote is no goal, only . . . a deception; a goal must be closer – at the very least the labourer's wage, or pleasure in work performed.

The one thing that we may be sure of is the reality of the sacrifice, the dying and the dead. But the ideal for the sake of which they die remains unrealised. The eggs are broken, and the habit of breaking them grows, but the omelette remains invisible. Sacrifices for short-term goals, coercion, if men's plight is desperate enough and truly requires such measures, may be justified. But holocausts for the sake of distant goals, that is a cruel mockery of all that men hold dear, now and at all times.

VI

If the old perennial belief in the possibility of realising ultimate harmony is a fallacy, and the positions of the thinkers I have appealed to – Machiavelli, Vico, Herder, Herzen – are valid, then, if we allow that Great Goods can collide, that some of them cannot live together, even though others can – in short, that one cannot have everything, in principle as well as in practice – and if human creativity may depend upon a variety of mutually exclusive choices: then, as Chernyshevsky and Lenin once asked, 'What is to be done?' How do we choose between possibilities? What and how much must we sacrifice to what? There is, it seems to me, no clear reply. But the collisions, even if they cannot be avoided, can be softened. Claims can be balanced, compromises can be reached: in concrete situations not every claim is of equal force – so much liberty and so much equality; so much for sharp moral condemnation, and so much for understanding a given human situation; so much for the full force of the law, and so much for the prerogative of mercy; for feeding the hungry, clothing the naked, healing the sick, sheltering the homeless. Priorities, never final and absolute, must be established.

The first public obligation is to avoid extremes of suffering. Revolutions, wars, assassinations, extreme measures may in desperate situations be required. But history teaches us that their consequences are seldom what is anticipated; there is no guarantee, not even, at times, a high enough probability, that such acts will lead to improvement. We may take the risk of drastic action, in personal life or in public policy, but we must always be aware, never forget, that we may be mistaken, that certainty about the effect of such measures invariably leads to avoidable suffering of the innocent. So we must engage in what are called trade-offs – rules, values, principles must yield to each other in varying degrees in specific situations. Utilitarian solutions are sometimes wrong, but, I suspect, more often beneficent. The best that can be done, as a general rule, is to maintain a precarious equilibrium that will prevent the occurrence of desperate situations, of intolerable choices – that is the first requirement for a decent society; one that we can always strive for, in the light of the limited range of our knowledge, and even of our imperfect understanding of individuals and societies. A certain humility in these matters is very necessary.

This may seem a very flat answer, not the kind of thing that the idealistic young would wish, if need be, to fight and suffer for, in the cause of a new and nobler society. And, of course, we must not dramatise the incompatibility of values – there is a great deal of broad agreement among people in different societies over long stretches of time about what is right and wrong, good and evil. Of course traditions, outlooks, attitudes may legitimately differ; general principles may cut across too much human need. The concrete situation is almost everything. There is no escape: we must decide as we decide; moral risk cannot, at times, be avoided. All we can ask for is that none of the relevant factors be ignored, that the purposes we seek to realise should be seen as elements in a total form of life, which can be enhanced or damaged by decisions.

But, in the end, it is not a matter of purely subjective judgement: it is dictated by the forms of life of the society to which one belongs, a society among other societies, with values held in common, whether or not they are in conflict, by the majority of mankind throughout recorded history. There are, if not universal values, at any rate a minimum without which societies could scarcely survive. Few today would wish to defend slavery or ritual murder or Nazi gas chambers or the torture of human beings for the sake of pleasure or profit or even political good – or the duty of children to denounce their parents, which the French and Russian revolutions demanded, or mindless killing. There is no justification for compromise on this. But on the other hand, the search for perfection does seem to me a recipe for bloodshed, no better even if it is demanded by the sincerest of idealists, the purest of heart. No more rigorous moralist than Immanuel Kant has ever lived, but even he said, in a moment of illumination, 'Out of the crooked timber of humanity no straight thing was ever made.' To force people into the neat uniforms demanded by dogmatically believed-in schemes is almost always the road to inhumanity. We can only do what we can: but that we must do, against difficulties.

Of course social or political collisions will take place; the mere conflict of positive values alone makes this unavoidable. Yet they can, I believe, be minimised by promoting and preserving an uneasy equilibrium, which is constantly threatened and in constant need of repair – that alone, I repeat, is the precondition for decent societies and morally acceptable behaviour, otherwise we are bound to lose our way. A little dull as a solution, you will say? Not the stuff of which calls to heroic action by inspired leaders are made? Yet if there is some truth in this view, perhaps that is sufficient. An eminent American philosopher of our day once said, 'There is no *a priori* reason for supposing that the truth, when it is discovered, will necessarily prove interesting.' It may be enough if it is truth, or even an approximation to it; consequently I do not feel apologetic for advancing this. Truth, said Tolstoy, in the novel with which I began, is the most beautiful thing in the entire world. I do not know if this is so in the realm of ethics, but it seems to me near enough to what most of us wish to believe not to be too lightly set aside.

THE DECLINE OF
UTOPIAN IDEAS IN THE WEST

THE IDEA of a perfect society is a very old dream, whether because of the ills of the present, which lead men to conceive of what their world would be like without them – to imagine some ideal state in which there was no misery and no greed, no danger or poverty or fear or brutalising labour or insecurity – or because these Utopias are fictions deliberately constructed as satires, intended to criticise the actual world and to shame those who control existing regimes, or those who suffer them too tamely; or perhaps they are social fantasies – simple exercises of the poetical imagination.

Broadly speaking, western Utopias tend to contain the same elements: a society lives in a state of pure harmony, in which all its members live in peace, love one another, are free from physical danger, from want of any kind, from insecurity, from degrading work, from envy, from frustration, experience no injustice or violence, live in perpetual, even light, in a temperate climate, in the midst of infinitely fruitful, generous nature. The main characteristic of most, perhaps all, Utopias is the fact that they are static. Nothing in them alters, for they have reached perfection: there is no need for novelty or change; no one can wish to alter a condition in which all natural human wishes are fulfilled.

The assumption on which this is based is that men have a certain fixed, unaltering nature, certain universal, common, immutable goals. Once these goals are realised, human nature is wholly fulfilled. The very idea of universal fulfilment presupposes that human beings as such seek the same essential goals, identical for all, at all times, everywhere. For unless this is so, Utopia cannot be Utopia, for then the perfect society will not perfectly satisfy everyone.

Most Utopias are cast back into a remote past: once upon a time there was a golden age. So Homer talks about the happy Phaeacians, or about the blameless Ethiopians among whom Zeus loves to dwell, or sings of the Isles of the Blest. Hesiod talks about the golden age, succeeded by progressively worse ages, descending to the terrible times in which he lived himself. Plato speaks, in the *Symposium*, of the fact that men were once – in a remote and happy past – spherical in shape, and then broke in half, and ever since each hemisphere is trying to find its appropriate mate for the purpose of once again becoming rounded and perfect. He speaks also of the happy life in Atlantis, gone, gone for ever as a result of some natural disaster. Virgil speaks about *Saturnia regna*, the Kingdom of Saturn, in which all things were good. The Hebrew Bible speaks of an earthly paradise, in which Adam and Eve were created by God and led blameless, happy, serene lives – a situation which might have gone on for ever, but was brought to a wretched end by man's disobedience to his maker. When, in the last century, the poet Alfred Tennyson spoke of a kingdom 'Where falls not hail, or rain, or any snow, Nor ever wind blows loudly', this reflects a long, unbroken tradition, and looks back to the Homeric dream of eternal light shining upon a windless world.

These are poets who believed that the golden age is in a past which can never return. Then there are the thinkers who believe that the golden age is still to come. The Hebrew prophet Isaiah tells us that 'in the last days' men 'shall beat their swords into plowshares, and their spears into pruninghooks: nation shall not lift up sword against nation, neither shall they learn war any more . . . The wolf also shall dwell with the lamb, and the leopard shall lie down with the kid . . . the desert shall rejoice, and blossom as the rose . . . and sorrow and sighing shall flee away.' Similarly, St Paul speaks of a world in which there will be neither Jew nor Greek, neither male nor female, neither bond nor free. All men shall be equal, and perfect in the sight of God.

What is common to all these worlds, whether they are conceived of as an earthly paradise or something beyond the grave, is that they display a static perfection in which human nature is finally fully realised, and all is still and immutable and eternal.

This ideal can take social and political forms, both hierarchical and democratic. In Plato's Republic there is a rigid, unified hierarchy of three classes, based on the proposition that there are three types of human nature, each of which can be fully realised and which together form an interlocking, harmonious whole. Zeno the Stoic conceives an anarchist society in which all rational beings live in perfect peace, equality and happiness without the benefit of institutions. If men are rational, they do not need control; rational beings have no need of the state, or of money, or of law-courts, or of any organised, institutional life. In the perfect society men and women shall wear identical clothes and 'feed in a common pasture'. Provided that they are rational, all their wishes will necessarily be rational too, and so capable of total harmonious realisation. Zeno was the first Utopian anarchist, the founder of a long tradition which has had a sudden, at times violent, flowering in our own time.

The Greek world generated a good many Utopias after the city-state showed the first signs of decline. Side by side with the satirical Utopias of Aristophanes there is the plan for a perfect state of Theopompus. There is the Utopia of Euhemerus, in which happy men live on islands in the Arabian Sea, where there are no wild animals, no winter, no spring, but an eternal, gentle, warm summer, where fruits fall into men's mouths from the trees, and there is no need for labour. These men live in a state of unceasing bliss on islands divided by the sea from the wicked, chaotic mainland in which men are foolish, unjust and miserable.

There may have been attempts to put this into practice. Zeno's disciple Blossius of Cumae, a Roman Stoic, probably preached a social egalitarianism which may have been derived from the earlier communist Iambulus. He was accused of inspiring anti-Roman revolts of a communist type, and was duly investigated, indeed 'grilled', by a senatorial committee which accused him of spreading subversive ideas – not unlike the McCarthy investigations in the United States. Blossius, Aristonicus, Gaius Gracchus were accused – the story ends with the execution of the Gracchi. However, these political consequences are merely incidental to my topic. During the Middle Ages there is a distinct decline in Utopias, perhaps because according to Christian faith man cannot achieve perfection by his own unaided efforts; divine grace alone can save him – and salvation cannot come to him while he is on this earth, a creature born in sin. No man can build a lasting habitation in this vale of tears: for we are all but pilgrims here below, seeking to enter a kingdom not of this earth.

The constant theme which runs through all Utopian thought, Christian and pagan alike, is that once upon a time there was a perfect state, then some enormous disaster took place: in the Bible it is the sin of disobedience – the fatal eating of the forbidden fruit; or else it is the Flood; or wicked giants came and disturbed the world, or men in their arrogance built the Tower of Babel and were punished. So too in Greek mythology the perfect state was broken by some disaster, as in the story of Prometheus, or of Deucalion and Pyrrha, or of Pandora's box – the pristine unity is shivered, and the rest of human history is a continuous attempt to piece together the fragments in order to restore serenity, so that the perfect state may be realised once again. Human stupidity or wickedness or weakness may prevent this consummation; or the gods may not permit it; but our lives are conceived, particularly in the thought of Gnostics and in the visions of the mystics, as an agonised effort to piece together the broken fragments of the perfect whole with which the universe began, and to which it may yet return. This is a persistent idea which goes through European thought from its earliest beginnings; it underlies all the old Utopias and has deeply influenced western metaphysical, moral and political ideas. In this sense utopianism – the notion of the broken unity and its restoration – is a central strand in the whole of western thought. For this reason it might be not unprofitable to try to reveal some of the main assumptions which appear to underlie it.

Let me put them in the form of three propositions, a kind of three-legged stool on which the central tradition of western political thought seems to me to rest. I shall, I fear, simplify these matters too much, but a mere sketch is not a book, and oversimplification is – I can only hope – not always falsification, and often serves to crystallise the issues. The first proposition is this: to all genuine questions there can only be one correct answer, all the other answers being incorrect. If there is no correct answer to it, then the question cannot be a genuine one. Any genuine question must, at least in principle, be answerable, and if this is so, only one answer can be correct. No one question, provided it is clearly stated, can have two answers which are different and yet both correct. The grounds of the correct answers must be true; all other possible answers must embody, or rest on, falsehood, which has many faces. That is the first cardinal assumption.

The second assumption is that a method exists for the discovery of these correct answers. Whether any man knows or can, in fact, know it, is another question; but it must, at least in principle, be knowable, provided that the right procedure for establishing it is used.

The third assumption, and perhaps the most important in this context, is that all the correct answers must, at the very least, be compatible with one another. That follows from a simple, logical truth: that one truth cannot be incompatible with another truth; all correct answers embody or rest on truths; therefore none of the correct answers, whether they are answers to questions about what there is in the world, or what men should do, or what men should be – in other words, whether they answer questions concerned with facts or with values (and for thinkers who believe this third proposition, questions of value are in some sense questions of fact) – can ever be in conflict with one another. At best, these truths will logically entail one another in a single, systematic, interconnected whole; at the very least, they will be consistent with one another: that is, they will form a harmonious whole, so that when you have discovered all the correct answers to all the central questions of human life and put them together, the result will form a kind of scheme of the sum of knowledge needed to lead a – or rather the – perfect life.

It may be that mortal men cannot attain to such knowledge. There may be many reasons for this. Some Christian thinkers would maintain that original sin makes men incapable of such knowledge. Or perhaps we lived in the light of such truths once, in the Garden of Eden before the age of sin, and then this light failed us because we tasted of the fruit of the Tree of Knowledge, knowledge which, as our punishment, is bound to remain incomplete during life on earth. Or perhaps we shall know it all one day, whether before or after the death of the body. Or again, it may be that men shall never know it: their minds may be too weak, or the obstacles offered by intractable nature may be too great, to make such knowledge possible. Perhaps only the angels can know it, or perhaps only God knows it; or, if there is no God, then one must express this belief by saying that in principle such knowledge can be conceived, even if no one has ever achieved it or is ever likely to do so. For, in principle, the answer must be knowable; unless this is so, the questions would not be genuine; to say of a question that it is in principle unanswerable is not to understand what kind of question it is – for to understand the nature of a question is to know what kind of answer could be a correct answer to it, whether we know it to be correct or not; hence the range of possible answers to it must be conceivable; and one in this range must be the correct one. Otherwise, for rationalist thinkers of this type, rational thought would end in insoluble puzzles. If this is ruled out by the very nature of reason, it must follow that the pattern of the sum (perhaps of an infinity) of the correct solutions of all possible problems will constitute perfect knowledge.

Let me continue with this argument. It is asserted that unless we can conceive of something perfect, we cannot understand what is meant by imperfection. If, let us say, we complain about our condition here on earth by pointing to conflict, misery, cruelty, vice – 'the misfortunes, follies, crimes of mankind' – if, in short, we declare our state to be short of perfect, this is intelligible only by comparison with a more perfect world; it is by measuring the gap between the two that we can measure the extent by which our world falls short. Short of what? The idea of that of which it falls short is the idea of a perfect state. This, I think, is what underlies Utopian thought, and indeed a great deal of western thought in general; in fact it seems central to it, from Pythagoras and Plato onwards.

At this point it may be asked where, if all this is the case, the solutions are to be sought: who are the authorities who can show the rest of us the right path for theory and practice? On this (as might have been expected) there has, in the west, been little agreement. Some have told us that the true answers are to be found in sacred texts, or given by inspired prophets, or by priests who are the authorised interpreters of these texts. Others deny the validity of revelation or prescription or tradition, and say that only accurate knowledge of nature yields the true answers – to be obtained by controlled observation, experiment, the application of logical and mathematical techniques. Nature is not a temple, but a laboratory, and hypotheses must be testable by methods which any rational being can learn and apply and communicate and check; science, they declare, may not answer all the questions we wish to put, but what it cannot answer no other method will supply: it is the only reliable instrument we have or will ever have. Again, some tell us that only the experts know: men gifted with mystical vision, or metaphysical insight and speculative power, or scientific skills; or men endowed with natural wisdom – sages, men of lofty intellect. But others deny this and declare that the most important truths are accessible to all men: every man who looks within his own heart, his own soul, will understand himself and the nature which surrounds him, will know how to live and what to do, provided he has not been blinded by the baleful influence of others – men whose natures have been perverted by bad institutions. That is what Rousseau would have said: truth is to be sought not in the ideas or behaviour of corrupt dwellers in sophisticated cities, but is more likely to be found in the pure heart of a simple peasant, or of an innocent child – and Tolstoy in effect echoed this; and this view has adherents today, despite the work of Freud and his disciples.

There is almost no view about the sources of true knowledge that has not been passionately held and dogmatically asserted in the course of conscious meditation about this problem in the Hellenic and Judaeo-Christian tradition. About the differences between them great conflicts have broken out and bloody wars have been fought, and no wonder, since human salvation was held to depend upon the right answer to these questions – the most agonising and crucial issues in human life. The point I wish to make is that all sides assumed that these questions could be answered. The all but universal belief which this amounts to is that these answers are, as it were, so much hidden treasure; the problem is to find the path to it. Or, to use another metaphor, mankind has been presented with the scattered parts of a jigsaw puzzle: if you can put the pieces together, it will form a perfect whole which constitutes the goal of the quest for truth, virtue, happiness. That, I think, is one of the common assumptions of a great deal of western thought.

This conviction certainly underlay the Utopias which pro-liferated so richly during the European Renaissance in the fif-teenth century, when there was a great rediscovery of the Greek and Latin classics, which were thought to embody truths forgot-ten during the long night of the Middle Ages or suppressed or distorted by the monkish superstitions of the Christian ages of faith. The New Learning was based on the belief that knowl-edge, and only knowledge – the liberated human mind – could save us. This, in its turn, rested on the most fundamental of all rationalist propositions – that virtue was knowledge – uttered by Socrates, developed by Plato and his greatest disciple, Aristotle, and the principal Socratic schools of ancient Greece. For Plato the paradigm of knowledge was geometrical in character, for Aristotle biological; for various thinkers during the Renaissance it may have been neo-Platonic and mystical, or intuitive or mathematical, or organic or mechanical, but none doubted that knowledge alone offered spiritual and moral and political salvation. It was, I think, assumed that if men have a common nature, this nature must have a purpose. Man's nature could be fully realised if only he knew what he truly wanted. If a man can discover what there is in the world, and what his relationship is to it, and what he is himself – however he has discovered it, by whichever method, by whichever recommended or traditional path to knowledge – he will know what will fulfil him, what, in other words, will make him happy, just, virtuous, wise. To know what will liberate one from error and illusion, and truly understand all that as a spiritual and physical being one knows oneself to seek after, and yet, despite this, to refrain from acting accordingly, is not to be in one's right mind – to be irrational and perhaps not altogether sane. To know how to compass your ends and then not to try to do so is, in the end, not truly to understand your ends. To understand is to act: there is a certain sense in which these earlier thinkers anticipated Karl Marx in their belief in the unity of theory and practice.

Knowledge, for the central tradition of western thought, means not just descriptive knowledge of what there is in the universe, but as part and parcel of it, not distinct from it, knowledge of values, or how to live, what to do, which forms of life are the best and worthiest, and why. According to this doctrine – that virtue is knowledge – when men commit crimes they do so because they are in error: they have mistaken what will, in fact, profit them. If they truly knew what would profit them, they would not do these destructive things – acts which must end by destroying the actor, by frustrating his true ends as a human being, by blocking the proper development of his faculties and powers. Crime, vice, imperfection, misery, all arise from ignorance and mental indolence or muddle. This ignorance may be fomented by wicked people who wish to throw dust in the eyes of others in order to dominate them, and who may, in the end, as often as not, be taken in by their own propaganda.

'Virtue is knowledge' means that if you know the good for man, you cannot, if you are a rational being, live in any way other than that whereby fulfilment is that towards which all desires, hopes, prayers, aspirations are directed: that is what is meant by calling them hopes. To distinguish reality from appearance, to distinguish that which will truly fulfil a man from that which merely appears to promise to do so, that is knowledge, and that alone will save him. It is this vast Platonic assumption, sometimes in its baptised, Christian form, that animates the great Utopias of the Renaissance, More's wonderful fantasy, Bacon's New Atlantis, Campanella's City of the Sun, and the dozen or so Christian Utopias of the seventeenth century – of which Fénelon's is only the best known. Absolute faith in rational solutions and the proliferation of Utopian writing are both aspects of similar stages of cultural development, in classical Athens and the Italian Renaissance and the French eighteenth century and in the two hundred years that followed, no less so in the present than in the recent or distant past. Even the early travellers' tales, which are held to have helped to open men's eyes to the variety of human nature and, therefore, to discredit the belief in the uniformity of human needs and consequently in the single, final remedy to all their ills, often seem to have had the opposite effect. The discovery, for example, of men in a savage state in the forests of America was used as evidence of a basic human nature, of the so-called natural man, with natural needs as they would have existed everywhere if men had not been corrupted by civilisation, by artificial man-made institutions, as a result of error or wickedness on the part of priests and kings and other power-seekers, who practised monstrous deceptions on the gullible masses, the better to dominate them and exploit their labour. The concept of the noble savage was part of the myth of the unsullied purity of human nature, innocent, at peace with its surroundings and itself, ruined only by contact with the vices of the corrupt culture of western cities. The notion that somewhere, whether in a real or imagined society, man dwells in his natural state, to which all men should return, is at the heart of primitivist theories; it is found in various guises in every anarchist and populist programme of the last hundred years, and has deeply affected Marxism and the vast variety of youth movements with radical or revolutionary goals.

As I have said, the doctrine common to all these views and movements is the notion that there exist universal truths, true for all men, everywhere, at all times, and that these truths are expressed in universal rules, the natural law of the Stoics and the medieval church and the jurists of the Renaissance, defiance of which alone leads to vice, misery and chaos. It is true that doubts were thrown on the idea by, for example, certain sophists and sceptics in ancient Greece, as well as by Protagoras, and Hippias, and Carneades and Pyrrhon and Sextus Empiricus, and in a later day by Montaigne and the Pyrrhonists of the seventeenth century, and above all by Montesquieu, who thought that different ways of life suited men in different environments and climates, with different traditions and customs. But this needs qualification. It is true that a sophist quoted by Aristotle thought that 'fire burns both here and in Persia, but what is thought just changes before our very eyes'; and that Montesquieu thinks that one should wear warm clothes in cold climates and thin garments in hot ones, and that Persian customs would not suit the inhabitants of Paris. But what this kind of plea for variety comes to is that different means are most effective in different circumstances towards the realisation of similar ends. This is true even of the notorious sceptic David Hume. None of these doubters wish to deny that the central human goals are universal and uniform, even though they may not be necessarily established *a priori*: all men seek food and drink, shelter and security; all men want to procreate; all men seek social intercourse, justice, a degree of liberty, means of self-expression, and the like. The means towards these ends may differ from country to country, and age to age, but the ends, whether alterable in principle or not, remain unaltered; this is clearly brought out by a high degree of family resemblance in the social Utopias of both ancient and modern times.

It is true that a rather graver blow against these assumptions was directed by Machiavelli, who suggested doubts about whether it was possible, even in principle, to combine a Christian view of life involving self-sacrifice and humility with the possibility of building and maintaining a powerful and glorious republic, which required not humility or self-sacrifice on the part of its rulers and citizens, but the pagan virtues of courage, vitality, self-assertion and, in the case of rulers, a capacity for ruthless, unscrupulous and cruel action where this was called for by the needs of the state. Machiavelli did not develop the full implications of this conflict of ideals – he was not a professional philosopher – but what he said caused great uneasiness in some of his readers for four and a half centuries. Nevertheless, broadly speaking, the issue he raised tended to be largely ignored. His works were pronounced immoral and condemned by the church, and not taken altogether seriously by the moralists and political thinkers who represent the central current of western thought in these fields.

To some degree, I think, Machiavelli did have some influence: on Hobbes, on Rousseau, on Fichte and Hegel, certainly on Frederick the Great of Prussia, who took the trouble of publishing a formal refutation of his views; most clearly of all on Nietzsche and those influenced by him. But, by and large, the most uncomfortable assumption in Machiavelli, namely that certain virtues and, even more, certain ideals may not be compatible – a notion which offends against the proposition that I have emphasised, that all true answers to serious questions must be compatible – that assumption was for the most part quietly ignored. No one seemed anxious to grapple with the possibility that the Christian and the pagan answers to moral or political questions might both be correct given the premises from which they start; that these premises were not demonstrably false, only incompatible; and that no single overarching standard or criterion was available to decide between, or reconcile, these wholly opposed moralities. This was found somewhat troubling by those who believed themselves to be Christians but wished to give unto Caesar what was Caesar's. A sharp division between public and private life, or politics and morality, never works well. Too many territories have been claimed by both. This has been and can be an agonising problem, and, as often happened in such cases, men were none too anxious to face it.

There was also another angle from which these assumptions were questioned. The assumptions, I repeat, are those of natural law: that human nature is a static, unaltering essence, that its ends are eternal, unaltering and universal for all men, everywhere, at all times, and can be known, and perhaps fulfilled, by those who possess the appropriate kind of knowledge.

When the new nation-states arose in the course, and partly as a result, of the Reformation in the sixteenth century in the west and north of Europe, some among the lawyers engaged in formulating and defending the claims and laws of these kingdoms – for the most part reformers, whether out of opposition to the authority of the Church of Rome, or, in some cases, to the centralising policies of the King of France – began to argue that Roman law, with its claim to universal authority, was nothing to them: they were not Romans; they were Franks, Celts, Norsemen; they had their own Frankish, Batavian, Scandinavian traditions; they lived in Languedoc; they had their Languedoc customs from time immemorial; what was Rome to them? In France they were descendants of Frankish conquerors, their ancestors had subdued the Gallo-Romans; they had inherited, they wished to recognise, only their own Frankish or Burgundian or Helvetic laws; what Roman law had to say was neither here nor there; it did not apply to them. Let the Italians obey Rome. Why should Franks, Teutons, descendants of Viking pirates, accept the dominion of a single, universal, foreign legal code? Different nations, different roots, different laws, different peoples, different communities, different ideals. Each had its own way of living – what right had one to dictate to the others? Least of all the Pope, whose claims to spiritual authority the reformers denied. This broke the spell of one world, one universal law, and consequently one universal goal for all men, everywhere, at all times. The perfect society which Frankish warriors, or even their descendants, conceived as their ideal might be very different from the Utopian vision of an Italian, ancient or modern, and wholly unlike that of an Indian or a Swede or a Turk. Henceforth, the spectre of relativism makes its dreaded appearance, and with it the beginning of the dissolution of faith in the very concept of universally valid goals, at least in the social and political sphere. This was accompanied, in due course, by a sense that there might be not only a historical or political but some logical flaw in the very idea of a universe equally acceptable to communities of different origin, with different traditions, character, outlook, concepts, categories, views of life.

But again, the implications of this were not fully spelt out, largely, perhaps, because of the enormous triumph at this very time of the natural sciences. As a result of the revolutionary discoveries of Galileo and Newton and the work of other mathematicians and physicists and biologists of genius, the external world was seen as a single cosmos, such that, to take the best-known example, by the application of relatively few laws the movement and position of every particle of matter could be precisely determined. For the first time it became possible to organise a chaotic mass of observational data into a single, coherent, perfectly orderly system. Why should not the same methods be applied to human matters, to morals, to politics, to the organisation of society, with equal success? Why should it be assumed that men belong to some order outside the system of nature? What holds good for material objects, for animals and plants and minerals, in zoology, botany, chemistry, physics, astronomy – all new sciences well on the way to being unified, which proceed from hypotheses about observed facts and events to testable scientific conclusions, and together form a coherent and scientific system – why should not this also apply to human problems? Why cannot one create a science or sciences of man and here also provide solutions as clear and certain as those obtained in the sciences of the external world?

This was a novel, revolutionary and highly plausible proposal which the thinkers of the Enlightenment, particularly in France, accepted with natural enthusiasm. It was surely reasonable to suppose that man has an examinable nature, capable of being observed, analysed, tested like other organisms and forms of living matter. The programme seemed clear: one must scientifically find out what man consists of, and what he needs for his growth and for his satisfaction. When one had discovered what he is and what he requires, one will then ask where this last can be found; and then, by means of the appropriate inventions and discoveries, supply men's wants, and in this way achieve, if not total perfection, at any rate a far happier and more rational state of affairs than at present prevails. Why does it not exist? Because stupidity, prejudice, superstition, ignorance, the passions which darken reason, greed and fear and lust for domination, and the barbarism, cruelty, intolerance, fanaticism which go with them, have led to the deplorable condition in which men have been forced to live too long. Failure, unavoidable or deliberate, to observe what there is in the world has robbed man of the knowledge needed to improve his life. Scientific knowledge alone can save us. This is the fundamental doctrine of the French Enlightenment, a great liberating movement which in its day eliminated a great deal of cruelty, superstition, injustice and obscurantism.

In due course this great wave of rationalism led to an inevitable reaction. It seems to me a historical fact that whenever rationalism goes far enough there often tends to occur some kind of emotional resistance, a 'backlash', which springs from that which is irrational in man. This took place in Greece in the fourth and third centuries BC, when the great Socratic schools produced their magnificent rationalistic systems: seldom, we are told by historians of Greek cults, did mystery religions, occultism, irrationalism, mysticisms of all kinds flourish so richly. So too the powerful and rigid edifice of Roman law, one of the great achievements of human civilisation, and, side by side with it, the great legal-religious structure of ancient Judaism were followed by a passionate, emotional resistance, culminating in the rise and triumph of Christianity. In the later Middle Ages there was, similarly, reaction to the great logical constructions of the schoolmen. Something not dissimilar occurred during the Reformation; and finally, following the triumphs of the scientific spirit in the west, a powerful counter-movement arose some two centuries ago.

This reaction came mainly from Germany. Something needs to be said about the social and spiritual situation in the Germany of that time. By the seventeenth century, even before the devastation of the Thirty Years War, German-speaking countries found themselves, for reasons which I do not have the competence to discuss, culturally inferior to their neighbours across the Rhine. During the entire seventeenth century, the French seemed to be dominant in every sphere of life, both spiritual and material. Their military strength, their social and economic organisation, their thinkers, scientists and philosophers, painters and composers, their poets, dramatists, architects – their excellence in the general arts of life – these placed them at the head of all Europe. Well might they be excused if then and later they identified civilisation as such with their own culture.

If, during the seventeenth century, French influence reached an unexampled height, there was a notable flowering of culture in other western countries also: this is plainly true of England in the late Elizabethan and Stuart period; it coincided with the golden age of Spain, and the great artistic and scientific renaissance in the Low Countries. Italy, if not perhaps at the height which it reached in the quattrocento, produced artists, and especially scientists, of rare achievement. Even Sweden in the far north was beginning to stir.

The German-speaking peoples could not boast of anything similar. If you ask what were the most distinguished contributions made to European civilisation in the seventeenth century by the German-speaking lands, there is little enough to tell: apart from architecture and the isolated genius of Kepler, original talent seemed to flow only in theology; the poets, scholars, thinkers, seldom rose above mediocrity; Leibniz seems to have few native predecessors. This can, I believe, be explained, at least in part, by the economic decline and political divisions in Germany; but I am concerned only to stress the facts themselves. Even though the general level of German education remained quite high, life and art and thought remained profoundly provincial. The attitude to the German lands of the advanced nations of the west, particularly of the French, seemed to be a kind of patronising indifference. In due course the humiliated Germans began feebly to imitate their French models. and this, as often happens, was followed by a cultural reaction. The wounded national consciousness asserted itself, sometimes in a somewhat aggressive fashion.

This is a common enough response on the part of backward nations who are looked on with too much arrogant contempt, with too great an air of conscious superiority, by the more advanced societies. By the beginning of the eighteenth century some among the spiritual leaders in the devout, inward-looking German principalities began to counter-attack. This took the form of pouring contempt on the worldly success of the French: these Frenchmen and their imitators elsewhere could boast of only so much empty show. The inner life, the life of the spirit, concerned with the relation of man to man, to himself, to God – that alone was of supreme importance; the empty, materialistic French wiseacres had no sense of true values – of what alone men lived by. Let them have their arts, their sciences, their *salons*, their wealth and their vaunted glory. All this was, in the end, dross – the perishable goods of the corruptible flesh. The *philosophes* were blind leaders of the blind, remote from all conception of what alone truly mattered, the dark, agonising, infinitely rewarding descent into the depths of man's own sinful but immortal soul, made in the semblance of divine nature itself. This was the realm of the devout, inward vision of the German soul.

Gradually this German self-image grew in intensity, fed by what might be called a kind of nationalist resentment. The philosopher, poet, critic, pastor Johann Gottfried Herder was perhaps the first wholly articulate prophet of this attitude, and elevated this cultural self-consciousness into a general principle. Beginning as a literary historian and essayist, he maintained that values were not universal; every human society, every people, indeed every age and civilisation, possesses its own unique ideals, standards, way of living and thought and action. There are no immutable, universal, eternal rules or criteria of judgement in terms of which different cultures and nations can be graded in some single order of excellence, which would place the French – if Voltaire was right – at the top of the ladder of human achievement and the Germans far below them in the twilight regions of religious obscurantism and within the narrow limits of provincialism and dim-witted rural existence. Every society, every age, has its own cultural horizons. Every nation has its own traditions, its own character, its own face. Every nation has its own centre of moral gravity, which differs from that of every other: there and only there its happiness lies – in the development of its own national needs, its own unique character.

There is no compelling reason for seeking to imitate foreign models, or returning to some remote past. Every age, every society, differs in its goals and habits and values from every other. The conception of human history as a single universal process of struggle towards the light, the later stages and embodiments of which are necessarily superior to the earlier, where the primitive is necessarily inferior to the sophisticated, is an enormous fallacy. Homer is not a primitive Ariosto; Shakespeare is not a rudimentary Racine (these are not Herder's examples). To judge one culture by the standards of another argues a failure of imagination and understanding. Every culture has its own attributes, which must be grasped in and for themselves. In order to understand a culture, one must employ the same faculties of sympathetic insight with which we understand one another, without which there is neither love nor friendship, nor true human relationships. One man's attitude towards another is, or should be, based on perceiving what he is in himself, uniquely, not what he has in common with all other men; only the natural sciences abstract what is common, generalise. Human relations are founded on recognition of individuality, which can, perhaps, never be exhaustively described, still less analysed; so it is with understanding communities, cultures, epochs, and what they are and strive for and feel and suffer and create, how they express themselves and see themselves and think and act.

Men congregate in groups because they are conscious of what unites them — bonds of common descent, language, soil, collective experience; these bonds are unique, impalpable and ultimate. Cultural frontiers are natural to men, spring from the interplay of their inner essence and environment and historical experience. Greek culture is uniquely and inexhaustibly Greek; India, Persia, France are what they are, not something else. Our culture is our own; cultures are incommensurable; each is as it is, each of infinite value, as souls are in the sight of God. To eliminate one in favour of another, to subjugate a society and destroy a civilisation, as the great conquerors have done, is a monstrous crime against the right to be oneself, to live in the light of one's own ideal values. If you exile a German and plant him in America, he will be unhappy; he will suffer because people can be happy, can function freely, only among those who understand them. To be lonely is to be among men who do not know what you mean. Exile, solitude, is to find yourself among people whose words, gestures, handwriting are alien to your

own, whose behaviour, reactions, feelings, instinctive responses, and thoughts and pleasures and pains, are too remote
from yours, whose education and outlook, the tone and quality
of whose lives and being, are not yours. There are many things
which men do have in common, but that is not what matters
most. What individualises them, makes them what they are,
makes communication possible, is what they do not have in
common with all the others. Differences, peculiarities,
nuances, individual character are all in all.

This is a novel doctrine. Herder identified cultural differences and cultural essence and the very idea of historical
development very differently from Voltaire. What, for him,
makes Germans German is the fact that the way in which they
eat or drink, dispense justice, write poetry, worship, dispose of
property, get up and sit down, obtain their food, wear their
clothes, sing, fight wars, order political life, all have a certain
common character, a qualitative property, a pattern which is
solely German, in which they differ from the corresponding
activities of the Chinese or the Portuguese. No one of these
peoples or cultures is, for Herder, superior to any of the others,
they are merely different; since they are different, they seek
different ends; therein is both their specific character and their
value. Values, qualities of character, are not commensurable: an
order of merit which presupposes a single measuring-rod is, for
Herder, evidence of blindness to what makes human beings
human. A German cannot be made happy by efforts to turn him
into a second-rate Frenchman. Icelanders will not be made
happy by life in Denmark, or Europeans by emigrating to
America. Men can develop their full powers only by continuing
to live where they and their ancestors were born, to speak their
language, live their lives within the framework of the customs
of their society and culture. Men are not self-created: they are
born into a stream of tradition, above all of language, which
shapes their thoughts and feelings, which they cannot shed or
change, which forms their inner life. The qualities which men
have in common are not sufficient to ensure the fulfilment of a

man's or a people's nature, which depends at least as much on
the characteristics due to the place, the time and the culture to
which men uniquely belong; to ignore or obliterate these
characteristics is to destroy men's souls and bodies equally. 'I am
not here to think, but to be, feel, live!' For Herder every action,
every form of life, has a pattern which differs from that of every
other. The natural unit for him is what he calls *das Volk*, the
people, the chief constituents of which are soil and language, not
race or colour or religion. That is Herder's lifelong sermon – after
all, he was a Protestant pastor – to the German-speaking peoples.

But if this is so, if the doctrine of the French Enlightenment –
and indeed, the central western assumption, of which I have
spoken, that all true values are immutable and timeless and
universal – needs revising so drastically, then there is something
radically wrong with the idea of a perfect society. The basic
reason for this is not to be found among those which were
usually advanced against Utopian ideas – that such a society
cannot be attained because men are not wise or skilful or
virtuous enough, or cannot acquire the requisite degree of
knowledge, or resolution, or, tainted as they are with original
sin, cannot attain perfection in this life – but is altogether
different. The idea of a single, perfect society of all mankind
must be internally self-contradictory, because the Valhalla of
the Germans is necessarily different from the ideal of future life
of the French, because the paradise of the Muslims is not that of
Jews or Christians, because a society in which a Frenchman
would attain to harmonious fulfilment is a society which to a
German might prove suffocating. But if we are to have as many
types of perfection as there are types of culture, each with its
ideal constellation of virtues, then the very notion of the
possibility of a single perfect society is logically incoherent.
This, I think, is the beginning of the modern attack on the
notion of Utopia, Utopia as such.

The romantic movement in Germany, which owed a great
deal to the influence of the philosopher Fichte, contributed its
own powerful impetus to this new and genuinely revolutionary

Weltanschauung. For the young Friedrich Schlegel, or Tieck, or Novalis, values, ethical, political, aesthetic, are not objectively given, not fixed stars in some Platonic firmament, eternal, immutable, which men can discover only by employing the proper method – metaphysical insight, scientific investigation, philosophical argument or divine revelation. Values are generated by the creative human self. Man is, above all, a creature endowed not only with reason but with will. Will is the creative function of man. The new model of man's nature is conceived by analogy with the new conception of artistic creation, no longer bound by the objective rules drawn from idealised universal nature ('la bella natura') or by the eternal truths of classicism, or natural law, or a divine lawgiver. If one compares classical doctrines – even those of such late neoclassical, somewhat Platonist, theorists as Joshua Reynolds or Jean-Philippe Rameau – with those of their romantic opponents, this emerges clearly. Reynolds, in his famous lectures on the Great Style, said in effect that, if you are painting a king, you must be guided by the conception of royalty. David, King of Israel, may in life have been of mean stature and have had physical defects. But you may not so paint him, because he is a king. Therefore you must paint him as a royal personage; and royalty is an eternal, immutable attribute, unitary and equally accessible to the vision of all men, at all times, everywhere; somewhat like a Platonic 'idea', beyond the reach of the empirical eye, it does not alter with the passage of time or difference of outlook, and the business of the painter or sculptor is to penetrate the veil of appearance, to conceive of the essence of pure royalty, and convey it on canvas, or in marble or wood or whatever medium the artist chooses to use. Similarly, Rameau was convinced that the business of a composer was to use sound to evince harmony – the eternal mathematical proportions which are embodied in the nature of things, in the great cosmos – not given to the mortal ear, yet that which gives the pattern of musical sounds the order and beauty which the inspired artist creates – or rather reproduces, 'imitates' – as best he can.

Not so those who are influenced by the new romantic doctrine. The painter creates; he does not copy. He does not imitate; he does not follow rules; he makes them. Values are not discovered, they are created; not found, but made by an act of imaginative, creative will, as works of art, as policies, plans, patterns of life are created. By whose imagination, whose will? Fichte speaks of the self, the ego; as a rule he identifies it with a transcendent, infinite, world-spirit of which the human individual is a mere spatiotemporal, mortal expression, a finite centre which derives its reality from the spirit, to perfect union with which it seeks to attain. Others identified this self with some other superpersonal spirit or force – the nation, the true self in which the individual is only an element; or, again, the people (Rousseau comes near to doing this) or the state (as Hegel does); or it is identified with a culture, or the *Zeitgeist* (a conception greatly mocked by Goethe in his *Faust*), or a class which embodies the progressive march of history (as in Marx), or some other, equally impalpable, movement or force or group. This somewhat mysterious source is held to generate and transform values which I am bound to follow because, to the degree to which I am, at my best or truest, an agent of God, or of history, or progress, or the nation, I recognise them as my own. This constitutes a sharp break with the whole of previous tradition, for which the true and the beautiful, the noble and the ignoble, the right and the wrong, duty, sin, ultimate good, were unalterable, ideal values and, like their opposites, created eternal and identical for all men; in the old formula, *quod semper*, *quod ubique, quod ab omnibus*: the only problem was how to know them and, knowing, realise or avoid them, do good and eschew evil.

But if these values are not uncreated, but generated by my culture or by my nation or by my class, they will differ from the values generated by your culture, your nation, your class; they are not universal, and may clash. If the values generated by Germans are different from values generated by Portuguese, if the values generated by the ancient Greeks are different from those of modern Frenchmen, then a relativity deeper than any enunciated by the sophists or Montesquieu or Hume will destroy the single moral and intellectual universe. Aristotle, Herder declared, is 'theirs' – Leibniz is 'ours'. Leibniz speaks to us Germans, not Socrates or Aristotle. Aristotle was a great thinker, but we cannot return to him: his world is not ours. So, three-quarters of a century later, it was laid down that if my true values are the expression of my class – the bourgeoisie – and not of their class – the proletariat – then the notion that all values, all true answers to questions, are compatible with each other cannot be true, since my values will inevitably clash with yours, because the values of my class are not the values of yours. As the values of the ancient Romans are not those of modern Italians, so the moral world of medieval Christianity is not that of liberal democrats, and, above all, the world of the workers is not that of their employers. The concept of a common good, valid for all mankind, rests on a cardinal mistake.

The notion that there exists a celestial, crystalline sphere, unaffected by the world of change and appearance, in which mathematical truths and moral or aesthetic values form a perfect harmony, guaranteed by indestructible logical links, is now abandoned, or at best is ignored. That is at the heart of the romantic movement, the extreme expression of which is the self-assertion of the individual creative personality as the maker of its own universe; we are in the world of rebels against convention, of the free artists, the Satanic outlaws, the Byronic outcasts, the 'pale and fevered generation' celebrated by German and French romantic writers of the early nineteenth century, the stormy Promethean heroes who reject the laws of their society, determined to achieve self-realisation and free self-expression against whatever odds.

This may have been an exaggerated, and at times hysterical, type of romantic self-preoccupation, but the essence of it, the roots from which it grew, did not vanish with the waning of the first wave of the romantic movement, and became the cause of permanent unease, indeed anxiety, in the European consciousness, as it has remained to this day. It is clear that the notion of a harmonious solution of the problems of mankind, even in principle, and therefore of the very concept of Utopia, is incompatible with the interpretation of the human world as a battle of perpetually new and ceaselessly conflicting wills, individual or collective. Attempts were made to stem this dangerous tide. Hegel, and after him Marx, sought to return to a rational historical scheme. For both there is a march of history – a single ascent of mankind from barbarism to rational organisation. They concede that history is the story of struggles and collisions, but these will ultimately be resolved. They are due to the particular dialectic of self-development of the world-spirit, or of technological progress, which creates division of labour and class war; but these 'contradictions' are the factors which themselves are indispensable to the forward movement that will culminate in a harmonious whole, the ultimate resolution of differences in unity, whether conceived as an infinite progress towards a transcendent goal, as in Hegel, or an attainable rational society, as in Marx. For these thinkers history is a drama in which there are violent contenders. Terrible tribulations occur, collisions, battles, destruction, appalling suffering; but the story has, must have, a happy ending. For Utopian thinkers in this tradition, the happy ending is a timeless serenity, the radiance of a static, conflict-free society after the state has withered away and all constituted authority has vanished – a peaceful anarchy in which men are rational, cooperative, virtuous, happy and free. This is an attempt to have the best of both worlds: to allow for inevitable conflict, but to believe that it is at once unavoidable and a temporary stage along the path to the total self-fulfilment of mankind.

Nevertheless, doubts persist, and have done so since the challenge thrown out by the irrationalists. That is the disturbing heritage of the romantic movement; it has entered the modern consciousness despite all efforts to eliminate or circumnavigate it, or explain it away as a mere symptom of the do not recognise them, they must be lying or deceiving themselves, or else that they have in some way lost the power of moral discrimination, and are to that extent abnormal. When such canons seem less universal, less profound, less crucial, we call them, in descending order of importance, customs, conventions, manners, taste, etiquette, and concerning these we not only permit but actively expect wide differences. Indeed we do not look on variety as being itself disruptive of our basic unity; it is uniformity that we consider to be the product of a lack of imagination, or of philistinism, and in extreme cases a form of slavery.

The common moral – and therefore also political – foundations of our conduct, so far from being undermined by the wars and the degradation of human personality that we have witnessed in our time, have emerged as something more broadly and deeply laid than they seemed to be during the first forty years of this century. I say 'our' conduct; I mean by this the habits and outlook of the western world. Asia and Africa are today boiling cauldrons of disruptive nationalism, as Germany and perhaps France still were after Britain and Holland and Scandinavia had attained relative equilibrium. Humanity does not seem to march with an even step, the crises of national development are not synchronised. Nevertheless, after the violent aberrations of the recent European experience, there are symptoms of recovery: of a return, that is to say, to normal health – the habits, traditions, above all the common notions of good and evil, which reunite us to our Greek and Hebrew and Christian and humanist past; transformed by the romantic revolt, but essentially in reaction against it. Our values today tend to be, increasingly, the old universal standards which distinguish civilised men, however dull, from barbarians, however gifted. When we resist aggression, or the destruction of liberty under despotic regimes, it is to these values that we appeal. And we appeal to them without the slightest doubt that those to whom we speak, no matter under what regime they live, do in fact understand our language; for it is clear, from all evidence, whether they pretend otherwise or not, that in fact they do so. The spokesmen of despotism may profess (it may be not always sincerely) that the brutalities and repression which they practise are designed to make these same values shine the more strongly in the new world which they are about to build. If this does not ring true, it is at any rate not cynicism but hypocrisy: an attempt to seem virtuous; a tribute to the restored prestige of humanism.

This was not so in the 20s and 30s of our century, when totalitarians of both the right and left affected to reject humanistic values as such – the good and the bad together – and did not say, as they now say more and more frequently, that they were serving them better than we. This seems to me genuine gain, genuine progress towards an international order, based on a recognition that we inhabit one common moral world. Upon this our hope must rest.

THE APOTHEOSIS
OF THE ROMANTIC WILL

The Revolt against the Myth of an Ideal World

I

THE HISTORY of ideas is a comparatively new field of knowledge, and still tends to be looked at with some suspicion in a good many academic quarters. Yet it has uncovered interesting facts. Among the most striking is the chronology of some of our most familiar concepts and categories, at any rate in the western world. We discover with some surprise how recently some of them emerged: how strange some of our apparently most deeply rooted attitudes might have seemed to our ancestors. I do not mean by this ideas based upon specific scientific and technological discoveries and inventions unknown to them, or new hypotheses about the nature of matter, or the history of societies remote from us in time or space, or the evolution of the material universe, or the springs of our own behaviour, and the part played in it by insufficiently examined unconscious and irrational factors. I mean something at once more pervasive and less easily traceable to specific causes: changes in widely accepted, consciously followed, secular values, ideals, goals, at any rate in western civilisation.

Thus no one today is surprised by the assumption that variety is, in general, preferable to uniformity – monotony, uniformity, are pejorative words – or, to turn to qualities of character, that integrity and sincerity are admirable independently of the truth or validity of the beliefs or principles involved; that warm-hearted idealism is nobler, if less expedient, than cold realism; or tolerance than intolerance, even though these virtues can be taken too far and lead to dangerous consequences; and so on. Yet this has not long been so; for the notion that One is good, Many – diversity – is bad, since the truth is one, and only error is multiple, is far older, and deeply rooted in the Platonic tradition. Even Aristotle, who accepts that human types differ from each other, and that therefore elasticity in social arrangements is called for, accepts this as a fact, without regret but without any sign of approval; and, with very few exceptions, this view seems to prevail in the classical and medieval worlds, and is not seriously questioned until, say, the sixteenth century.

Again, what Catholic in, let us say, the sixteenth century would say 'I abhor the heresies of the reformers, but I am deeply moved by the sincerity and integrity with which they hold and practise and sacrifice themselves for their abominable beliefs'? On the contrary, the deeper the sincerity of such heretics, or unbelievers – Muslims, Jews, atheists – the more dangerous they are, the more likely to lead souls to perdition, the more ruthlessly should they be eliminated, since heresy – false beliefs about the ends of men – is surely a poison more dangerous to the health of society than even hypocrisy or dissimulation, which at least do not openly attack the true doctrine. Only truth matters: to die in a false cause is wicked or pitiable.

Here, then, there is no common ground between views that prevailed even as late as the sixteenth or seventeenth century and modern liberal attitudes. Who in the ancient world or the middle ages even spoke of the virtues of diversity in life or thought? But when a modern thinker like Auguste Comte wondered why, when we do not allow freedom of opinion in mathematics, we should allow it in morals and politics, his very question shocked J. S. Mill and other liberals. Yet most of these beliefs, which are part of modern liberal culture (and today under attack from both the right and the left on the part of those who have reverted to an older view) – these beliefs are relatively novel, and draw their plausibility from a deep and radical revolt against the central tradition of western thought. This revolt, which seems to me to have become articulate in the second third of the eighteenth century, principally in Germany, has shaken the foundations of the old, traditional establishment, and has affected European thought and practice profoundly and unpredictably. It is perhaps the largest shift in European consciousness since the Reformation, to which, by twisting, circuitous paths, its origins can be traced.

II

If I may be permitted an almost unpardonable degree of simplification and generalisation, I should like to suggest that the central core of the intellectual tradition in the west has, since Plato (or it may be Pythagoras), rested upon three unquestioned dogmas:

(*a*) that to all genuine questions there is one true answer and one only, all others being deviations from the truth and therefore false, and that this applies to questions of conduct and feeling, that is, to practice, as well as to questions of theory or observation – to questions of value no less than to those of fact;

(*b*) that the true answers to such questions are in principle knowable;

(*c*) that these true answers cannot clash with one another, for one true proposition cannot be incompatible with another; that together these answers must form a harmonious whole: according to some they form a logical system each ingredient of which logically entails and is entailed by all the other elements; according to others, the relationship is that of parts to a whole, or, at the very least, of complete compatibility of each element with all the others.

There has, of course, been wide disagreement about the exact paths leading to these, often hidden, truths. Some have believed (and believe) that they are to be found in sacred texts, or their interpretation by appropriate experts – priesthoods, inspired prophets and seers, the doctrine and tradition of a church; some put their faith in other kinds of experts, philosophers, scientists, privileged observers of one kind or another, men who may, perhaps, have undergone a special spiritual training, or alternatively simple men, free from the corruption and sophistication of cities – peasants, children, 'the people', beings whose souls are pure. Others, again, have taught that these truths are accessible to all men provided their minds are not befuddled by wiseacres or deliberate deceivers. Nor has there been agreement about the right road to the truth. Some have appealed to nature, others to revelation; some to reason, others to faith or intuition or observation or deductive and inductive disciplines, hypothesis and experiment; and so on.

Even the most notorious sceptics accepted some part of this: the Greek sophists distinguished between nature and culture and believed that differences of circumstances, environment, temperament, accounted for the variety of laws and customs. But even they believed that ultimate human ends were much the same everywhere, for all men seek to satisfy natural wants, desire security, peace, happiness and justice. Nor did Montesquieu or Hume, for all their relativism, deny this; the former's faith in absolute principles such as freedom and justice and the latter's faith in nature and custom led them to similar conclusions. Moralists, anthropologists, relativists, utilitarians, Marxists, all assumed common experience and common ends in virtue of which human beings were human – too sharp a deviation from such standards pointed to perversion or mental sickness or madness.

Again, opinions differed about the conditions in which these truths were discoverable: some thought that men, because of original sin, or innate lack of ability, or natural obstacles, could never know the answers to every question, or perhaps any of them fully; some thought that there had been perfect knowledge before the Fall, or before the Flood or some other disaster that had befallen men – the building of the tower of Babel, or primitive accumulation of capital and the class war that resulted from it, or some other breach in the original harmony; others believed in progress – that the Golden Age lay not in the past but in the future; still others believed that men were finite, doomed to imperfection and error on this earth, but would know the truth in life beyond the grave; or else that only the angels could know it; or only God himself. These differences led to deep divisions and destructive wars, since nothing less than the question of eternal salvation was at issue. But what none of the contending parties denied was that these fundamental questions were in principle answerable; and that a life formed according to the true answers would constitute the ideal society, the Golden Age, inasmuch as the very notion of human imperfection was intelligible only as a falling short of the perfect life. Even if we did not, in our fallen state, know of what it consisted, we knew that if only the fragments of the truth by which we lived could be fitted together like a jigsaw puzzle the resultant whole, translated into practice, would constitute the perfect life. This could not be so if the questions turned out to be in principle unanswerable, or if more than one answer to the same question was equally true, or, worse still, if some of the true answers proved to be incompatible with each other, if values clashed and could not, even in principle, be reconciled. But this would entail that the universe was in the end irrational in character – a conclusion which reason, and faith that wished to live in peace with reason, could not but reject.

All the Utopias known to us are based upon the discoverability and harmony of objectively true ends, true for all men, at all times and places. This holds of every ideal city, from Plato's Republic and his Laws, and Zeno's anarchist world community, and the City of the Sun of Iambulus, to the Utopias of Thomas More and Campanella, Bacon and Harrington and Fénelon. The communist societies of Mably and Morelly, the state capitalism of Saint-Simon, the Phalanstères of Fourier, the various combinations of anarchism and collectivism of Owen and Godwin, Cabet, William Morris and Chernyshevsky, Bellamy, Hertzka and others (there is no lack of them in the nineteenth century)

rest on the three pillars of social optimism in the west of which I
have spoken: that the central problems – the *massimi problemi* –
of men are, in the end, the same throughout history; that they
are in principle soluble; and that the solutions form a harmonious whole. Man has permanent interests, the character of which
the right method can establish. These interests may differ from
the goals which men actually seek, or think that they seek,
which may be due to spiritual or intellectual blindness or
laziness, or the unscrupulous machinations of self-seeking
knaves – kings, priests, adventurers, power-seekers of all kinds
– who throw dust in the eyes of fools and ultimately their own.
Such illusions may also be due to the destructive influence of
social arrangements – traditional hierarchies, the division of
labour, the capitalist system – or again to impersonal factors,
natural or the unintended consequences of human nature, which
can be resisted and abolished. Once men's true interests can be
made clear, the claims which they embody can be satisfied by
social arrangements founded on the right moral directions,
which make use of technical progress or, alternatively, reject it
in order to return to the idyllic simplicity of humanity's earlier
days, a paradise which men have abandoned, or a golden age
still to come. Thinkers from Bacon to the present have been
inspired by the certainty that there must exist a total solution:
that in the fullness of time, whether by the will of God or by
human effort, the reign of irrationality, injustice and misery
will end; man will be liberated, and will no longer be the
plaything of forces beyond his control – savage nature, or the
consequences of his own ignorance or folly or vice; that this
springtime in human affairs will come once the obstacles,
natural and human, are overcome, and then at last men will
cease to fight each other, unite their powers and cooperate to
adapt nature to their needs (as the great materialist thinkers
from Epicurus to Marx have advocated) or their needs to nature
(as the Stoics and modern environmentalists have urged). This is
common ground to the many varieties of revolutionary and
reformist optimism, from Bacon to Condorcet, from the

Communist Manifesto to modern technocrats, communists, anarchists and seekers after alternative societies.

It is this great myth – in Sorel's sense of the word – that came under attack towards the end of the eighteenth century by a movement at first known in Germany as *Sturm und Drang*, and later as the many varieties of romanticism, nationalism, expressionism, emotivism, voluntarism and the many contemporary forms of irrationalism of both the right and the left familiar to everyone today. The prophets of the nineteenth century predicted many things – domination by international cartels, by collectivist regimes both socialist and capitalist, by military-industrial complexes, by scientific élites, preceded by *Krise*, *Kriege*, *Katastrophen*, wars and holocausts – but what none of them, so far as I know, predicted was that the last third of the twentieth century would be dominated by a world-wide growth of nationalism, enthronement of the will of individuals or classes, and the rejection of reason and order as being prison-houses of the spirit. How did this begin?

III

It is customary to say that in the eighteenth century rational views and respect for coherent intellectual systems were succeeded by sentimentality and introspection and the celebration of feeling, as instanced by the bourgeois English novel, the *comédie larmoyante*, the addiction to self-revelation and self-pity of Rousseau and his disciples, and his onslaughts on the clever but morally empty or corrupt intellectuals of Paris, with their atheism and calculating utilitarianism, which did not take into account the need for love and free self-expression of the un-perverted human heart; and that this discredited the hollow pseudo-classicism of the age and opened the gate to unbridled emotionalism. There is some truth in this, but on the one hand Rousseau, like the objects of his scorn, identified nature and reason, and condemned mere irrational 'passion'; and on the other, emotion has never been absent from human relationships and art. The Bible, Homer, the Greek tragedians, Catullus, Virgil, Dante, French classical tragedy are full of profound emotion. It was not the human heart or human nature as such that were ignored or suppressed in the central tradition of European art, but this did not prevent continuous concern with form and structure, an emphasis on rules for which rational justification was sought. In art, as in philosophy and politics, there was for many centuries a conscious appeal to objective standards, of which the most extreme form was the doctrine of eternal prototypes, immutable Platonic or Christian patterns, in terms of which both life and thought, theory and practice, tended to be judged. The aesthetic doctrine of mimesis, which unites the ancient, medieval and Renaissance worlds with the Great Style of the eighteenth century, presupposes that there exist universal principles and eternal patterns to be incorporated or 'imitated'. The revolt which (at least temporarily) overthrew it was directed not merely against the decayed formalism and pedantry of chilly neoclassicism – it went much further, for it denied the reality of universal truths, the eternal forms which knowledge and creation, learning and art and life, must learn to embody if they are to justify their claims to represent the noblest flights of human reason and imagination. The rise of science and empirical methods – what Whitehead once called 'the revolt of matter' – only substituted one set of forms for another; it shook faith in the *a priori* axioms and laws provided by theology or Aristotelian metaphysics, and put in their place laws and rules validated by empirical experience, in particular by a spectacularly increased capacity to fulfil Bacon's programme – to predict and control nature, and men as natural beings.

The 'revolt of matter' was not a rebellion against laws and rules as such, nor against old ideals – the reign of reason, of happiness and knowledge; on the contrary, the domination of mathematics and analogies made from it to other provinces of human thought, the faith in salvation by knowledge, were never so strong as they were during the Enlightenment. But by the end of the eighteenth century and the beginning of the nineteenth we find violent scorn for rules and forms as such – passionate pleas for the freedom of self-expression of groups, movements, individuals, whithersoever this might carry them. Idealistic students in German universities, affected by the romantic currents of the age, thought nothing of such goals as happiness, security, or scientific knowledge, political and economic stability and social peace, and indeed looked upon such things with contempt. For the disciples of the new philosophy suffering was nobler than pleasure, failure was preferable to worldly success, which had about it something squalid and opportunist, and could surely be bought only at the cost of betraying one's integrity, independence, the inner light, the ideal vision within. They believed that it was the minorities, above all those who suffered for their convictions, that had the truth in them, and not the mindless majorities, that martyrdom was sacred no matter in what cause, that sincerity and authenticity and intensity of feeling, and, above all, defiance – which involved perpetual struggle against convention, against the oppressive forces of church and state and philistine society, against cynicism and commercialism and indifference – that these were sacred values, even if, and perhaps because, they were bound to fail in the degraded world of masters and slaves; to fight, and if need be die, was brave and right and honourable, whereas to compromise and survive was cowardice and betrayal. These men were champions not of feeling against reason, but of another faculty of the human spirit, the source of all life and action, of heroism and sacrifice, nobility and idealism both individual and collective – the proud, indomitable, untrammelled human will. If the exercise of it caused suffering, led to conflict, was incompatible with an untroubled, harmonious life, or the achievement of artistic perfection, serene and undisturbed by the dust and din of the battle for the fullness of life; if the revolt of Prometheus against the Olympian gods doomed him to eternal torment, then so much the worse for Olympus, down with the view of perfection which can be purchased only at the price of putting chains on the free, independent will, the unbridled imagination, the wild wind of inspiration which goeth where it listeth. Independence, defiance by individuals and groups and nations, pursuit of goals not because they are universal but because they are mine, or those of my people, my culture – this was the outlook of a minority even among the German romantics, echoed by still fewer in the rest of Europe: nevertheless, they set their stamp on their time and on ours. No great artist, no national leader in the nineteenth century was wholly free from their influence. Let me return to some of its roots in the years before the French Revolution.

IV

No thinker was more opposed to undisciplined enthusiasm, emotional turbulence, *Schwärmerei* – vague, unfocused fervour and yearning – than Immanuel Kant. A scientific pioneer himself, he set himself to give a rational explanation and justification of the methods of the natural sciences, which he rightly looked upon as the major achievement of the age. Nevertheless, in his moral philosophy he did lift the lid of a Pandora's box, which released tendencies which he was among the first, with perfect honesty and consistency, to disown and condemn. He maintained, as every German schoolboy used to know, that the moral worth of an act depended on its being freely chosen by the agent; that if a man acted under the influence of causes which he could not and did not control, whether external, such as physical compulsion, or internal, such as instincts or desires or passions, then the act, whatever its consequences, whether they were good or bad, advantageous or harmful to men, had no moral value, for the act had not been freely chosen, but was simply the effect of mechanical causes, an event in nature, no more capable of being judged in ethical terms than the behaviour of an animal or a plant. If the determinism that reigns in nature – on which, indeed, the whole of natural science is based – determines the acts of a human agent, he is not truly an agent, for to act is to be capable of free choice between alternatives; and free will must in that case be an illusion. Kant is certain that freedom of the will is not illusory but real. Hence the immense emphasis that he places on human autonomy – on the capacity for free commitment to rationally chosen ends. The self, Kant tells us, must be 'raised above natural necessity', for if men are ruled by the same laws as those which govern the material world 'freedom cannot be saved', and without freedom there is no morality.

Kant insists over and over again that what distinguishes man is his moral autonomy as against his physical heteronomy – for his body is governed by natural laws, not issuing from his own inner self. No doubt this doctrine owes a great deal to Rousseau, for whom all dignity, all pride rest upon independence. To be manipulated is to be enslaved. A world in which one man depends upon the favour of another is a world of masters and slaves, of bullying and condescension and patronage at one end, and obsequiousness, servility, duplicity and resentment at the other. But whereas Rousseau supposes that only dependence on other men is degrading, for no one resents the laws of nature, only ill will, the Germans went further. For Kant, total dependence on non-human nature – heteronomy – was incompatible with choice, freedom, morality. This exhibits a new attitude to nature, or at least the revival of an ancient Christian antagonism to it. The thinkers of the Enlightenment and their predecessors in the Renaissance (save for isolated antinomian mystics) tended to look upon nature as divine harmony, or as a great organic or artistic unity, or as an exquisite mechanism created by the divine watchmaker, or else as uncreated and eternal, but always as a model from which men depart at their cost. The principal need of man is to understand the external world and himself and the place that he occupies in the scheme of things: if he grasps this, he will not seek after goals incompatible with the needs of his nature, goals which he can follow only through some mistaken conception of what he is in himself, or of his relations to other men or the external world. This is equally true of rationalists and empiricists, Christian naturalists and pagans and atheists, both in the Renaissance and after – of Pico and Marsilio Ficino, of Locke and Spinoza, Leibniz and Gassendi; for them God is nature is God, nature is not, as it is for Augustine or Calvin, in conflict with the spirit, a source of temptation and debasement. This world view reaches its clearest expression in the writings of the French philosophers of the eighteenth century, Helvétius and Holbach, d'Alembert and Condorcet, the friends of nature and the sciences, for whom man is subject to the same kind of causal laws as animals and plants and the inanimate world, physical and biological laws, and in the case of men psychological and economic too, established by observation and experiment, measurement and verification. Such notions as the immortal soul, a personal God, freedom of the will, are for them metaphysical fictions and illusions. But they are not so for Kant.

The German revolt against France and French materialism has social as well as intellectual roots. Germany in the first half of the eighteenth century, and for more than a century before, even before the devastation of the Thirty Years War, had little share in the great renaissance of the west – her cultural achievement after the Reformation is not comparable to that of the Italians in the fifteenth and sixteenth centuries, of Spain and England in the age of Shakespeare and Cervantes, of the Low Countries in the seventeenth century, least of all of France, the France of poets, soldiers, statesmen, thinkers, which in the seventeenth century dominated Europe both culturally and politically, with only England and Holland as her rivals. What had the provincial German courts and cities, what had even Imperial Vienna, to offer?

This sense of relative backwardness, of being an object of patronage or scorn to the French with their overweening sense of national and cultural superiority, created a sense of collective humiliation, later to turn into indignation and hostility, that sprang from wounded pride. The German reaction at first is to imitate French models, then to turn against them. Let the vain but godless French cultivate their ephemeral world, their material gains, their pursuit of glory, luxury, ostentation, the witty trivial chatter of the *salons* of Paris and the subservient court at Versailles. What is the worth of the philosophy of atheists or smooth, worldly *abbés* who do not begin to understand the true nature, the real purposes of men, their inner life, man's deepest concerns – his relation to the soul within him, to his brothers, above all to God – the deep, the agonising questions of man's being and vocation? Inward-looking German pietists abandoned French and Latin, turned to their native tongue, and spoke with scorn and horror of the glittering generalities of French civilisation, the blasphemous epigrams of Voltaire and his imitators. Still more contemptible were the feeble imitators of French culture, the caricature of French customs and taste in the little German principalities. German men of letters rebelled violently against the social oppression and stifling atmosphere of German society, of the despotic and often stupid and cruel German princes and princelings and their officials who crushed or degraded the humbly born, particularly the most honest and gifted men among them, in the three hundred courts and governments into which Germany was then divided.

This surge of indignation formed the heart of the movement that, after the name of a play by one of its members, was called *Sturm und Drang*. Their plays are filled with cries of despair or savage indignation, titanic explosions of rage or hatred, vast destructive passions, unimaginable crimes which dwarf the scenes of violence even in Elizabethan drama; they celebrate passion, individuality, strength, genius, self-expression at whatever cost, against whatever odds, and usually end in blood and crime, their only form of protest against a grotesque and odious social order. Hence all these violent heroes – the *Kraftmenschen*, *Kraftschreiber*, *Kraftkerls*, *Kraftknaben* – who march hysterically through the pages of Klinger, Schubart,

Leisewitz, Lenz, and even the gentle Carl Philipp Moritz; until life began to imitate art, and the Swiss adventurer Christoph Kaufmann, a self-proclaimed follower of Christ and Rousseau, who so impressed Herder, Goethe, Hamann, Wieland, Lavater, swept through the German lands with a band of unkempt followers, denouncing polite culture, and celebrating anarchic freedom, transported by wild and mystical public exaltation of the flesh and the spirit.

Kant abhorred this kind of disordered imagination, and, still more, emotional exhibitionism and barbarous conduct. Although he too denounced the mechanistic psychology of the French Encyclopedists as destructive of morality, his notion of the will is that of reason in action. He saves himself from subjectivism, and indeed irrationalism, by insisting that the will is truly free only so far as it wills the dictates of reason, which generate general rules binding on all rational men. It is when the concept of reason becomes obscure (and Kant never succeeded in formulating convincingly what this signified in practice), and only the independent will remains man's unique possession whereby he is distinguished from nature, that the new doctrine becomes infected by the 'stürmerisch' mood. In Kant's disciple, the dramatist and poet Schiller, the notion of freedom begins to move beyond the bounds of reason. Freedom is the central concept of Schiller's early works. He speaks of 'the legislator himself, the God within us', of 'high, demonic freedom', 'the proud demon within the man'. Man is most sublime when he resists the pressure of nature, when he exhibits 'moral independence of natural laws in a condition of emotional stress'. It is will, not reason – certainly not feeling, which he shares with animals – that raises him above nature, and the very disharmony which may arise between nature and the tragic hero is not entirely to be deplored, for it awakens man's sense of his independence. This is a clean break from Rousseau's invocations to nature and eternal values, no less than from Burke or Helvétius or Hume, with their sharply differing views. In Schiller's early plays it is the individual's resistance to external force, social or natural, that is celebrated. Nothing, perhaps, is more striking than the contrast between the values of the leading champion of the German *Aufklärung*, Lessing, in the 1760s, and those of Schiller in the early 80s of the century. Lessing, in his play *Minna von Barnhelm*, written in 1768, describes a proud Prussian officer, accused of a crime of which he is innocent, who disdains to defend himself and prefers poverty and disgrace to fighting for his rights; he is high-minded, but also headstrong; his pride makes it impossible to stoop to quarrels with his detractors, and it is his mistress Minna who, by a display of skill, tact and good sense manages to rescue him from his condition and cause him to be rehabilitated. Major Tellheim, because of his absurd sense of humour, is represented as heroic but somewhat ridiculous; it is the worldly wisdom of Minna that saves him and turns what might have been a tragic end into an amiable comedy. But Karl Moor in Schiller's *Robbers* is this same Tellheim lifted to a great tragic height: he has been betrayed by his unworthy brother, disinherited by his father, and is determined for his own sake, and that of other victims of injustice, to be avenged upon odious, hypocritical society. He forms a robber band, he pillages and murders, he kills the love he bears his mistress – he must be free to wreak his hatred, to pour destruction on the hateful world which has turned him into a criminal. In the end he gives himself up to the police for punishment, but he is a noble criminal, raised far above the degraded society which has ignored his personality, and Schiller writes a moving epitaph upon his tomb.

The distance which divides Karl Moor from Lessing's Tellheim is eighteen years: it was in that period that the revolt known as *Sturm und Drang* reached its height. In his later works Schiller, like Coleridge and Wordsworth and Goethe, came to terms with the world, and preached political resignation rather than revolt. Yet even in a later phase he returns to the notion of will as sheer defiance of nature and convention. Thus in discussing Corneille's *Médée* he tells us that when Medea, to avenge herself on Jason, who had abandoned her, killed her children by him, she is a true tragic heroine because with superhuman will-power she defied the force of circumstance and nature, crushed natural feeling, did not allow herself to become a mere animal, driven hither and thither by unresisted passion, but, in her very crime, exhibited the freedom of a self-directed personality, triumphant over nature, even though this freedom was turned to wholly evil ends. Above all, one must act and not be acted upon; Phaethon, he tells us, drove Apollo's horses wildly, to his doom, but he drove and was not driven. To surrender one's freedom is to surrender oneself, to lose one's humanity.

Rousseau says this too, yet he is sufficiently a son of the Enlightenment to believe that there are eternal truths graven on the hearts of all men, and it is only a corrupt civilisation that has robbed them of the ability to read them. Schiller too supposes that there was once a unity of thought and will and feeling – that man was once unbroken – then possessions, culture, luxury inflicted the fatal wound. This again is the myth of a paradise from which we are driven by some disastrous breach with nature, a paradise to which the Greeks were closer than we are. Schiller too struggles to reconcile the will, man's inborn freedom, his vocation to be his own master, with the laws of nature and history; he ends by believing that man's only salvation is in the realm of art, where he can achieve independence of the causal treadmill where, in Kant's words, man is a mere turnspit, acted upon by external forces. Exploitation is evil inasmuch as it is the using of men as means to ends that are not their own, but those of the manipulator, the treatment of free beings as if they were things, tools, the deliberate denial of their humanity. Schiller oscillates between singing hymns to nature, which, in his Hellenic childhood, was at one with man, and an ominous sense of her as a destroyer; 'she treads them in the dust, the significant and the trivial, the noble and the base – she preserves a world of ants, but men, her most glorious creation, she crushes in her giant's arms . . . in one frivolous hour'.

Nowhere was German *amour propre* more deeply wounded than in East Prussia, still semi-feudal and deeply traditionalist; nowhere was there deeper resentment of the policy of modernisation which Frederick the Great conducted by importing French officials who treated his simple and backward subjects with impatience and open disdain. It is not surprising, therefore, that the most gifted and sensitive sons of this province, Hamann, Herder, and Kant too, are particularly vehement in opposing the levelling activities of these morally blind imposers of alien methods on a pious, inward-looking culture. Kant and Herder at least admire the scientific achievements of the west: Hamann rejects these too. This is the very spirit in which Tolstoy and Dostoevsky, a century later, wrote about the west, and, as often as not, is a response of the humiliated, a form of sour grapes – a sublime form of it, perhaps, but still sour grapes – the pretence that what one cannot achieve oneself is not worth striving for. This is the bitter atmosphere in which Herder writes: 'I am not here to think, but to be, feel, live!' The sages of Paris reduce both knowledge and life to systems of contrived rules, the pursuit of external goods, for which men prostitute themselves, and sell their inner freedom, their authenticity; men, Germans, should seek to be themselves, instead of imitating – aping – strangers who have no connection with their own real natures and memories and ways of life. A man's powers of creation can only be exercised fully on his own native heath, living among men who are akin to him, physically and spiritually, those who speak his language, amongst whom he feels at home, with whom he feels that he belongs. Only so can true cultures be generated, each unique, each making its own peculiar contribution to human civilisation, each pursuing its own values in its own way, not to be submerged in some general cosmopolitan ocean which robs all native cultures of their particular substance and colour, of their national spirit and genius, which can only flourish on its own soil, from its own roots, stretching far back into a common past. Civilisation is a garden made rich and beautiful by the variety of its flowers, delicate plants which great conquering empires – Rome, Vienna, London – trample and crush out of existence.

This is the beginning of nationalism, and even more of populism. Herder upholds the value of variety and spontaneity, of the different, idiosyncratic paths pursued by peoples, each with its own style, ways of feeling and expression, and denounces the measuring of everything by the same timeless standards – in effect, those of the dominant French culture, which pretends that its values are valid for all time, universal, immutable. One culture is no mere step to another. Greece is not an antechamber to Rome. Shakespeare's plays are not a rudimentary form of the tragedies of Racine and Voltaire. This has revolutionary implications. If each culture expresses its own vision and is entitled to do so, and if the goals and values of different societies and ways of life are not commensurable, then it follows that there is no single set of principles, no universal truth for all men and times and places. The values of one civilisation will be different from, and perhaps incompatible with, the values of another. If free creation, spontaneous development along one's own native lines, not inhibited or suppressed by the dogmatic pronouncements of an élite of self-appointed arbiters, insensitive to history, is to be accorded supreme value; if authenticity and variety are not to be sacrificed to authority, organisation, centralisation, which inexorably tend to uniformity and the destruction of what men hold dearest – their language, their institutions, their habits, their form of life, all that has made them what they are – then the establishment of one world, organised on universally accepted rational principles – the ideal society – is not acceptable. Kant's defence of moral freedom and Herder's plea for the uniqueness of cultures, for all the former's insistence on rational principles and the latter's belief that national differences need not lead to collisions, shook – some might say undermined – what I have called the three pillars of the main western tradition.

Subverted this tradition in favour of what? Not of the reign of feeling, but of the assertion of the will – the will to do what is universally right in Kant, but something which cuts even deeper in the case of Herder: the will to live one's own regional, local life, to develop one's own *eigentümlich* values, to sing one's own songs, to be governed by one's own laws in one's own home, not to be assimilated to a form of life that belongs to all and therefore to no one. Freedom, Hegel once observed, is *bey sich selbst seyn* – to be at home, not to be impinged upon by what is not one's own, by alien obstacles to self-realisation whether on the part of individuals or civilisations. The idea of the earthly paradise, of a golden age for the whole of mankind, of one life which all men live in peace and brotherhood, the Utopian vision of thinkers from Plato to H. G. Wells, is not compatible with this. This denial of monism was to lead, in due course, on the one hand to the conservatism of Burke and Möser; on the other, to romantic self-assertion, nationalism, the worship of heroes and leaders, and in the end to Fascism and brutal irrationalism and the oppression of minorities. But all that was still to come: in the eighteenth century the defence of variety, opposition to universalism, is still cultural, literary, idealistic and humane.

V

Fichte drives this still further. Inspired both by Kant and less obviously by Herder, an admirer of the French Revolution, but disillusioned by the Terror, humiliated by the misfortunes of Germany, speaking in defence of reason and harmony – words used by now in more and more attenuated and elusive senses – Fichte is the true father of romanticism, above all in his celebration of will over calm, discursive thought. A man is made conscious of being what he is – of himself as against others or the external world – not by thought or contemplation, since the purer it is, the more a man's thought is in its object, the less conscious of itself it will be as a subject; self-awareness springs from encountering resistance. It is the impact on me of what is external to me, and the effort to resist it, that makes me know that I am what I am, aware of my aims, my nature, my essence, as opposed to what is not mine; and since I am not alone in the world, but connected by a myriad strands, as Burke has taught us, to other men, it is this impact that makes me understand what my culture, my nation, my language, my historical tradition, my true home, have been and are. I carve out of external nature what I need, I see it in terms of my needs, temperament, questions, aspirations: 'I do not accept what nature offers because I must,' Fichte declares, 'I believe it because I will.'

Descartes and Locke are evidently mistaken – the mind is not a wax tablet upon which nature imprints what she pleases, it is not an object, but a perpetual activity which shapes its world to respond to its ethical demands. It is the need to act that generates consciousness of the actual world: 'We know because we are called upon to act, not the other way about.' A change in my notion of what should be will change my world. The world of the poet (this is not Fichte's language) is different from the world of the banker, the world of the rich is not the world of the poor; the world of the Fascist is not the world of the liberal, the world of those who think and speak in German is not the world of the French. Fichte goes further: values, principles, moral and political goals, are not objectively given, not imposed on the agent by nature or a transcendent God; 'I am not determined by my end: the end is determined by me.' Food does not create hunger, it is my hunger that makes it food. This is new and revolutionary.

Fichte's concept of the self is not wholly clear: it cannot be the empirical self, which is subject to the causal necessitation of the material world, but an eternal, divine spirit outside time and space, of which empirical selves are but transient emanations; at other times Fichte seems to speak of it as a super-personal self in which I am but an element – the Group – a culture, a nation, a church. These are the beginnings of political anthropomorphism, the transformation of state, nation, progress, history, into super-sensible agents, with whose unbounded will I must identify my own finite desires if I am to understand myself and my significance, and be what, at my best, I could and should be. I can only understand this by action: 'Man shall be and do something', 'We must be a quickening source of life, not an echo of it or an annex to it.' The essence of man is freedom, and although there is talk of reason, harmony, the reconciliation of one man's purpose to that of another in a rationally organised society, yet freedom is a sublime but dangerous gift: 'Not nature but freedom itself produces the greatest and most terrible disorder of our race . . . man is the cruellest enemy of man.' Freedom is a double-edged weapon; it is because they are free that savages devour each other. Civilised nations are free, free to live in peace, but no less free to fight and make war; 'culture is not a deterrent of violence but its tool'. He advocates peace, but if it is to be a choice between freedom, with its potentiality of violence, or the peace of subjection to the forces of nature, he unequivocally prefers – and indeed thinks it is the essence of man not to be able to avoid preferring – freedom. Creation is of man's essence; hence the doctrine of the dignity of labour, of which Fichte is virtually the author – labour is the impressing of my creative personality upon the material brought into existence by this very need, it is a means for expressing my inner self – the conquest of nature and the attainment of freedom for nations and cultures is the self-realisation of the will: 'Sublime and living will! Named by no name, compassed by no thought!'

Fichte's will is dynamic reason, reason in action. Yet it was not reason that seems to have impressed itself upon the imagination of his listeners in the lecture-halls of Jena and Berlin, but dynamism, self-assertion; the sacred vocation of man is to transform himself and his world by his indomitable will. This is something novel and audacious: ends are not, as had been thought for more than two millennia, objective values, discoverable within man or in a transcendent realm by some special faculty. Ends are not discovered at all, but made, not found but created. A Russian writer asked later in the nineteenth century, 'Where is the dance before I have danced it?' Where is the picture before I have painted it? Where indeed? Joshua Reynolds thought that it dwelt in some super-sensuous empyrean of eternal Platonic forms which the inspired artist must discern and labour to embody as best he can in the medium in which he works – canvas, or marble, or bronze. But the answer the Russian implies is that before the work of art is created it is nowhere, that creation is creation out of nothing – an aesthetics of pure creation which Fichte applies to the realms of ethics, of all action. Man is not a mere compounder of pre-existent elements; imagination is not memory; it literally generates, as God generated the world. There are no objective rules, only what we make.

Art is not a mirror held up to nature, the creation of an object according to the rules, say, of harmony or perspective, designed to give pleasure. It is, as Herder taught, a means of communication, of self-expression for the individual spirit. What matters is the quality of this act, its authenticity. Since I, the creator, cannot control the empirical consequences of what I do, they are not part of me, do not form part of my real world. I can control only my own motives, my goals, my attitude to men and things. If another man causes me damage, I may suffer physical pain, but I shall not suffer grief unless I respect him, and that is within my control. 'Man is the inhabitant of two worlds', one of which, the physical, I can afford to ignore; the other, the spiritual, is in my power. That is why worldly failure is unimportant, why worldly goods – riches, security, success, fame – are trivial in contrast with what alone counts, my respect for myself as a free being, my moral principles, my artistic or human goals; to give up the latter for the former is to compromise my honour and independence, my real life, for the sake of something outside it, part of the empirical-causal treadmill, and this is to falsify what I know to be the truth, to prostitute myself, to sell out – for Fichte and those who followed him the ultimate sin.

From here it is no great distance to the worlds of Byron's gloomy heroes – satanic outcasts, proud, indomitable, sinister –

Manfred, Beppo, Conrad, Lara, Cain – who defy society and suffer and destroy. They may, by the standards of the world, be accounted criminal, enemies of mankind, damned souls: but they are free; they have not bowed the knee in the House of Rimmon; they have preserved their integrity at a vast cost in agony and hatred. The Byronism that swept Europe, like the cult of Goethe's *Werther* half a century earlier, was a form of protest against real or imaginary suffocation in a mean, venal and hypocritical milieu, given over to greed, corruption and stupidity. Authenticity is all: 'the great object in life is sensation,' Byron once said – 'to feel that we exist – even though in pain'. His heroes are like Fichte's dramatisation of himself, lonely thinkers: 'There was in him a vital scorn of all. He stood a stranger in this breathing world.' The attack on everything that hems in and cramps, that persuades us that we are part of some great machine from which it is impossible to break out, since it is a mere illusion to believe that we can leave the prison – that is the common note of the romantic revolt. When Blake says 'A Robin Red breast in a Cage / Puts all Heaven in a Rage', the cage is the Newtonian system. Locke and Newton are devils; 'Reasoning' is 'secret Murder'; 'Art is the Tree of Life . . . Science is the Tree of Death.' 'The Tree of Knowledge has robbed us of the Tree of Life,' said Hamann a generation earlier, and this is literally echoed by Byron. Freedom involves breaking rules, perhaps even committing crimes. This note was earlier sounded by Diderot (and perhaps by Milton in his conception of Satan, and in Shakespeare's *Troilus*); Diderot conceived of man as the theatre of an unceasing civil war between an inner being, the natural man, struggling to get out of the outer man, the product of civilisation and convention. Diderot drew analogies between the criminal and the genius, solitary and savage beings, who break rules and defy conventions and take fearful risks, unlike the *hommes d'esprit* who scatter their wit elegantly and agreeably, but are tame and lack the sacred fire. 'Action – action is the soul of the world, not pleasure . . . Without action all feeling and knowledge is nothing but postponed death.' And again, 'God brooded over the void and a world arose'; 'Clear a space! Destroy! Something will arise! Oh God-like feeling!' This is Lenz, the most authentic voice of the *Sturm und Drang*, half a century before Byron: what matters is the intensity of the creative impulse, the depth of nature from which it springs, the sincerity of one's beliefs, readiness to live and die for a principle, which counts for more than the validity of the conviction or the principle themselves.

Voltaire and Carlyle both wrote about Muhammad. Voltaire's play is simply an attack on obscurantism, intolerance, religious fanaticism; when he speaks of Muhammad as a blind and destructive barbarian, he means, as everyone knew, the Roman Church, for him the greatest obstacle to justice, happiness, freedom, reason – universal goals which satisfy the deepest demands of all men at all times. When, a century later, Carlyle deals with the same subject, he cares only about Muhammad's character, the stuff of which he is made, and not his doctrines or their consequences: he calls him 'a fiery mass of life cast up from the great bosom of nature herself', possessed of 'a deep, great, genuine sincerity'. 'Heart! Warmth! Blood! Humanity! Life!' These are Herder's words. The attack on Voltaire and the 'second-rate' shallow talk in France was mounted by the Germans in the last third of the eighteenth century. Half a century later the goal of rational happiness, especially in its Benthamite version, is rejected contemptuously by the new, romantic generation in continental Europe, for whom pleasure is but 'tepid water on the tongue'; the phrase is Hölderlin's, but it could just as well have been uttered by Musset or Lermontov. Goethe, Wordsworth, Coleridge and even Schiller made their peace with the established order. So in due course, did Schelling and Tieck, Friedrich Schlegel and Arnim and a good many other radicals. But in their earlier years these men celebrated the power of the will to freedom, to creative self-expression, with fateful consequences for the history and outlook of the years that followed. One form of these ideas was the new image of the artist, raised above other men not only by his genius but by his heroic readiness to live and die for the sacred vision within him. It was this same ideal that animated and transformed the concept of nations or classes or minorities in their struggles for freedom at whatever cost. It took a more sinister form in the worship of the leader, the creator of a new social order as a work of art, who moulds men as the composer moulds sounds and the painter colours – men too feeble to rise by their own force of will. An exceptional being, the hero and genius to whom Carlyle and Fichte paid homage, can lift others to a level beyond any which they could have reached by their own efforts, even if this can be achieved only at the cost of the torment or death of multitudes.

For more than two millennia the view prevailed in Europe that there existed an unalterable structure of reality, and the great men were those who understood it correctly either in their theory or their practice – the wise who knew the truth, or the men of action, rulers and conquerors, who knew how to achieve their goals. In a sense the criterion of greatness was success based on getting the answer right. But in the age of which I speak the hero is no longer the discoverer, or the winner in the race, but the creator, even, or perhaps all the more, if he was destroyed by the flame within him – a secularised image of the saint and martyr, of the life of sacrifice. For in the life of the spirit there were no objective principles or values – they were made so by a resolve of the will which shaped a man's or a people's world and its norms; action determined thought, not vice versa. 'To know is to impose a system, not to register passively,' said Fichte; and 'laws are not drawn from facts, but from our own self'. One categorises reality as the will dictates. If the empirical facts prove recalcitrant, one must put them in their place, in the mechanical treadmill of causes and effects, which have no relevance to the life of the spirit – to morality, religion, art, philosophy, the realm of ends, not means.

For these thinkers ordinary life, the common notion of reality, and in particular the artificial constructions of the natural sciences and practical techniques – economic, political, sociological – no less than that of common sense, are a baseless, utilitarian fabrication, what Georges Sorel later called 'la petite science', something invented for their own convenience by technologists and ordinary men, not reality itself. For Friedrich Schlegel and Novalis, for Wackenroder and Tieck and Chamisso, above all for E. T. A. Hoffmann, the tidy regularities of daily life are but a curtain to conceal the terrifying spectacle of true reality, which has no structure, but is a wild whirlpool, a perpetual *tourbillon* of the creative spirit which no system can capture: life and motion cannot be represented by immobile, lifeless concepts, nor the infinite and unbounded by the finite and the fixed. A finished work of art, a systematic treatise, are attempts to freeze the flowing stream of life; only fragments, intimations, broken glimpses can begin to convey the perpetual movement of reality. The prophet of *Sturm und Drang*, Hamann, had said that the practical man was a somnambulist, secure and successful because he was blind; if he could see, he would go mad, for nature is 'a wild dance', and the irregulars of life – outlaws, beggars, vagabonds, the visionary, the sick, the abnormal – are closer to it than French philosophers, officials, scientists, sensible men, pillars of the enlightened bureaucracy: 'The tree of knowledge has robbed us of the tree of life.' The early German romantic plays and novels are inspired by an attempt to expose the concept of a stable, intelligible structure of reality which calm observers describe, classify, dissect, predict, as a sham and a delusion, a mere curtain of appearances designed to protect those not sensitive or brave enough to face the truth from the terrifying chaos beneath the false order of bourgeois existence. 'The irony of the cosmos plays with us all, the visible is about us like carpets with shimmering colours and patterns . . . beyond the carpets is a region populated by dreams and delirium, none dare lift the carpet and peer beyond the curtain.'

Tieck, who wrote this, is the originator of the Novel and the Theatre of the Absurd. In *William Lovell* everything turns out to be its opposite: the personal turns out to be impersonal; the living is discovered to be the dead; the organic, the mechanical; the real, the artificial; men seek freedom and fall into the blackest slavery. In Tieck's plays there is a deliberate attempt to confound the imaginary and the real: characters in the play (or in a play within the play) criticise the play, complain about the plot, and about the equipment of the theatre; members of the audience expostulate and demand that the illusion, on which all drama rests, be preserved; they are in turn answered sharply by the play's characters from the stage, to the bewilderment of the real audience; at times musical keys and dynamic tempi engage in dialogues with each other. In *Prince Zerbino*, when the Prince despairs of reaching the end of his journey he orders the play to be turned backwards – the events to be replayed in reverse order, to unhappen – the will is free to order what it pleases. In one of Arnim's plays an old nobleman complains that his legs are growing longer and longer: this is the result of boredom; the old man's inner state is externalised; moreover, his boredom itself is a symbol of the death throes of the old Germany. As a perceptive contemporary Russian critic has remarked, this is full-blown expressionism long before its triumph a century later, in the Weimar period.

The attack upon the world of appearances at times takes surrealist forms: in one of Arnim's novels the hero finds that he has wandered into a beautiful lady's dreams, is invited by her to sit in one of her chairs, wishes to escape from the dream that is not his, sees that the chair remains empty, and feels great relief. Hoffmann carried this war upon the objective world, upon the very notion of objectivity, to its outer limits: old women who turn into brass door-knockers, or State Councillors who step into brandy glasses, are dissipated into alcoholic fumes, float over the earth, then recoagulate themselves and return to their armchairs and dressing-gowns – these are not innocent flights of fancy but spring from a deranged imagination in which the will is uncontrolled and the real world proves to be a phantasmagoria. After this, the way lies clear for Schopenhauer's world tossed hither and thither by a blind, aimless, cosmic will, for

Dostoevsky's underground man, and Kafka's lucid nightmares, for Nietzsche's evocation of the *Kraftmenschen* condemned in Plato's dialogues – Thrasymachus, or Callicles – who see no reason against sweeping aside the cobwebs of laws and conventions if they obstruct their will to power, for Baudelaire's 'Enivrez-vous sans cesse!', 'Let the will become intoxicated by drugs or pain, dreams or sorrow, no matter by what', but let it break its chains.

Neither Hoffmann nor Tieck sets out, any more than Pascal or Kierkegaard or Nerval, to deny the truths of science, or even those of common sense, at their own level – that is, as categories required for limited purposes, medical or technological or commercial. This was not the world which mattered; they conceived true reality as distinct from the irrelevant surface of things – the world without frontiers or barriers, within or without, shaped and expressed by art, by religion, by metaphysical insight, by all that is involved in personal relationships – this was the world in which the will is supreme, in which absolute values clashed in irreconcilable conflict, the 'nocturnal world' of the soul, the source of all imaginative experience, all poetry, all understanding, all that men truly live by. It is when scientifically minded rationalists claimed to be able to explain and control this level of experience in terms of their concepts and categories, and declared that conflict and tragedy arose only from ignorance of fact, inadequacies of method, the incompetence or ill will of rulers and the benighted condition of their subjects, so that in principle, at least, all this could be put right, a harmonious, rationally organised society established, and the dark sides of life be made to recede like an old, insubstantial, scarcely remembered nightmare, that the poets and the mystics and all those who are sensitive to the individual, unorganisable, untranslatable aspects of human experience tended to rebel. Such men react against what appears to them to be the maddening dogmatism and smooth *bon sens* of the *raisonneurs* of the Enlightenment and their modern successors. Nor, despite the brilliant and heroic efforts of both Hegel and

Marx to integrate the tensions, paradoxes and conflicts of human life and thought into new syntheses of successive crises and resolutions – the dialectic of history or cunning of reason (or of the process of production) leading to an ultimate triumph of reason and realisation of human potentialities – have the terrible doubts injected by these indignant critics ever been stilled.

I do not mean that these doubts have in fact prevailed, at least in the realm of ideology. Even if belief in the happy innocence of our first ancestors – *Saturnia regna* – has largely waned, faith in the possibility of a golden age still to come has remained unimpaired, and indeed spread far beyond the western world. Both liberals and socialists, and many who put their trust in rational and scientific methods designed to effect a fundamental social transformation, whether by violent or gradual methods, have held this optimistic belief with mounting intensity during the last hundred years. The conviction that once the last obstacles – ignorance and irrationality, alienation and exploitation, and their individual and social roots – have been eliminated, true human history, that is, universal harmonious cooperation, will at last begin is a secular form of what is evidently a permanent need of mankind. But if it is the case that not all ultimate human ends are necessarily compatible, there may be no escape from choices governed by no overriding principle, some among them painful, both to the agent and to others. From this it would follow that the creation of a social structure that would, at the least, avoid morally intolerable alternatives, and at the most promote active solidarity in the pursuit of common objectives, may be the best that human beings can be expected to achieve, if too many varieties of positive action are not to be repressed, too many equally valid human goals are not to be frustrated.

But a course demanding so much skill and practical intelligence – the hope of what would be no more than a better world, dependent on the maintenance of what is bound to be an unstable equilibrium in need of constant attention and repair – is evidently not inspiring enough for most men, who crave a bold, universal, once-and-for-all panacea. It may be that men cannot face too much reality, or an open future, without a guarantee of a happy ending – providence, the self-realising spirit, the hidden hand, the cunning of reason or of history, or of a productive and creative social class. This seems borne out by the social and political doctrines that have proved most influential in recent times. Yet the romantic attack on the system-builders – the authors of the great historical libretti – has not been wholly ineffective. Whatever the political theorists may have taught, the imaginative literature of the nineteenth century, and of ours too, which expresses the moral outlook, conscious and unconscious, of the age, has (despite the apocalyptic moments of Dostoevsky or Walt Whitman) remained singularly unaffected by Utopian dreams. There is no vision of final perfection in Tolstoy, or Turgenev, in Balzac or Flaubert or Baudelaire or Carducci. Manzoni is perhaps the last major writer who still lives in the afterglow of a Christian-liberal, optimistic eschatology. The German romantic school and those it influenced, directly and indirectly, Schopenhauer, Nietzsche, Wagner, Ibsen, Joyce, Kafka, Beckett, the existentialists, whatever fantasies of their own they may have generated, do not cling to the myth of an ideal world. Nor from his wholly different standpoint does Freud. Small wonder that they have all been duly written off as decadent reactionaries by Marxist critics. Some indeed, and those not the least gifted or perceptive, are justly so described. Others were, and are, the very opposite: humane, generous, life-enhancing, openers of new doors.

One is not committed to applauding or even condoning the extravagances of romantic irrationalism if one concedes that, by revealing that the ends of men are many, often unpredictable, and some among them incompatible with one another, the romantics have dealt a fatal blow to the proposition that, all appearances to the contrary, a definite solution of the jigsaw puzzle is, at least in principle, possible, that power in the service of reason can achieve it, that rational organisation can bring about the perfect union of such values and counter-values as individual liberty and social equality, spontaneous self-expression and organised, socially directed efficiency, perfect knowledge and perfect happiness, the claims of personal life and the claims of parties, classes, nations, the public interest. If some ends recognised as fully human are at the same time ultimate and mutually incompatible, then the idea of a golden age, a perfect society compounded of a synthesis of all the correct solutions to all the central problems of human life, is shown to be incoherent in principle. This is the service rendered by romanticism and in particular the doctrine that forms its heart, namely, that morality is moulded by the will and that ends are created, not discovered. When this movement is justly condemned for the monstrous fallacy that life is, or can be made, a work of art, that the aesthetic model applies to politics, that the political leader is, at his highest, a sublime artist who shapes men according to his creative design, and that this leads to dangerous nonsense in theory and savage brutality in practice, this at least may be set to its credit: that it has permanently shaken the faith in universal, objective truth in matters of conduct, in the possibility of a perfect and harmonious society, wholly free from conflict or injustice or oppression – a goal for which no sacrifice can be too great if men are ever to create Condorcet's reign of truth, happiness and virtue, bound 'by an indissoluble chain' – an ideal for which more human beings have, in our time, sacrificed themselves and others than, perhaps, for any other cause in human history.

THE BENT TWIG

On the Rise of Nationalism

I

THE RICH development of historical studies in the nineteenth century transformed men's views about their origins and the importance of growth, development and time. The causes of the emergence of the new historical consciousness were many and diverse. Those most often given are the rapid and profound transformation of human lives and thought in the west by the unparalleled progress of the natural sciences since the Renaissance, by the impact on society of new technology and, in particular, the growth of large-scale industry; the disintegration of the unity of Christendom and the rise of new states, classes, social and political formations, and the search for origins, pedigrees, connections with, or return to, a real or imaginary past. All of this culminated in the most transforming event of all – the French Revolution, which exploded, or at the very least profoundly altered, some of the most deeply rooted presuppositions and concepts by which men lived. It made men acutely conscious of change and excited interest in the laws that governed it.

All these are truisms that need no restating; nor does the corollary, no less platitudinous, that the theories claiming to account for social change in the past could not be confined to it: if they were valid at all, they must work equally well for the

A somewhat different treatment of the topic of this essay is to be found in 'Nationalism: Past Neglect and Present Power', reprinted in *Against the Current* (see p: v above, note 1).

future. Prophecy, which had hitherto been the province of religion and the preserve of mystics and astrologers, moved from preoccupation with the apocalyptic books of the Bible – the four Great Beasts of the Book of Daniel or of the Revelation of St John – and other occult regions, and became the province of philosophers of history and the fathers of sociology. It seemed reasonable to assume that the realm of historical change could be dealt with by the same kind of powerful new weapons as those which had unlocked the secrets of the external world in so astonishing a fashion.

Nor did this prove to be an altogether idle hope. Some of the historical prophets of the late eighteenth and nineteenth centuries, even the visionary among them, proved to have a firmer grasp of reality than their theological predecessors. Some thinkers of the Enlightenment were optimistic, some less hopeful. Voltaire and Rousseau were equally clear about the very different worlds they wished to see, but wondered gloomily whether human folly and vice would ever permit their realisation. Melchior Grimm thought it would take centuries to improve human nature. Turgot and Condorcet were the most sanguine: Condorcet was sure that the application of mathematical methods – in particular social statistics – to social policy would usher in that reign of truth, happiness and virtue, bound 'by an indissoluble chain', that would put an end for ever to the reign of cruelty, misery and oppression whereby kings and priests and their wretched tools had kept mankind in subjection for so long.

What these men believed was not absurd. The new scientific methods did put vast new power in the hands of those who knew how to organise and rationalise the new society. The bright new world that Condorcet conceived in the darkness of his prison cell was that very world of 'sophisters [i.e. Condorcet's rational men], economists and calculators' which Burke, who had perceived its coming no less clearly, had lamented only three years before. This great mutation did in due course come to pass, even though its consequences turned out very differently from Condorcet's dreams. So, too, Condorcet's disciple Saint-Simon, at the beginning of the century, correctly foretold the revolutionary role to be played by the union of applied science, finance and industrial organisation, and, still more accurately, the replacement of religious by secular propaganda, into the service of which artists and poets would be drafted as they had once worked for the glory of the church. And he wrote lyrical but acutely prophetic chapters about the vast increase of social human power, in particular over nature, that was in process of realisation. His secretary and collaborator Auguste Comte saw that to achieve this a species of secular religion, organised by an authoritarian church dedicated to rational, but not liberal or democratic, ideals would be needed.

Events have proved him right. The transformation in our own century of political and social movements into monolithic bodies, imposing a total discipline upon their followers, exercised by a secular priesthood claiming absolute authority, both spiritual and lay, in the name of unique scientific knowledge of the nature of men and things, has in fact occurred, and on a vaster scale than even that most fanatical systematiser seems to have imagined. This was duly echoed by the fathers of science fiction, Jules Verne and H. G. Wells. Jules Verne confined himself to brilliant predictions of technological discoveries and inventions. Wells is the last preacher of the morality of the Enlightenment, of the faith that the great mass of prejudice and ignorance and superstition, and the absurd and repressive rules in which it is embodied, economic, political, racial and sexual, would be destroyed by the new élite of scientific planners. It was this type of approach that seemed so vulgar and dehumanising to Victorian romantics, Carlyle or Disraeli or Ruskin. It alarmed even so rational a thinker as John Stuart Mill, who wished to believe in scientific method, but perceived in Comte's authoritarian arrangements a menace to both individual liberty and democratic government, and so became involved in a conflict of values which he was never able to resolve.

'The government of persons will be succeeded by the administration of things': this Saint-Simonian formula was common to Comte and Marx. Marx became convinced that this would be brought about by the true motor of all social change – the productive forces of society, the relationships of which were the primary factors that determined, and were as a rule disguised by, outer forms – 'the superstructure' – of social relationships. These included legal and social institutions as well as ideas in men's heads, ideologies that consciously or unconsciously performed the task of defending the status quo, that is, the power of the class in control, against the historical forces embodied in the victims of the prevailing system, which in the end would prove victorious. Whatever his errors, no one can today deny that Marx displayed unique powers of prognosis in identifying the central trend at work – the concentration and centralisation of capitalist enterprise – the inexorable trend towards ever-increasing size on the part of big business, then in its embryo, and the sharpening social and political conflicts that this involved. He also set himself to unmask the conservative and liberal, patriotic and humanitarian, religious and ethical disguises in which some of the most brutal manifestations of these conflicts, and their social and intellectual consequences, would be concealed.

These were genuinely prophetic thinkers. And there were others. The unsystematic and wayward Bakunin predicted more accurately than his great rival Marx the circumstances in which the revolutions by the dispossessed would occur. He saw that they were liable to develop not in the most industrialised societies on an ascending curve of economic progress, but on the contrary, where the majority of the population was near subsistence level, and had least to lose by an upheaval, that is, in the most backward regions of the world, inhabited by primitive peasants in conditions of desperate poverty, where capitalism was weakest – Spain, Russia. This doctrine was reformulated later but never attributed to anarchist inspiration by later Marxists such as Parvus (Helphand) and Trotsky.

These were the optimists. But by the early 1830s the first

pessimists begin. The poet Heine warned the French in 1832 that one fine day their German neighbours, fired by a terrible combination of absolutist metaphysics, historical memories and resentments, fanaticism and savage strength and fury, would fall upon them, and would destroy the great monuments of western civilisation: 'Implacable Kantians . . . with axe and sword will uproot the soil of our European life in order to tear out the roots of the past . . . armed Fichteans will appear', restrained neither by fear nor by greed, like those 'early Christians, whom neither physical torture nor physical pleasure could break'. The most terrible of all will be Schelling's disciples, the Philosophers of Nature, who, isolated and un-approachable beyond the barriers of their own obsessive ideas, will identify themselves with the elemental forces of 'the demonic powers of ancient German pantheism'. When these metaphysically intoxicated barbarians get going, then let the French beware: the French Revolution will seem like a peaceful idyll.

Who can say that this, too, has not come to pass in a form far more horrible than any conceived even in Wagner's most sinister moments? A few decades later Jakob Burckhardt fore-told the inevitability of the military-industrial complex that would, or at any rate might, dominate the decadent countries of the west. There follow the fears of Max Weber, and all the black Utopias of Zamyatin, Aldous Huxley, Orwell, and the long row of blood-chilling Cassandras, half satirists, half prophets, of our day. Some of these vaticinations were pure predictions; others, like those of Marxists and of the Francophobe neo-pagans who terrified Heine, can be regarded as to some extent self-fulfilling.

These are examples of genuinely successful diagnoses and prognoses of the direction in which western society was moving. Besides these there have been all those justly forgotten Utopias – from Plato to Fourier or Cabet or Bellamy or Hertzka – embalmed in the pages of the more voluminous histories of socialist doctrines. On the other side, there were the liberal and technocratic or neo-medieval fantasies, which rest either on a return to a pre-capitalist and pre-industrial type of *Gemeinschaft*, or, alternatively, on the construction of one single, technocratically organised, managerial, Saint-Simonian world. But in all this great array of elaborate, statistically supported serious futurology mingled with free fantasy, there took place one movement which dominated much of the nineteenth century, for which no significant future was predicted, a movement so familiar to us now, so decisive both within, and in relationships between, nations, that it is only by some effort of the imagination that one can conceive of a world in which it played no part. Its existence and its power (especially outside the English-speaking world) seem to us so self-evident today that it appears strange to have to draw attention to it as a phenomenon the prophets before our day, and in our time too, virtually ignored; in the case of the latter, at times with consequences fatal to themselves and those who believed them. This movement is nationalism.

II

No social or political thinker in the nineteenth century was unaware of nationalism as a dominant movement of his age. Nevertheless, in the second half of the century, indeed up to the First World War, it was thought to be waning. Consciousness of national identity may well be as old as social consciousness itself. But nationalism, unlike tribal feeling or xenophobia, to which it is related, but with which it is not identical, seems scarcely to have existed in ancient or classical times. There were other foci of collective loyalty. It seems to emerge at the end of the Middle Ages in the west, particularly in France, in the form of the defence of customs and privileges of localities, regions, corporations and, of course, states, and then of the nation itself, against the encroachment of some external power – Roman law or papal authority – or against related forms of universalism – natural law and other claims of supranational authority. Its emergence as a coherent doctrine may perhaps be placed and dated in the last third of the eighteenth century in Germany, more particularly in the conceptions of the *Volksgeist* and *Nationalgeist*, in the writings of the vastly influential poet and philosopher Johann Gottfried Herder.

The roots of this go back to the beginnings of the eighteenth century, and indeed before it, at any rate in East Prussia, where it grew and whence it spread. Herder's thought is dominated by his conviction that among the basic needs of men, as elemental as that for food or procreation or communication, is the need to belong to a group. More fervently and imaginatively than Burke, and with a wealth of historical and psychological examples, he argued that every human community had its own unique shape and pattern. Its members were born in a stream of tradition which shaped their emotional and physical development no less than their ideas. Indeed, distinctions between reason, imagination, emotion, sensation, were for him largely artificial. There was a central historically developing pattern that characterised the life and activity of every identifiable community and, most deeply, that unit which, by his own time, had come to be the nation. The way in which a German lived at home and the way in which he conducted his public life, German song and German legislation – the collective genius, not attributable to individual authors, that created the myths and legends, the ballads and historical chronicles – was the same as that which made the style of Luther's Bible, or the arts and crafts and images and categories of thought of the Germans of his own time. The way in which Germans spoke or dressed or moved had more in common with the way in which they built their cathedrals, or organised their civic lives – a central German essence, as it were, an identifiable pattern and quality – than it had with analogous activities among the inhabitants of China or Peru.

Human customs, activities, forms of life, art, ideas, were (and must be) of value to men not in terms of timeless criteria, applicable to all men and societies, irrespective of time and place, as the French *lumières* taught, but because they were their own, expressions of their local, regional, national life, and spoke to them as they could speak to no other human group. This is why men withered in exile, that is what nostalgia ('the noblest of pains') was a yearning for. To understand the Bible one must imaginatively enter into the life of the Judaean shepherds of primitive times; to understand the Eddas, the savage struggle with the elements of a barbarous northern race. Everything valuable was unique.

Universalism, by reducing everything to the lowest common denominator which applies to all men at all times, drained both lives and ideals of that specific content which alone gave them point. Hence Herder's implacable crusade against French universalism, and his concept and glorification of individual cultures – Indian, Chinese, Norse, Hebrew – and his hatred of the great levellers, Caesar and Charlemagne, Romans, Christian knights, British empire-builders and missionaries, who eliminated native cultures and replaced them with their own historically, and therefore spiritually, foreign and oppressive to their victims. Herder and his disciples believed in the peaceful coexistence of a rich multiplicity and variety of national forms of life, the more diverse the better. Under the impact of the French revolutionary and Napoleonic invasions, cultural or spiritual autonomy, for which Herder had originally pleaded, turned into embittered and aggressive nationalist self-assertion.

The origins of cultural change and national attitudes are difficult to establish. Nationalism is an inflamed condition of national consciousness which can be, and has on occasion been, tolerant and peaceful. It usually seems to be caused by wounds, some form of collective humiliation. It may be that this happened in German lands because they had remained on the edges of the great renaissance of western Europe. The late sixteenth century, a great creative age, far from spent even in Italy, the culture of which had risen to an unparalleled height a hundred years before, was marked by an immense upsurge of creative activity in France, in England, in Spain, in the Low

Countries. German towns and principalities, both those dominated by the imperial power of Vienna and those outside it, were by comparison profoundly provincial. They excelled only in architecture and, perhaps, Protestant theology. The terrible devastation of the Thirty Years War doubtless made this cultural gap even wider. To be the object of contempt or patronising tolerance on the part of proud neighbours is one of the most traumatic experiences that individuals or societies can suffer. The response, as often as not, is pathological exaggeration of one's real or imaginary virtues, and resentment and hostility towards the proud, the happy, the successful. This, indeed, characterised much German feeling about the west, more especially about France, in the eighteenth century.

The French dominated the western world, politically, culturally, militarily. The humiliated and defeated Germans, particularly the traditional, religious, economically backward East Prussians, bullied by French officials imported by Frederick the Great, responded, like the bent twig of the poet Schiller's theory, by lashing back and refusing to accept their alleged inferiority. They discovered in themselves qualities far superior to those of their tormentors. They contrasted their own deep, inner life of the spirit, their own profound humility, their selfless pursuit of true values – simple, noble, sublime – with the rich, worldly, successful, superficial, smooth, heartless, morally empty French. This mood rose to fever pitch during the national resistance to Napoleon, and was indeed the original exemplar of the reaction of many a backward, exploited, or at any rate patronised society, which, resentful of the apparent inferiority of its status, reacted by turning to real or imaginary triumphs and glories in its past, or enviable attributes of its own national or cultural character. Those who cannot boast of great political, military or economic achievements, or a magnificent tradition of art or thought, seek comfort and strength in the notion of the free and creative life of the spirit within them, uncorrupted by the vices of power or sophistication.

There is much of this in the writings of the German

romantics, and, after them, of the Russian Slavophils, and many an awakener of the national spirit in central Europe, Poland, the Balkans, Asia, Africa. Hence the value of a real or imaginary rich historical past to inferiority-ridden peoples, for it promises, perhaps, an even more glorious future. If no such past can be invoked, then its very absence will be ground for optimism. We may today be primitive, poor, even barbarian, but our very backwardness is a symptom of our youth, our unexhausted vital power; we are the inheritors of the future which the old, worn-out, corrupt, declining nations, for all their vaunted present-day superiority, can no longer hope for. This messianic theme is sounded strongly by Germans, then by Poles and Russians, and after that, in our time, by many states and nations which feel that they have not yet played their part (but soon will) in the great drama of history.

III

This attitude, almost universal among the developing nations, is plain to the most untutored eye today. But in the home of political prophecy, the nineteenth century, when the future was discerned through many historical, sociological and philosophical telescopes, it was evidently not plain at all. The great masters did not foretell the huge proliferation of national pride, indeed did not predict it at all. Hegel, in his emphasis on 'historic', as opposed to 'unhistoric', nations as the carriers of the ever-forward-thrusting cosmic *Geist*, may have flattered the self-esteem of western and northern Europe or fed the ambitions of those who sought German or Nordic unity and power. But he was no less opposed than Metternich to the wild, violent, emotional nationalism of Francophobe and anti-Semitic students, with their chauvinism and book-burnings, which seemed to him barbarous excesses, as they did to Goethe, who forbade his son to fight against the French. To trace to Hegel's writings the fierce nationalism of later German writers who derive from them is certainly unjust. Even the fanatical early chauvinists – the Jahns, the Arndts, the Goerreses, and indeed Fichte, who is in part responsible for this mood, with his paeans to the uncontaminated German language as a vehicle for the uniquely liberating German mission in the world – even they did not consciously view nationalism as the dominant force in the future of Europe, still less of mankind. They were merely struggling to liberate their nations from disabling dynastic or foreign or sceptical influences. Jahn and Arndt and Körner are German chauvinists, but they are not theorists of nationalism as such, still less prophets of its universal sway; inferior nations, indeed, are not entitled to it.

The rationalists and liberals, and of course the early socialists, virtually ignore nationalism. For them it is a mere sign of immaturity, an irrational relic of, or retrogressive return to, a barbarous past: fanatics like Maistre (who for all his ultra-montanism was an early believer in natural 'integralism') or Fries or Gobineau or Houston Stewart Chamberlain and Wagner, or, later, Maurras, Barrès, Drumont, are not taken seriously until the Boulanger and Dreyfus affairs; these, in their turn, are regarded as temporary aberrations, due to the abnormal mood following on defeat in war, which will make way once again for the return of sanity, reason and progress. These thinkers, who look to the past for strength, do not play the part of social seers: with varying degrees of pessimism, they seek to revive a national spirit that has been undermined, perhaps fatally, by the enemy – liberals, Freemasons, scientists, atheists, sceptics, Jews. With a great effort something may yet be saved. But they believe that it is the other, 'destructive' tendencies which work against the national spirit that are there in menacing strength and hold the field and must be resisted, if only to preserve islands of purity and strength and 'integral' life. Gobineau is the most pessimistic of these, and in any case he is concerned with race rather than nations, Treitschke the most hopeful – reflecting, no doubt, their respective national moods.

As for Marx and Engels, for them, I need hardly repeat, it is the emergence of classes, economically determined by the division of labour and accumulation of capital, and the war between these classes, that account for social change in human history. Nationalism, like religion, is a temporary phenomenon which, generated by the ascendancy of the bourgeoisie, is one of the self-sustaining spiritual weapons against the proletariat. If, too often, it penetrates the masses, it does so as a form of 'false consciousness' which disguises their true condition from them and breeds illusions that provide them with deceptive comfort in their benighted state. After the end of the conditions that have given rise to it – the class war – nationalism, like religion, will evaporate together with other politically potent and historically conditioned illusions. It may acquire a certain independent influence of its own, as many such by-products of the evolution of productive forces do, but it cannot survive the destruction of its primary source, the capitalist system.

This tenet became a dogma for every school of Marxism. No matter how wide the disagreements on other issues, this was common ground, from the peaceful gradualism of Eduard Bernstein to the most left-wing members of the Bolshevik Party. The belief that nationalism was a reactionary bourgeois ideology was tantamount to the belief that it was doomed. At most, national risings on the part of colonial peoples against their imperialist masters might be considered as historically determined, a tactical step on the road to the true socialist revolution which could not be too far behind. Even so, a national rising was one thing, and nationalism another. It was this belief that caused such disappointment and indignation to the internationalist left, led by Lenin, Karl Liebknecht and their friends, when the socialist parties in the belligerent countries, instead of proclaiming a general strike which should have stopped the war in 1914, joined the national colours and went to war against each other. It was this that caused Rosa Luxemburg to protest against the very formation of a national state by the Poles at the end of the war. The October

Revolution, it is fair to say, was genuinely anti-nationalist in character.

The contrast, enunciated in some quarters, between Lenin as the authentic voice of Russian feeling, as against the 'rootless cosmopolitanism' of men like Trotsky or Zinoviev or Radek, has no foundation. Lenin looked on the Russian Revolution as the breaking of the weakest link in the capitalist chain, whose value consisted in precipitating the world revolution, since, as Marx and Engels were convinced, communism in one country could not survive. Events decreed otherwise, but the doctrine itself was altered only under Stalin. The initial mood among the early Bolsheviks was genuinely anti-nationalist: so much so that Bolshevik critics in Russia vied with each other in disparaging the glories of their own national literature – Pushkin, for example – in order to express their contempt for national tradition as a central bourgeois value.

There was a similar mood among the leaders of the abortive communist revolutions that followed in Hungary and Munich. 'National-chauvinism', 'social-chauvinism' became terms of abuse, battle-cries used to crush autonomous movements in some of the non-Russian provinces of the old Russian empire. But after this, the genuine internationalist phase was over. Every revolution and upheaval thereafter contained a nationalist component. The rise of Fascism or National Socialism was interpreted by Marxist theorists as the final and extreme, but desperate, resistance on the part of capitalism in these countries against the inevitable victory of international socialism. The systematic underestimate of the strength of totalitarian or authoritarian nationalist movements, and their triumph in central and north-eastern Europe, the Iberian peninsula and elsewhere, was due to ideologically caused miscalculation.

The economic autarky which followed the great crisis of 1931, plausibly enough interpreted as a culmination of the internal contradictions of the capitalist system, was, whatever else it might indicate, a form of acute economic nationalism, which outlived its putative economic causes and gravely obstructed the advance of the enlightenment, whether liberal or socialist. What followed in the newly liberated territories in Asia and Africa seems to support the view that after the 1920s neither socialism nor any other political movement in the post-war world could be successful unless it came arm in arm not only with anti-imperialism but with pronounced nationalism.

IV

The rise of nationalism is today a world-wide phenomenon, probably the strongest single factor in the newly established states, and in some cases among the minority populations of the older nations. Who, in the nineteenth century, would have predicted the rise of acute nationalism in Canada, in Pakistan (indeed, the very possibility of Pakistan itself would have met with considerable scepticism among Indian nationalist leaders a hundred years ago), or in Wales or Brittany or Scotland or the Basque country? It might be said that this is an automatic psychological accompaniment of liberation from foreign rule – a natural reaction, on Schiller's 'bent twig' theory, against oppression or humiliation of a society that possesses national characteristics. In most of these cases the desire for national independence is intertwined with social resistance to exploitation. This kind of nationalism is, perhaps, as much a form of social or class resistance as of purely national self-assertion, creating a mood in which men prefer to be ordered about, even if this entails ill-treatment, by members of their own faith or nation or class, to tutelage, however benevolent, on the part of ultimately patronising superiors from a foreign land or alien class or milieu.

So too, it may be that no minority that has preserved its own cultural tradition or religious or racial characteristics can indefinitely tolerate the prospect of remaining a minority for ever, governed by a majority with a different outlook or habits. And this may indeed account for the reaction of wounded pride, or the sense of collective injustice, which animates, for example, Zionism or its mirror-image, the movement of the Palestinian Arabs, or such 'ethnic' minorities as Negroes in the United States or Irish Catholics in Ulster, the Nagas in India and the like. Certainly contemporary nationalism seldom comes in its pure, romantic form as it did in Italy or Poland or Hungary in the early nineteenth century, but is connected far more closely with social and religious and economic grievances. Yet it seems undeniable that the central feeling is deeply nationalistic. More ominous still (and even more rarely, if indeed ever, foreseen a century ago), racial hatreds seem to be at the core of the most hideous expressions of violent collective emotion of this kind: genocide and near-genocide in India, in the Sudan, in Nigeria and Burundi, indicate that, no matter what other factors may be present in such explosive situations, they always possess a national or racialist core, which other factors may exacerbate, but which they do not generate, and without which they do not combine into the socially and politically critical mass. Passionate nationalism appears to be the *sine qua non* of contemporary revolutions.

Whatever may be the explanation of this phenomenon, which, in its own way, is just as menacing as the other dangers that loom over mankind – pollution or over-population or the nuclear holocaust – its rise is incompatible with nineteenth-century notions of the relative unimportance of race or nationality or even culture, as opposed to, say, class or economic competition, or of psychological and anthropological factors as against sociological or economic ones. Yet these were the assumptions upon which predictions of the emergence of a rational society, whether founded upon the principles of liberal individualism or on technocratic centralisation, once rested. Unanticipated outbreaks of such dissimilar, yet equally nationalist movements in the communist societies of our day – from the Hungarian resistance in 1956 to anti-Semitism and nationalism in Poland, and indeed in the Soviet Union itself –

seem, to say the least, to weaken the orthodox Marxist thesis.[1]
Yet they certainly cannot be described, as they sometimes are by
those who are embarrassed by them, as mere relics and survivals
of an earlier ideology. Neither Nagy in Hungary nor Moczar in
Poland, despite the vast differences of their purposes, were in
any sense bourgeois nationalists.

[1] The attitude of the founders of Marxism to national or local patriotism,
autonomist movements, self-determination of small states and the like, is
not in doubt. Apart from the direct implications of their theory of social
development, their attitude to Danish resistance to Prussia over Schleswig-
Holstein, to the Italian fight for unity and independence (when Marx in his
despatches to the *New York Times* so sharply differed from the pro-Italian
Lassalle), to the efforts by the Czechs to defend their culture from German
hegemony, and even to the outcome of the Franco-Prussian War, is quite
clear. The charge brought by the Swiss anarchist leader James Guillaume
against Marx, of supporting Pan-Germanism, was only a piece of absurd
propaganda during the 1914–18 war. Like other historicists who believe in a
single progressive universal civilisation, Marx regarded national or regional
loyalties as irrational resistance by lower forms of development, which
history would render obsolete. In this sense German civilisation (and the
developed workers' organisation in it) represented a more advanced stage of
(admittedly capitalist) development than, say, Danish or Bohemian or any
other *Kleinstaaterei*. Similarly, it was more desirable from the point of view of
the International Workingmen's Movement that the Germans – with their
superior workers' organisations – should win rather than the French, riddled
with Proudhonism, Bakuninism etc.; there is no trace of nationalism in
Marx's conception of the stages of world progress towards communism and
beyond it. It is all the more significant, therefore, that the creation of states
founded on Marxist doctrines should, nevertheless, display acute national
feeling. A particularly sharp expression of this is contained in the report
presented to the National Conference of the Romanian Communist Party by
its leader Nicolae Ceauşescu on 19 July 1972: 'Some people think that the
nation is a concept which is historically obsolete, and that the policy of
national unity and the development of the nation, particularly in the
conditions of the building of socialism, is indeed a wrong policy, represents
an expression of narrow-minded nationalism. Sometimes it is even said that
this policy is opposed to socialist internationalism . . . With respect to the
national problem in socialist conditions, we have to say that the victory of the
new order has opened up the way to achieving true national unity, to
strengthening and developing the nation on a new basis . . . The dialectical
process of bringing together [different] nations presupposes their strong
affirmation [of their nationhood] . . . Between national and international

In the face of this, faith in countervailing forces – in multinational corporations which, whatever their relationship with class war and social conflict, at any rate do cross national borders, or in the United Nations as a barrier to unbridled chauvinism – seems about as realistic (at least so far as lands outside western Europe are concerned) as Cobden's belief that the development of free trade throughout the world would of itself ensure peace and harmonious co-operation between nations. One is also reminded of Norman Angell's apparently unanswered argument a short while before 1914 that the economic interests of modern capitalist states alone made large-scale wars impossible.

V

What we are seeing, it seems to me, is a world reaction against the central doctrines of nineteenth-century liberal rationalism itself, a confused effort to return to an older morality. The lines of battle in the eighteenth and nineteenth centuries were more or less clearly drawn. On one side stood the supporters of tradition, of political and social hierarchies, whether 'natural' or hallowed by history, or belief in, and obedience to, divine, or at any rate transcendent, authority. These were men who believed that the operations of untrammelled reason must be kept within bounds and should, above all, be prevented from questioning

---

interests not only is there no contradiction, but, on the contrary, there is a full dialectical unity' (*Scînteia* [the organ of the Central Committee of the Romanian Communist Party], 20 July 1972, p. 8).

The fact that Ceauşescu, perhaps the most impeccably Leninist-Stalinist of all recent leaders of communist states, should have chosen to make a doctrinal issue of what has, in practice, for many years been the line of many communist governments and parties in the east and west is surely of some importance. The conflict between Marxist discipline and nationalist forces, which is a fairly constant factor in contemporary communism – indeed, the entire topic of Marxism and nationalism, both its theoretical aspects and in practice – deserves closer study than it has obtained.

the validity of the laws and customs and ancient ways of life – those impalpable and unanalysable bonds that hold society together and alone preserve the moral health of states and individuals. This is the faith in the 'integral' community which critical examination by sceptical intellectuals, using rationalist methods, can only discredit in theory and undermine, and in the end disintegrate, in practice. On the other side stood the unswerving champions of reason, who rejected faith in tradition, intuition, transcendent sources of authority as mere smoke-screens to justify irrationality, ignorance, bias, fear of the truth in matters of theory, and stupidity, injustice, oppression and the corrupt power of Bentham's sinister interests in practice.

The party of progress, liberal or socialist, appealed to the methods of reason, especially the methods employed in the natural sciences, by which any rational being could verify the truth of a principle, or the effectiveness of a policy, or the reliability of the evidence on which these conclusions were founded. He could test such claims for himself by the use of techniques open to anyone, at any time, anywhere, without appeal to special faculties or mystical intuition with which only a chosen few were mysteriously endowed – magical ways of knowing for which infallibility was often claimed. Each side knew its enemies: on the right stood monarchists and conservatives, clericals and authoritarians, nationalists and imperialists, men whom their opponents called reactionaries and obscurantists; on the other side, rationalists, scientific materialists, sceptical intellectuals, egalitarians and positivists of many hues. Whatever the differences within each group, whether about ends or about means, the main lines of division between them were clearly discernible; and in spite of mixed and intermediate positions, each side was conscious of where it belonged, and who its natural allies and opponents were.

There is a sense in which, in our time, Burke's 'sophisters, economists and calculators', the rationalists, the Victorian progressives, have won. Condorcet once observed that all real issues of the future could be decided on the basis of rational calculation of utilitarian consequences. *Calculemus* was to be the new watchword, the key to the solution of both social and personal problems. This method, with its stress on systems analysis, cost-effectiveness, reduction to statistical and quantitative terms, reliance on the authority and power of organisation and experts, is today the common property of both sides. The application of technological techniques in organising the lives and productive activities of human beings is the policy of governments, of industrial enterprises, indeed of all large-scale economic (and cultural) activities in capitalist and communist states alike. Scientific knowledge and scientific organisation, which alone have succeeded in revealing the secrets of nature, animate and inanimate, can surely be made to rationalise social life and so bring about the maximum satisfaction of discoverable human needs, provided that the system is organised by disinterested experts.

Physicists and biologists, geographers and urban and rural planners, psychologists and anthropologists, mathematicians and engineers (including Stalin's 'engineers of human souls'), specialists of every kind, can be, and to a larger degree have been, harnessed into the service of those who, sometimes with pure motives and a fanatical devotion to what they see as the cause of reason and human happiness, are determined to make the best use possible of available resources, natural and artificial, human and non-human. Marxists, or inhabitants of underdeveloped countries, may protest against the use of such methods in their own interest by the class enemy, internal or external, capitalists, 'neo-colonialists', imperialists. But they do not protest against the technological approach itself, and indeed seek to adapt and perfect it for the promotion of their own interests. It is against this that a world-wide protest has begun.

The effectiveness of this revolt (for such it seems to be), since it is still in its early beginnings, is hard to foretell. It springs from the feeling that human rights, rooted in the sense of human beings as specifically human, that is, as individuated, as possessing wills, sentiments, beliefs, ideals, ways of living of their own, have been lost sight of in the 'global' calculations and vast extrapolations which guide the plans of policy-planners and executives in the gigantic operations in which governments, corporations and interlocking élites of various kinds are engaged. Quantitative computation cannot but ignore the specific wishes and hopes and fears and goals of individual human beings. This must always be so, whenever policies for large numbers must be devised, but it has today gone very far indeed.

There is a growing number among the young of our day who see their future as a process of being fitted into some scientifically well-constructed programme, after the data of their life-expectancy and capacities and utilisability have been classified, computerised, and analysed for conduciveness to the purpose, at the very best, of producing the greatest happiness of the greatest number. This will determine the organisation of life on a national or regional or world scale, and this without undue attention to, or interest in (since this is not needed for the completion of the task), their individual characters, ways of life, wishes, quirks, ideals. This moves them to gloom and fury or despair. They wish to be and do something, and not merely to be acted upon, or for, or on behalf of. They demand recognition of their dignity as human beings. They do not wish to be reduced to human material, to being counters in a game played by others, even when it is played, at least in part, for the benefit of these counters themselves. A revolt breaks out at all levels.

The dissident young opt out or attack universities, intellectual activities, organised education, because they identify them with this huge and dehumanising machinery. Whether they know it or not, what they are appealing to is some species of natural law, or Kantian absolutism, which forbids the treatment of human beings as means to ends, no matter how benevolently this is conceived. Their protests sometimes take rational forms, at other times violently irrational ones, mostly exhibitionistic and often hysterical attempts to defy the ruling powers, to insult them into awareness of the totalitarian effect of such policies, whether intended or unintended (the authentic Marxist component of such protests, the denunciation of exploitation and class rule, is not, as a rule, the dominant note). They protest against the destructive effect on individuals of global planning, of the substitution of figures and curves for the direct perception of actual human beings for whose ostensible good all this is being done, especially of those remote from them, whose lives the planners seek to determine, sometimes by exceedingly brutal means, hidden from their own sight by the opaque medium of impersonal statistics.

In industrial or post-industrial societies the protest is that of individuals or groups whose members do not wish to be dragged along by the chariot-wheels of scientific progress, interpreted as the accumulation of material goods and services and of utilitarian arrangements to dispose of them. In poor or ex-colonial territories the desire of the majority to be treated as equals of their former masters – as full human beings – often takes the form of nationalist self-assertion. The cry for individual and national independence – the demand not to be interfered with or dictated to or organised by others – springs from the same sense of outraged human dignity. It is true that the movement for national independence at times itself leads to the creation of larger units, to centralisation, and often to the suppression by the new élite of its own fellow citizens, and it can lead to the crushing of various minorities, ethnic, political, religious. At other times it is inspired by the opposite ideal – escape from huge impersonal authority that ignores ethnic, regional and religious differences, a craving for 'natural' units of 'human' size.

But the original impulse, the desire *fare da se*, appears to be the same in both cases; it is the *se* that varies. The self that seeks liberty of action, determination of its own life, can be large or small, regional or linguistic; today it is liable to be collective and national or ethnic-religious rather than individual; it is always resistant to dilution, assimilation, depersonalisation. It is the very triumph of scientific rationalism everywhere, the great eighteenth-century movement for the liberation of men from superstition and ignorance, from the selfishness and greed of kings, priests and oligarchies, above all from the vagaries of natural forces, that, by a curious paradox, has imposed a yoke that, in its turn, evoked an all-too-human cry for independence from its rule. It is a cry for room in which men can seek to realise their natures, quirks and all, to live lives free from dictation or coercion from teachers, masters, bullies and persuaders and dominators of various kinds. No doubt to do entirely as one likes could destroy not only one's neighbours but oneself. Freedom is only one value among others, and cannot be realised without rules and limits. But in the hour of revolt this is inevitably forgotten.

VI

Antinomianism is nothing new. Mutiny against the life of the barracks – suffocation in 'closed' societies – against the laws and institutions that are felt to be unjust or oppressive or corrupt or indifferent to some of the deepest aspirations of human beings, occur in the history of every long-lived state and church and social order. Sometimes these institutions, whatever their official professions and ideologies, are felt to favour a particular class or group at the expense of others, whom they seek, consciously or unconsciously, to deceive or coerce into conformity. At other times the system is felt to be mechanically self-perpetuating and the reasons for its existence, even if once valid, seem to have become obsolete. Its supporters delude men (and are themselves deluded) into supposing that human arrangements, which may have originally responded to real needs, are objective necessities, laws of nature (at least human nature) which it is idle and irrational to seek to alter. Diderot spoke of the war within each human being, of the natural man seeking to liberate himself from the artificial man, who is compounded of social conventions, irrational pressures and the 'interested error' of the ruling class which rational criticism would blow sky-high but upon which contemporary society rests.

Protest against this takes the form sometimes of a nostalgic longing for earlier times, when men were virtuous or happy or free, or dreams of a golden age in the future, or of a restoration of simplicity, spontaneity, natural humanity, the self-subsistent rural economy, in which man, no longer dependent on the whims of others, can recover moral (and physical) health. The result would presumably be the reign of those eternal values which all but the hopelessly corrupt can easily recognise simply by looking within themselves; this is what Rousseau and Tolstoy and a good many peaceful anarchists and their modern followers still believe. Populist movements in the nineteenth century which idealised peasants, or the poor, or the 'true' nation, very different from its self-appointed bureaucratic rulers, represented attempts of this kind – a return to 'the people' in order to escape from a world of false values, 'inauthentic' lives, organisation men, or Ibsen's or Chekhov's crushed or repressed beings, where human capacity for love and friendship, justice and creative work, enjoyment, curiosity, pursuit of the truth, has been aborted and frustrated. Some wish to improve contemporary society by reforms. Others feel, as the anabaptists of the sixteenth century may have felt, that the corruption has gone too far, that the wicked must be destroyed root and branch, in the hope that a new and pure society will arise miraculously upon its ruins.

These are extreme cases, chosen to illustrate the predicament at its most characteristic. It is with this mood and this predicament that nationalism is connected. It too is a pathological form of a self-protective resistance. Rousseau, the most spell-binding voice of this general revolt, told the Poles to resist encroachment by the Russians by obstinately clinging to their national institutions, their clothes, their habits, their ways of life – not to conform, not to assimilate; the claims of universal humanity were incarnated, for the time being, in their resistance. There is something of the same attitude in the Russian populists of the last century. It is to be found among those hitherto suppressed peoples or minorities – those ethnic groups which feel humiliated or oppressed, to whom nationalism represents the straightening of bent backs, the recovery of a freedom that they may never have had (it is all a matter of ideas in men's heads), revenge for their insulted humanity.

This is less acutely felt in societies which have enjoyed political independence for long periods. The west has, by and large, satisfied that hunger for recognition, the desire for the *Anerkennung* which Hegel analysed very memorably; it is lack of this that, more than any other cause, seems to lead to nationalist excesses. Nationalism to many liberals and socialists in the west appears to be mere chauvinism or imperialism, part and parcel of the ideology of that very establishment which has robbed the victims of their birthright. What could be more paradoxical or more pathetic than that they should seek to realise the very values of the monstrous system which has reduced them to poverty and degradation? Is this not one of the best illustrations of the Marxist thesis that one of the greatest wrongs the ruling class does to its subjects is to blind them to their true interest, to infect them with its ideology, dictated by its own interests, as if they were identical with those of the oppressed?

In fact, nationalism does not necessarily and exclusively militate in favour of the ruling class. It animates revolts against it too, for it expresses the inflamed desire of the insufficiently regarded to count for something among the cultures of the world. The brutal and destructive side of modern nationalism needs no stressing in a world torn by its excesses. Yet it must be recognised for what it is – a world-wide response to a profound and natural need on the part of newly liberated slaves – 'the decolonised' – a phenomenon unpredicted in the Europe-centred society of the nineteenth century. How did the possibility of this development come to be ignored? To this question I volunteer no answer.

INDEX

INDEX

Compiled by Douglas Matthews